Gender, Migration and Categorisation

# Gender, Migration and Categorisation

Making Distinctions between Migrants
in Western Countries, 1945-2010

*Marlou Schrover & Deirdre M. Moloney (eds)*

IMISCOE Research

AMSTERDAM UNIVERSITY PRESS

Cover illustration: Hungarian refugees Rozsa and Imre Tölgyesi at home in Numansdorp, 1958. Habetler Collection, IISG Amsterdam

Cover design: Studio Jan de Boer BNO, Amsterdam
Layout: Hanneke Kossen, Amsterdam

Amsterdam University Press English-language titles are distributed in the US and Canada by the University of Chicago Press.

ISBN      978 90 8964 573 9
e-ISBN   978 90 4852 175 3 (pdf)
e-ISBN   978 90 4852 176 0 (ePub)
NUR      741 / 763

© Marlou Schrover and Deirdre M. Moloney / Amsterdam University Press, Amsterdam 2013

# Table of contents

# 1 Introduction

## Making a difference

*Marlou Schrover and Deirdre Moloney*

## Introduction

All people are equal, according to Thomas Jefferson, but all migrants
are not. States differentiate explicitly between *categories of migrants*
(e.g., colonial, refugee, labour and family), and they differentiate implicitly according to *categories of analysis*, such as gender, class, religion
and ethnicity. The relationship between gender and categorisation is
twofold. In the first place, the ability to move between the categories
of migrants is different for men and for women. Secondly, ideas about
gender, together with those from other categories of analysis (e.g., class,
religion and ethnicity), shape debates in the media and policies, as this
volume makes clear. The contributions in this volume describe and analyse how in a number of countries – France, the USA, Turkey, Canada,
Mexico, the Netherlands, Sweden and Denmark – distinctions between
migrants were made and justified in policies and in public debates. The
countries examined are similar enough to make valuable comparisons,
while being sufficiently varied to lead to interesting conclusions. Each
of the countries has significant and diverse groups of migrant populations. Several have large groups of migrants from earlier colonial or
neo-colonial relationships with other societies; and all have developed
important policies on migration and refugees, at least since the mid
20th century. Several of the major migrant groups have religious traditions that differ from those of the majority population, which often
leads to conflict and controversies about national identities and social
roles. About half of the countries have encouraged multiculturalism,
while the other countries have not.

All authors except Schacher examine the period after the Second
World War. Schacher analyses the Armenian refugee issue in the 1920s,
pointing out striking continuities with more recent debates. All authors
focus on gender as the primary analytical category. In the conclusion,
we make comparisons between the countries and between the catego-

ries of migrants examined. All authors address the intersection of gender with other categories of analysis.

We have selected our subjects for four major reasons. In the first place, (re-)categorisations and processes of (re-)labelling can best be studied at nodal points: moments of debate (Laclau & Mouffe 1985). It is at such times that boundaries are redrawn or justified. Secondly, changes in categorisation typically occur only following longer periods of debate, or after repeated debate. Debates in the media generally lead to policy changes only later (if at all). Thirdly, in order to look at how authorities differentiate between categories of migrants (colonial, refugee, labour and family) it is necessary to study debates that relate to these different categories of migrants holistically rather than to look at each in isolation. Lastly, since we want to focus on gender, this is part of the debates chosen, preferably in combination with other categories of analysis, such as class, ethnicity and religion.

The past six decades have witnessed extensive debates on three issues, as we will show in this volume. These are who is a 'refugee', who is 'family' and 'multiculturalism'. We focus on these debates. Generally speaking, scholars, policymakers, politicians and journalists distinguish four main categories of migrants: postcolonial migrants, refugees or asylum seekers, labour migrants and family migrants (migrants who are motivated to cross borders for family reunification or formation). In practice, however, these categories are not static or mutually exclusive. Among, for example, the Portuguese migrants who in the 1970s came to North-Western Europe as guest workers were people fleeing the Salazar regime and the draft for the Mozambique and Angola wars. Many Spanish guest workers opposed the Franco regime. They left their country for political reasons as much as for economic reasons. Guest workers from Morocco left during the so-called 'years of lead', the repressive regime of King Hassan ii. They were escaping both poverty and repression. Turkish guest workers sought to escape the 1970s political coups, and ethnic and religious tensions in Eastern Turkey, while many Greek guest workers fled the Regime of the Colonels. They preferred, however, to come within the framework of guest-worker migration, rather than apply for asylum. This changed after 1975, when labour migration was restricted because the guest-worker regime had come to an end. Christians and Kurds from Turkey then started to apply for asylum. As opportunities for labour migration diminished, refugee migration increased, and migration for family reunification and formation became more important. Categories of migrants are like communicating vessels: migrants change categories, and the bureaucrats who decide on entry or residence might allocate them to different categories.

When one route closes, another may open. We analyse when and why this happens. Opportunities to use a different route, furthermore, differ according to gender. Migrant men, for instance, were more likely than migrant women to be accused of 'misusing' the possibilities for family migration when they moved from the category of labour migrants to that of family migrants.

People tend to think in categories because simplification makes the social world understandable and manageable (Boyd & Richerson 1987). According to Bourdieu (1980), categorisation is a struggle to impose definitions of divisions within society and, hence, of making and unmaking social groups. Categorisation does not describe social order but rather shapes and reshapes power relations, according to Foucault (1980). We define categorisation as the grouping of individuals into collective entities that come with rights (or the denial thereof). Authoritative institutions, states above all, use formalised categorisations that are artificial (Brubaker, Loveman & Stamatov 2004: 33). Foucault's (1988, 1991) notion of governmentality depends on these categorisations (Burchell, Gordon & Miller 1991). Governmentality does not refer to the government, but to the many heterogeneous and pervasive ways in which the conduct of individuals and groups is shaped and directed. We define governmentality as practices (mentalities, rationalities and techniques) through which subjects are governed, and the techniques and strategies by which a society is rendered governable. The discursive mechanisms act as technologies of governance by which groups are constituted as a problem in need of a policy response (Gray 2006). Discursive mechanisms make issues visible so that they can be governed (Wiebel 2010: 16). States have the authority to decide who is who and to differentiate rights accordingly (Bourdieu 1994). In doing so, they create gender differences. Categorisation is used to legitimise differences within policies and between groups of people. Categorisations are constantly renewed with the intention to exclude or deny rights (mostly) or to include and grant rights (rarely). Categorisation results in debates and a constant redrawing of boundaries; we address these in this volume. Scholars, as a rule, tend to follow the categorisations that policymakers use. In part, this is the result of the source material that is available and organised according to these categorisations. We take a different approach. By looking at different categories of migrants we analyse how migrants move between categories, how and why policy implementers use categories, and how use of these categories differs according to gender.

In this volume all authors use similar research methods; we trace and analyse public and policy debates in policy documents, parliamentary papers, non-governmental organisation (NGO) archives, court cases and newspaper articles. Policymakers fear public unrest, which as a rule means media coverage. Courts and lawyers know that via media coverage and political debates individual cases can become precedents. We place this public sphere – defined by Habermas (1989) as the theatre for deliberation and debating – centre stage in this volume. We trace how concepts were introduced and used, how demarcations were made and justified, how changes occurred over time, and how these aspects differed according to gender. We show that personification was used as a strategy to change labels, and the ways in which precedent cases were drawn on to force decisions in other cases. By personification, we mean that one person – often a woman or a child – is made the figurehead of a campaign that aims to change policy and frequently leads to (re-) categorisation. Personification as a strategy has had different outcomes for migrant men and women, as we will show.

This introductory chapter accomplishes two things. First, it provides an overview of the literature on gender and migration. It also presents an overview of the literature on three themes that have led to extensive public and political debate: refugee migration, family migration and multiculturalism. Our overview on these themes is not extensive, since Schacher, Walaardt, Boyd & Nowak, and Oxford, in their respective chapters, provide overviews of the literature on refugee migration; Raissiguier, Van Walsum, Legêne & Jones, and Oxford do so for 'family'; and Cederberg, Andreassen, and Schrover do so for multiculturalism.

There is now a very large literature on gender and migration, and it is not possible, or useful, to offer a synthesis of it. There are, obviously, many differences between migrant men and women. As a result, there is not *one* unified theory of gender and migration (Donato et al. 2006; Sinke 2006). Differences according to gender have been observed, for instance, regarding the trajectories that migrants follow, the networks they use, the ties that they maintain, their employment niches, and the opportunities and restrictions they encounter. Theories have been developed that aim to explain all these differences. These theories are discussed in the first part of this chapter. We add to this body of theory by focusing on gender, migration and categorisation in the public sphere. This is addressed in the second part of this chapter and developed further in our concluding chapter.

The literature on gender and migration can be grouped into seven clusters.

1   Most studies on gender and migration are about women and migration, rather than comparing migrant men and migrant women. Women's roles and femininity are addressed, but men's roles and masculinity rarely are.
2   The concept of intersectionality was introduced several decades ago to emphasise that categories of power and identity – such as class, gender and ethnicity – intersect. The concept has been advocated, but has rarely been applied empirically.
3   The literature pays ample attention to the feminisation of migration, which is presented as a new phenomenon. This occurs without offering much proof and without making clear what feminisation means.
4   Some authors address differences between migrant men and women when it comes to migration patterns, networks and transnational ties.
5   The literature on gender and migration focuses on the private sphere and family, and pays less attention to the work sphere. When the work sphere is addressed, much of that literature concentrates on domestic servants. Furthermore there is an emphasis on prostitution and related issues.
6   There is a rather large literature on gender, citizenship and residency status.
7   In recent years, there has been a shift in the academic literature toward debates about headscarves and veiling which closely follows shifts in political and public discourse.

We address these seven points at some length below. Thereafter, we introduce the core element of this volume: categorisation, differentiation and defining in relationship to gender and migration. Specifically, we present the three issues that we earlier mentioned as having led to extensive public and political debates in recent decades. The issue of who is a 'refugee' is taken up in the main part of this volume by Schacher, by Walaardt, by Boyd & Nowak, and by Oxford. Raissiguier, Van Walsum, Legêne & Jones, and Oxford examine who is 'family', and Cederberg, Andreassen, and Schrover look at debates on 'difference' within multicultural policy. Here, we suffice to highlight the fact that concepts, discourses, strategies, theories and debates travel across time, between categories of migrants, across gender boundaries and between countries (Said 1982; Bal 2002: 24). We will return to the added theoretical value of this point in the concluding chapter. There we also summarise our findings in an explanatory model.

## State of the art: The literature on gender and migration

### SEX AND GENDER; MASCULINITY AND FEMININITY

Since 'gender' has a variety of meanings, it is useful to clarify the term before proceeding. 'Gender' and 'sex' are frequently used as synonyms, with a preference for 'gender' over 'sex' (Haig 2004). 'Gender' is used when actually 'women' are meant (Lenz et al. 2002; Calavita 2006). This is confusing. It is therefore helpful to return to 1955, when Money first used the term 'gender' – which was at that time a grammatical concept – as a category of analysis because the concept 'sex' was inadequate for the description of social identities (Money 1955). 'Sex' relates to the identification of an individual based on his or her biological endowments and functions. Gender is the constitutive element of social relationships, and particularly relationships of power, based on perceived differences between the sexes (Scott 1986).

Gender is concerned with the ascription of social characteristics such as 'womanly', 'manly', 'feminine' and 'masculine'. It is a normative concept, and relates to behaviour that is expected of men or women. Theories on gender emphasise the need to look at who has the power to define which differences are relevant. Gender roles are internalised and institutionalised (in laws and regulations). Gender refers to the construction, organisation and maintenance of masculinity and femininity. Masculinity and femininity describe the roles that men and women are assigned, or assume, and roles that they are expected to perform, which affect how gender is institutionalised and embedded in laws and regulations. Ideas on this differ per country, and by context, and they often change over time. Migrants might adapt and change roles depending on whether they are with co-ethnics or others, or when visiting their country of origin. Roles are situational and fluid. Although masculinity and femininity, and thus gender are fluid constructions, a static male/female binary is implicitly or explicitly used in social life and entrenched in laws and policies (Scott 1986; Scott 1988, 1998; Calavita 2006). Gender is a constitutive element of social relationships, particularly of relationships of power, based on perceived differences between the sexes (Scott 1986: 1067). Characteristics change over time, are culturally variable, and are not necessarily linked to the sex of an individual (Browne 2007: 1).

Early studies on migration either focused on men or described migrants in genderless terms. Models were based on the (heterosexual) male experience, and similar mechanisms were assumed to influence the migration decisions of both men and women. Women were 'added' later, but without applying gender as an analytical category, and hence, without systematically explaining differences between migrant men and women. Much of the earlier research was descriptive. To compensate for the absence of women in early studies, research on gender and migration originally focused on women rather than on gender (Anthias & Yuval-Davis 1992; Lutz, Phoenix & Yuval-Davis 1995; Hondagneu-Sotelo 2000; Anthias & Lazaridis 2000; Knörr & Meier 2000; Sharpe 200l; Morokvasic, Erel & Shinozaki 2003; Oishi 2005; Donato et al. 2006; Piper 2007). These studies do contribute to our understanding of the gendered nature of migration, but the added value of an approach that compares men to women is widely acknowledged (Lenz et al. 2002; Morokvasic, Erel & Shinozaki 2003).

Rather surprisingly, the idea still prevails that studies about men and migration are not about gender. There was initially little comparison between femininity and masculinity. Recent studies, however, do examine masculinity and migration (Connell 1993; España-Maram 2006; McKay 2007; Hansen 2008; Nobil Ahmad 2008; Ryan & Webster 2008; Nobil Ahmad 2011). Walaardt in this volume looks at how masculinity and migration intersect.

## INTERSECTIONALITY

Gender is still mostly studied in isolation from other constructive elements of power and equality and also in isolation from other defining elements of identity, including social location, opportunity and experience (e.g., class and ethnicity). In reality, these categories intersect. The concept of intersectionality was introduced in the 1960s by the feminist movement to emphasise the interaction between categories of analysis (Davis 2008). The term was new, but the awareness that categories intersected was not. Hollingshead (1952: 685), for instance, observed that 'horizontal strata' 'transect' with 'vertical structures' 'based upon the social values that are attached to occupation, education, place of residence in the community, and associations'. They were 'combined into a complicated status system. The vertically differentiating factors of race, religion, and ethnic origin, when combined with the horizontally differentiating ones of occupation, education, place of residence and so on, produce a social structure that is highly compartmentalized.' Similarly, in her study of women's organisations in New Haven, Minnis (1953) found that women's organisations were born and existed in a complex pattern of interlocking strands of 'cleavage': race, religion, ethnicity and class. Hacker (1951) saw possibilities for 'fruitful analysis' if 'women's roles' were studied in combination with class and race.

Recent literature has emphasised the importance of simultaneously studying the multiple dimensions of durable social inequality (for an overview of the literature see Schrover & Yeo 2010). The concept of intersectionality emphasises that an interaction between power relations works to include or exclude people (Crenshaw 1989; Tilly 1998; McCall 2005; Boris 2005; Phoenix & Pattynama 2006; Sassen 2006; Davis 2008). Changes in power, equality (or inequality), and identity can thus be explained only when categories of exclusion and inclusion are studied together (McCall 2005).

In practice, it has proven difficult to think about two or more categories simultaneously. Rather than thinking from a cumulative perspective, as the theory of intersectionality stipulates, researchers tend to think first in terms of hierarchies, and then move towards answering questions, such as 'in this case does gender trump ethnicity' or vice versa. Furthermore, individuals' identity goes beyond merely their class, gender and ethnicity. People can be defined by their sexual orientation, familial role (mother/father, daughter/son, sister/brother), religion, nationality, ability/disability and age. Including an increasing number of categories, however, makes the concept of intersectionality cumbersome to use (McCall 2005; Boris 2005; Davis 2008). Not all differences are similarly important at all times. Which differences are (deemed to be) important depends on who is asking the question, as well as when and where it is asked. The reply to the question 'who are you?' differs depending on whether a potential employer or a lover is asking it. Identities are fluid, situational and relational. Migrants can switch between identities depending on, for instance, whether they are at that moment oriented towards the country of origin or settlement (Mahler & Pessar 2006). Nevertheless, it is possible to group and analyse identities and power relations by bracketing time, space and personal or institutional setting. Gender, class and ethnicity are generally accepted as key aspects of identity, and dimensions of durable social inequality (Tilly 1998; McCall 2005; Boris 2005; Davis 2008). Yet each of these categories are of more or less importance in different contexts. As the authors in this volume illustrate, it is possible to identify which categories are made important in political and public debates at certain points in time. Oxford's chapter illustrates this for sexuality, and Schacher does so for religion.

## FEMINISATION OF MIGRATION

Migration researchers and policymakers repeatedly claim that a feminisation of migration has taken place (see, e.g., Wihtol de Wenden 1998;

King & Zontini 2000; El-Cherkeh et al. 2004; Kawar 2004; Oso Casas & Garson 2005). Authors use phrases like 'women workers form the majority in movements as diverse as those of Cape Verdians to Italy, Filipinos to the Middle East and Thais to Japan' (Castles & Miller 2003: 7-9, 188). The countries mentioned are not chosen randomly, although the phrase 'as diverse as' might suggest this. These are the countries in which migrant women *do* outnumber men. Examples of precisely the opposite could as easily be given. In 2005 men outnumbered women among immigrants in Saudi Arabia (70% men), Cuba (73% men) and Bangladesh (86% men). Note that there is a difference between the first set of countries, which refers to emigrants from one country, and the second set, which speaks on immigrants (presumably from various countries) to one country.

In some countries, the number of documented migrant women *has* increased. Data are, however, difficult to interpret. In 1978, Singapore, for instance, introduced the Foreign Maids Scheme, which made it possible for women from the Philippines, Indonesia, Thailand, Burma, Sri Lanka, India and Bangladesh to enter Singapore as 'live-in' domestic workers. As a result, that country's migrant domestic worker population grew from 5,000 in 1978 to 150,000 in 2005 (Human Rights Watch 2005: 19). This does not necessarily mean that the actual number of migrant domestic workers increased. The scheme was introduced to counter the exploitation of foreign domestic workers, and registration was part of that effort. The data therefore partly reflect an increase in the number of *documented* domestic workers. Women who migrated to Singapore as domestic workers prior to 1978 were not registered. Women currently make up half of the migrant population in Singapore. There are no data available that allow us to compare the current percentage of migrant women with that of the past.

Frequently it remains unclear what authors mean when they use the term 'feminisation'. The term may indicate that women outnumber men in migration. Or it might suggest that the number of women now equals the number of men, while that was not the case in the past. It is also used to refer to (assumed) changes in migration: an increase in long-distance migration of women (as opposed to the mostly short-distance migration that was common in the past), or an increase in the number of women who are pioneers or single migrants (as opposed to the dependent migrants of the past). Authors generally offer no proof of feminisation, but simply observe that women today form about half of migrants. They then quickly move on to issues such as migrant women's health hazards, the problems of care workers, domestic servants and mail order brides, or prostitution, trafficking and illegality (Wihtol de Wenden 1998; Biemann 2002; Hoerder 2002: 517-519; Sassen 2003: 61; El-Cherkeh et al. 2004: 13; Yamanaka & Piper 2005; Dodson 2008: 152). As such, the feminisation of migration is linked to problems (Ryan 2002; Lepp 2002; Piper 2003; Dannecker 2005; Labadie-Jackson 2008).

Providing a historical overview of trends in international migration is difficult because many countries either lack a system of continuous registration of international migration or, if they have such a system, they do not process and publish the data. Only a handful of countries gather data on the inflow of foreigners (Zlotnik 1998; Jennissen 2004; Oso Casas & Garson 2005). Claims about the feminisation of migration are based on ambiguous data, weak statistical evidence or no statistics at all (Kempadoo & Doezema 1998; Lepp 2002). A lack of data does not prevent some authors from claiming that the feminisation of (labour) migration has become a well-established fact (Piper 2003: 726). Data that are presented are frequently highly selective. Authors write about feminisation of migration in Australia, for instance, but produce data on the percentage of women among the Asian-born Chinese only (and even those do not pass the 60% mark) (Ryan 2002: 96). Authors suggest increases when there are none (Alcalá 2006: 22). Graphs are presented with *y*-axes that start at 45% and terminate at 55% to emphasise increases (Orbeta & Abrigo 2009: 7 and 11; Donato et al. 2011). Data refer to labour migration only, or to the migration from specific countries, such as the Philippines. In fact, the Philippine government encourages the migration of women, and the percentage of migrant women is exceptionally high compared to other countries. Even in the Philippines, however, it did not exceed 60% in the period between 1993 and 2007 (Orbeta & Abrigo 2009: 7 and 11).

The percentages of women and men in migration *did* change during the last century. Fast economic growth in North-Western European countries between 1945 and 1975 led to guest-worker migration. Austria, Belgium, Denmark, Germany, Luxemburg, Sweden and the Netherlands actively recruited guest workers, while Southern European countries supplied labour. About 70% of the recruited guest workers were men. Eastern European countries recruited guest workers from Cuba, Mozambique and Vietnam. About 85% of these were men. Similarly, the US Bracero Program mainly recruited men (Rosas 2011). Earlier, around 1900, Chinese and Asian migrants to the USA and Canada were forbidden to bring wives. As a result, some ethnic groups developed into 'bachelor societies', including, for example, Chinese communities in California and Western Canada. These masculinisations of migration were not labelled as such at the time, or later.

The literature on the feminisation of migration presents the migration of women as new (Schrover 2013). Such novelty both calls for and justifies specific measures or policies aimed at migrant women. Yet, it is not so much the migration of women that has increased. Rather, there has been an increased focus on migrant women. In migration policies this heightened focus is used to justify restrictions and controls. In this volume, we show how juggling numbers and percentages is a favoured strategy in the problematisation of migration.

## MIGRATION PATTERNS, NETWORKS AND TIES

The differences in men's and women's migration patterns have often been explained using the concept of perceived profitability; that is, people move if a cost-benefit analysis points to gains (Stark 1991). This idea is used in the neo-classical, or push-pull, model and the family strategy model (Sjaastad 1962; Stark 1991). These models acknowledge that calculations and consequences of a decision can be different for men and women (Brettell 1986). The assumption is that, as a rule, men can earn more than women, and it is therefore advantageous to let men migrate. When women migrate in equal numbers to men, or in greater numbers, this is explained as a family strategy. It is also interpreted from a remittance perspective. Women may earn less than men but they might send more money home, meaning that it could be more profitable for families left behind if they migrate instead of men (Grasmuck & Pessar 1991; De Jong, Richter & Isarabhakdi 1995; Davis & Winters 2001; Curran 2012). The problem with these models is that it is difficult to assess profitability, because men and women do not have the same (access to) resources, the labour market, power, agency, interests, knowledge and networks. Those factors affect any cost-benefit analysis migrants might make. A decision to migrate is, furthermore, not necessarily a product of collectively made, rational, economic calculations. In some cases it is an individual decision made *outside* of and *against* the wishes of the household or family. Fostered within communities of young men, it is borne out of a lust for adventure, which is associated with locally entrenched masculine ideals (Nobil Ahmad 2008, 2011). Some migrations result in the creation of a culture of migration, in which (temporary) migration is seen as a standard stage of adult life. In Morocco, for instance, there are villages where migration is so common among men that those who do not migrate are ridiculed and equated with children, women or the elderly (De Haas & Van Rooij 2010: 45).

There is consensus among scholars of migration that women migrate through older, more mature networks than men do (Boyd 1989; Tacoli

1995). Migrant men and women have access to different networks, value those resources differently, have different exchange opportunities and develop different exchange relations (Moch & Fuchs 1993). Networks of immigrant men and women are not the same. Furthermore, non-kin networks of immigrant men and women seldom overlap (Ross 1983). Networks of women tend to be less formalised and less visible than those of men. Women are more inclined to form networks than men, because networks reduce their feelings of vulnerability (Accampo 1993). Immigrant men and women use their networks for different purposes. Women make frequent use of weak ties (Moch 2003b). Men move through the family network to find work, while women move through job networks to find a family (Bertaux-Wiame 1979). Women move and live in familial contexts more often than men (Schrover 2003), and they developed more kin-based networks. Men develop more non-kin networks. While this all may be true, the networks of men and women are not that different. Benhabib and Resnik (2009) point out that women's networks consist of dependent children, dependent elderly and the men they are involved with. They fail to point out that this is also largely true for migrant men, whose primary networks are equally formed by children, parents and partners.

Men tend to join or establish organisations that are oriented towards the country of origin, whereas women favour organisations that are aimed at the country of settlement (Jones-Correa 1998). Immigrant men experience status loss due to downward social mobility, which they compensate for by joining organisations where their (former) status is recognised and bolstered. Those immigrant women who did not work prior to their migration, but enter the workforce in the new country, experience a gain in status (ibid.).

The process of cumulative causation has been used to explain the migration of women via older networks (Massey 1990). Cumulative causation is the process whereby the propensity to migrate grows with each additional migrant. Networks and accumulated migrant experience demonstrate benefits, diminish familial resistance and increase security by providing information about and access to labour market opportunities. Networks make migration less risky for individuals by circulating information among potential migrants. As a result, the nature of migration changes over time. The initial high risk, resulting from a lack of information, declines when more family and friends migrate. Denser networks of migrants provide potential migrants with more and increasingly reliable information (DaVanzo 1978; Portes & Bach 1985). Tight knit networks, arising from physical and social proximity, make it easier to enforce trust and support (Portes & Sensenbrenner 1993). This facilitates the choice to migrate, making migration progressively more likely (Massey 1990). Thus, networks are thought to play a crucial role in reducing perceived vulnerability (Granovetter 1973; Grasmuck & Pessar 1991; Moch & Fuch 1993; Curran & Saguy 2001).

This network theory is related to theories on forms of embeddedness or modes of incorporation (Stewart 2005). Migrants may compensate for their lack of embeddedness or status in one sector – for instance, in the labour market – by increasing their embeddedness in another sector, for instance, by maintaining wide networks (Mahler & Pessar 2001; Pessar & Mahler 2003). Differences in how migrant men and women maintain ties with their countries of origin are explained by the fact that doing *kinwork,* or caring for the maintenance of family relations, is commonly characterised as women's work – though not only among migrants. Furthermore, differences in ties relate to status loss. In countries with larger numbers of emigrant women, there are discussions about the children who are left behind and about so-called transnational mothering (Yeates 2004; Mongaya Hoegsholm 2007; Pajnik & Bajt 2012). Rather surprisingly, this debate is not matched by similar debates about men who leave their children behind, or use of the concept of transnational fathering (Kraler et al. 2011).

The literature on migration patterns, networks and ties focuses on the choices and deliberations of migrants, and less on how states (both countries of origin and those of destination) create frameworks in which choices are made. The literature follows political categorisations and hardly discusses issues of choice or deliberation, strategies, networks and ties in the context of refugee migration. According to Boyd & Nowak, Schacher, and Walaardt in this volume, these frameworks are important, as migrants use strategies, networks and ties in different ways.

## THE PRIVATE SPHERE, PROSTITUTION AND RISK

Research on gender and migration places strong emphasis on family and household, suggesting that gender is enclosed in the private sphere. The literature on gender and migration reflects political ideas about the household as private and the labour market as a political domain (Palmary et al. 2012). Migration of women is mostly described from a family perspective (for a recent overview of the literature on family, gender and migration see Kraler et al. 2011), while men's migration is described from a labour perspective (Phizacklea 2003). If the migration of women is discussed in the context of work, it usually relates to domestic work and care (Henshall Momsen 1999; Ehrenreich & Hochschild 2002;

George 2005; Moya 2007 gives good overview of the literature). In the past, domestic work was important to migrant women, and it remains so today. The labour market is strongly segregated by gender and ethnicity (Schrover, Van der Leun & Quispel 2007). Migrant women and men both tend to cluster in a restricted number of sectors, but migrant women cluster in fewer sectors than men. The literature on domestic servants is characterised by discussions about restricted rights, poor labour conditions, abuse and exploitation (Constable 1997; Anderson 2000). Much less attention is given to the opportunities that this work offers to migrant women. The huge concentration of research has given domestic service a greater importance than it has in reality and diverts attention away from migrant women's work in other sectors.

There is an emphasis in the literature on women as trafficking victims (Phizacklea 1998; Soderlund 2005; Gould 2010). This literature shows great continuity since the 1850s, with its focal points on youth, innocence, whiteness, corruption and foreignness (Doezema 2005; Moloney 2012). Trafficking is used as a synonym for prostitution, which, in turn, is equated with abuse. The migration of women is described in terms of hardship and suffering, often dramatised with heart-breaking personal stories (Agustín 2003, 2005; Brennan 2004; Haynes 2004; Soderlund 2005; Outshoorn 2005; Doezema 2005). Recently, scholars have taken a critical stance towards this profusion of scholarship about trafficking, which is part of what Agustín (2007) calls 'a rescue industry'. Authors have pointed out that claims about the number of trafficked women, are based on poor and inadequate research, that all migration of women is regarded as trafficking, and that tragic stories are used to mobilise support for control and restrictions on the mobility of women (Fehér 2000; Kapur 2005; Brennan 2008; Wooditch, DuPont-Morales & Hummer 2009; Deane 2010; Weitzer 2010; Oude Breuil et al. 2011; Brysk 2011; Blanchette & Da Silva 2012). Previous scholars have emphasised that sex-trafficking discourse, involving innocent victims, violated borders and criminality, is part of problematising migration and is used to justify restrictive migration policies (Berman 2003), but that has not led to changes in the literature.

In part, the emphasis on victimhood of migrant women can be explained by a policy-driven, sameness-difference dilemma. Basically this conundrum involves the recognition that migrant women may be disadvantaged in comparison to migrant men (e.g., in laws or their application), but attempts to address inequalities – by politicians, lawyers and pressure groups – tend to backfire (Oxford 2005; Calavita 2006; see also Schrover, Cederberg, and Andreassen in this volume). It is difficult to escape from a sexualised-victimised image once it has been established (MacLeod & Saraga 1988; Connell 1997; Utas 2005). The (often unintended) result is that differences between men and women are accentuated, and the victimhood of women is emphasised. Sexualisation and victimisation have been used to legitimise government policies or the strategies of organisations (including migrant organisations and churches) (Connell 1990). Schrover, Cederberg, and Andreassen address this point in this volume.

Within this victimhood discourse, women are presented as vulnerable. Vulnerability is the subject of an entire field of study, which developed several decades ago, initially to explain how and why people move in and out of poverty (Beck 1992; Moser 1998; Alwang, Siegel & Jørgensen 2001; Bustamante 2002; Hogan & Marandola 2005). Later, ideas from the field of vulnerability studies were applied to migration research (Waddington & Sabates-Wheeler 2003). Vulnerability is – of course – a staple element in the construction of (Western) femininity, as is the construction of women as mothers and wives, while men are not constructed primarily as vulnerable, or as fathers and husbands. Raissiguier and Van Walsum, Legêne & Jones address this point in this volume.

In the victimhood discourse, women are portrayed as victims and men as perpetrators (Beck 1992; Moser 1998; Alwang, Siegel & Jørgensen 2001; Hogan & Marandola 2005; Stewart 2005). Since the 1980s, several authors have criticised this perspective because it works to disempower women and denies them agency (MacLeod & Saraga 1988; Connell 1997; Utas 2005). Recent authors have moved beyond the critique and point to the functionality of the continued use of that discourse. Some people base their identities on victimhood or injury (Brown 1995; Doezema 2001). That, in turn, results in a politics that seeks protection from the state, rather than power and freedom, and ultimately in a politics that reaffirms structures of domination. Other people profit from ascribing a victimhood identity. For instance, in the 1970s white middle-class Western women justified their own claims to equality by constructing 'third-world women' as helpless subjects of 'barbaric traditionalism'. The 'other' was seen as equal in Christian rhetoric, but not in reality (Doezema 2001). Schrover, Cederberg, and Andreassen in this volume describe how this has affected policies. If we look at who profits from a certain discourse and in what ways – as we do in this volume – we can understand how, why and by whom differences between migrant men and women were created, maintained and entrenched in laws and regulations. This volume discusses why policymakers, as well as certain migrants and immigrant organisations, had an interest in making differences. Many Western feminists eagerly bought into the construction of 'third-world women' as 'powerless', 'exploited' and 'sexually harassed' (Mohanty 1988). 'Third-world women' were, as a category, automatically and necessarily defined as religious, as well as oriented toward the family and the domestic sphere. Their victimisation played a role in the construction of a counter identity of 'Western' women, who were everything that 'third-world women' were not (Doezema 2001). Schrover, Boyd & Nowak, and Andreassen build on this idea in this volume.

Victimisation can be used as a successful strategy; it is possible to claim rights for women by presenting them as victims (see Schacher in this volume). The price of this success, however, is that migrant women come to be seen as vulnerable and in need of protection. The 'successful' use of the victimhood discourse explains a change in migration and integration policy that has taken place in the past decades (Roggeband & Verloo 2007). In the 1970s, integration policy stressed the rights of migrants as distinct from the rest of the people in the receiving society. In the 1990s, the diversity framework was replaced by a vulnerability framework, which focused on migrant women, as described by Schrover, Andreassen, and Cederberg in this volume.

## CITIZENSHIP AND RESIDENCY

There is a large literature about gender, citizenship and residency (see, e.g., Soysal 1994; Ackers 1996; Bredbenner 1998; Kofman et al. 2000; Sinha 2006; Lister et al. 2007; Pawley 2008; Benhabib & Resnik 2009; Rygiel 2011). There are two systems for delegating citizenship: via birth to a citizen (*jus sanguinis*), as in the case of Germany, for example, or via birth on national soil (*jus soli*), as, for instance, in the USA. While these definitions seem straightforward, they are not. Current political and public discourse equates citizenship with integration, civil society and active societal participation. The conflation of immigrant integration with citizenship has caused a shift from the state's control over its national borders to control of the borders of society (Schinkel 2008). This conflation of controlling borders with controlling society results from the definition of citizenship at two levels: the juridical level and the discursive level (membership of the nation-state and membership of society). People with juridical citizenship can be denied discursive citizenship. At the juridical (or formal) level, citizens have rights that non-citizens do not share (e.g., voting rights) (Marshall 1950). At the juridical level, a sharp distinction is made between citizens and non-citizens. Discursive (or moral) citizenship relates to being (seen as) part of a community or society and being a virtuous citizen (Kennedy 2005). In recent decades, the sovereignty of nation-states has eroded because of globalisation and the creation of larger political units such as the European Union. Yet, this has not reduced the discursive or moral importance attached to citizenship (Bader 1999). Discursive citizenship is a vague and flexible notion (Schinkel 2008). The distinction between internal and external borders can be sharp at the discursive level, but it is not static and it changes continuously over time.

In many countries, women automatically experienced a change in their nationality when they married men with a different nationality than their own (though this was not true for men) (Boris 2005; De Hart 2006). Many countries introduced so-called 'marriage rules' and 'derivative citizenship' in around 1900, consolidating earlier practices. Derivative citizenship is based on a gendered conception of belonging. Women marrying men outside of their community or nationality are often described in sexually disapproving terms, even if they are in a stable monogamous relationship. That judgement implies that by crossing one boundary – that of ethnicity – they also cross a boundary of moral acceptability (Stoler 1992, 1995; Breger & Hill 1998).

When countries changed rules regarding derivative citizenship (Studer 2001; De Hart 2006; Volpp 2006) discussions moved to dependent residency (Sterett 1997; Côté, Kérisit & Côté 2001). In the former, women derived citizenship from their husbands, while in the latter women derived the right to remain in a country through their husbands (although in theory husbands could also derive the right to remain through their wives). Discussions on dependent residency arose when possibilities for labour migration were reduced (Schrover et al. 2008; Schrover & Yeo 2010). Debates about derived citizenship were interwoven with those about multiculturalism as Cederberg, Andreassen, and Schrover show in this volume.

## Veiling

In recent years there has been an increase in the number of publications on headscarves and veils (with many publications coming out of the large VEIL project on values, equality and differences in liberal democracies (Molokotos Liederman 2000; McGoldrick 2006; Brems 2006; Winter 2008; Berghahn & Rostock 2009; Lettinga 2011; Rosenberger & Sauer 2012). The shift in the academic literature parallels changes in public and political debates about headscarves and veils, as reflected in the so-called 'burqa bans' introduced by countries in which very few women actually wear face-covering veils (Herrera & Moors 2003; Joppke 2007; Schrover in this volume). Current political arguments against veiling are remarkably similar to those used by British and French colonial authorities in their attempts to legitimise their colonial rule (Fanon 1965; Abu-Lughod 2002). Modernising, liberating and emancipating Islamic women, by forcing them to unveil, or allowing them to do so, was a key aspect of the colonisers' claim of moral superiority. In a similar fashion, the US 'war against terror' in Afghanistan was justified by emphasising the right of women to discard their burqas (Stabile & Kumar 2005; Van Walsum & Spijkerboer 2007; Bush 2010). The British and French unveiling campaigns were comparable to the 1927 Soviet *Hujum*, a campaign in Soviet Central Asia in which mass unveiling was meant to lead to the social and intellectual liberation of women (Kamp 2008). That campaign aimed to enforce and legitimise Soviet rule over Uzbekistan.

Rather surprisingly, current debates in Turkey run counter to debates in Western Europe. The Turkish government first outlawed the wearing of headscarves for women working in the public sector (as teachers, lawyers and politicians) in 1924, when Atatürk introduced the secular Turkish state (Gökariksel & Mitchell 2005). From the 1980s onwards, this ban increasingly led to debates. In Turkey some women harbour hopes that future membership in the EU might give Turkish women the right to wear headscarves if they wish. This intersects with the paradoxical situation in which Western feminists occasionally find themselves. While they generally favour women's choices, they find it very hard to view the wearing of headscarves or other veiling as a choice, despite what is said by the women who make this choice. They find themselves being accused of colonialist paternalism. Furthermore Western feminists find themselves allied with Western populist, right-wing politicians, who in the Western context, do not generally support women's rights (Winter 2006).

The move towards placing headscarves and veils at the centre of political debates is part of a shift towards minority integration policies. Yet, such policies have been labelled a failure in several European countries, which have moved on to issues of religion rather than class position, discrimination or socio-economic factors. This renders integration a personal choice and removes responsibly from authorities (Roggeband & Verloo 2007; see also Cederberg, Andreassen, and Schrover in this volume).

* * *

Overall the large literature on gender and migration reflects certain biases with great consistency. Countering some of those unbalances is long overdue. In this volume, we move away from attempts to take stock of differences between migrant men and migrant women, and from describing migrants or focusing on the private sphere. We look instead at political and public debates about categorisation, differentiation, and how and why boundaries have been drawn and redrawn. As pointed out earlier, our exploration focuses on three primary fields in which this boundary drawing has led to extensive debates: who is a 'refugee' (Schacher, Walaardt, Boyd & Nowak, and Oxford), who is 'family' (Raissiguier, Van Walsum, Legêne & Jones, and also partly in Oxford), and who has the right to be different according to multicultural policy (Cederberg, Andreassen, and Schrover). The sections that follow present a state of the art on these points.

## State of the art and contributions to the literature: Defining the true refugee

The 1951 Convention Relating to the Status of Refugees built on earlier, ad hoc policies, including those related to Jewish refugees in the 1930s and Armenian refugees in 1917. Policies regarding Armenians, described by Schacher in this volume, should be viewed in the context of more general developments. Since the 1880s, mobility from Europe has been affected by US restrictions on migration. US authorities wanted to prevent paupers and criminals from arriving by introducing controls and barriers at the borders, as well as in the countries of departure (Zolberg 2006). These developments are important for understanding how people fleeing the Armenian genocide from 1917 onwards, were received in the USA and elsewhere, as Schacher describes. Thirty years prior to the 1951 Refugee Convention, policies were not that different, nor were the responses to refugee migration, as Schacher illustrates. Some Armenian refugees were women travelling alone. As in the case of other migrant women travelling alone, this immediately raised suspicions regarding their involvement in prostitution and other immoral behaviour. Christian relief organisations in Turkey and the USA were well aware of this potential stigma and tried to steer clear of cases that might disadvantage the whole group of refugees.

Schacher contributes to the literature by emphasising four arguments, each of which recurred in later periods (as described by Walaardt, Boyd & Nowak, and Oxford in this volume). First, there was a strong fear among decision makers about setting precedents. People were allowed to enter if their case could be presented as an exceptional one. Armenian refugees were characterised as special, and different from the many other people adrift in the same period. Secondly, long before the 1951 definition of a refugee came to be accepted, there was a clear idea about who was an 'honest refugee'. Decision makers involved in the Armenian case were as suspicious as later decision makers. They feared they would be deceived by 'non-deserving refugees', who told fabricated stories, masterminded by their (us-based) advocates. Those fears were very similar to suspicions in later periods. Thirdly, policies phrased in gender-neutral terms, such as a literacy test, had divergent consequences for men and women. Women fleeing the Armenian genocide were, to a large extent, illiterate and were disadvantaged by the test. A vague reference in the rulings to religious persecution as the grounds for exemption dampened the gender-specific effects in practice. It further created differences between men and women in how policies were applied: religion surfaced more frequently in women's cases. Here, there are also clear similarities to later decades: bending the rules in cases involving women proved easier than changing the rules (Schrover 2009b). In the fourth place, civil servants and others were afraid of publicity. Deporting women – especially in the company of their children – led to negative publicity, even in this period when communication was slow. Negative publicity could be expected if Christian women were deported to a Muslim country, where, according to newspaper reports, Christians were being systematically discriminated against, killed and deported. Women were at risk of being kidnapped and raped, as well as being forced to marry a Muslim and convert to Islam. Anti-Islam rhetoric, deployed in later decades, was already in full force by 1917, and the stereotypes were the same as those used in pervasive 1990s flight and recue stories (De Hart 2001).

After the Second World War, feelings of guilt and a sense of failure towards Jewish refugees, combined with the geopolitical tensions of the Cold War, led to creation of an international refugee policy. This point has been addressed extensively in the large literature on refugees and asylum seekers (see, amongst others, Grahl-Madsen 1966, 1982-1983a, 1982-1983b, 1983; Holborn 1975; Takkenberg & Tahbaz 1989; Salomon 1991; Loescher 1993; Carruthers 2005). At the time there were still many displaced persons living in camps in Europe. At the Yalta Conference of 1945 it was agreed that displaced persons were to be repatriated to their countries of origin, but Western states refused to repatriate some of those who came from Eastern Europe during or after the war. The continued arrival of Eastern Europeans in the West served as a refutation of communist governments and their policies.

The 1951 Refugee Convention defined a refugee as follows:

any person who, owing to well-founded fear of being persecuted for reasons of race, religion, nationality, membership in a particular social group, or political opinion, exists outside the country of his nationality and is unable or, owing to such fear, is unwilling to return to that country; or who, not having a nationality and being outside the country of his former habitual residence as a result of such events, is unable or, owing to such fear, is unwilling to return to it (art. 1a).

The Convention's drafters conceived of flight motives as political, public and collective, rather than as personal and private.

From the 1950s to the 1970s, providing asylum to the victims of one's enemies demonstrated the antagonists' immoral value system, as Zolberg (2006: 18) emphasised. Over the past 50 years, the number of antagonists, and evils, has increased, changed and blurred. Politically, the benefits of a lenient refugee policy have become less obvious. That has reduced the willingness to deal with the refugee problem at an international level and resulted in a restrictive discourse. While asylum cases are no longer used to prove that capitalism trumps communism, they now highlight the failure of the newly decolonised, Islamic or third-world countries to protect their citizens. They are used to contrast a superior (enlightened) West against a failing Rest.

Walaardt, in this volume, adds to the literature by describing the arrival in the 1970s in the Netherlands of what he calls the 'New Refugees'. They sought asylum after Cold War rhetoric started to wane. They came from NATO countries (Portugal and the USA) and were fleeing right-wing, rather than left-wing regimes. The arrival of the New Refugees might have resulted in changes in policy, as they came from different countries than the earlier post-war refugees, and they had different claims and different lobby groups. Remarkably, however, policies hardly changed. Cold War refugees had been treated with suspicion and authorities feared setting precedents and the arrival of numerous others (as had earlier been the case for Armenian refugees). New Refugees encountered the same fears and restrictions. Men fleeing communism and those fleeing from military service in the colonial wars were similarly portrayed. Both groups were cast as masculine actors who had courageously opposed – in the eyes of many Dutch – detestable regimes. Both were cast in the image of protest heroes. Such heroic images of male refugees dominated the asylum discourse. Only decades later, with the migration of new groups of New Refugees, would public attention shift away from men and the hero-refugee and toward women and the victim-refugee.

Differences between men and women refugees or asylum seekers have been addressed in the literature. Under certain conditions, women are much less likely than men to be granted refugee status (cf. Spijkerboer 2000; Calavita 2006). Currently, discussions do not centre on whether the grounds *are* the same, but on whether they *should* be, and whether gender-related violence should be grounds for asylum. Gender or gender-related harm was absent from the 1951 definition as a category of persecution. Gender-related violence is understood in current discussions as something that affects women alone. If reference is made to men, it is to homosexuals (Oxford 2005). It is much more common for women than for men to be the victims of sexual violence. Those who have been victims of what is called accidental or arbitrary rape (which is seen as an unfortunate, but common, part of regular warfare) are not regarded as persecuted. Women who were raped in order to retrieve information about their families (such as the whereabouts of husbands or sons) were not granted asylum in the past. In recent years, there has been a change in asylum policies and laws. In the usa, immigrant women can gain asylum by proving they have been persecuted on account of female circumcision, honour killings, domestic violence, coercive family planning, forced marriages or repressive social norms. This is also true for some European countries, such as Germany. Asylum seekers in the usa stand a better chance of having their request approved if they mention female circumcisions at the hearings rather than explaining their role in a resistance movement. Stories about resistance are almost never acknowledged as grounds for women's asylum (while they are for men), whereas the mentioning of female circumcision is (Oxford 2005).

The drafters of the 1951 Convention did not conceptualise rape, female circumcision, domestic violence, enforced family policies, or compulsory veiling in their definition of rights. In fact, they did not conceive of women applying for refugee status based on gender issues at all. In recent decades, however, women have been granted refugee status for each of those reasons (Spijkerboer 2000; Oxford 2005; Calavita 2006). The Convention tried to target states that failed to protect, or denied protection to, a minority of their citizens. Today, refugees or asylum seekers arrive from states – including Liberia, Angola, Democratic Republic of the Congo, Somalia and Sierra Leone – where the government does not have the power to protect citizens. They come from African countries where states do not prevent their populations from leaving, as was earlier the case with Eastern European countries. Or they come from countries such as Afghanistan, where the state never extended civil rights to half of its citizens, simply because they are women.

Women took centre stage in human rights debates and in asylum cases for a few years. This volume adds to the literature by looking specifically at these debates. However, as Boyd & Nowak discuss in this volume, this focus on women was not long-lived, nor did it apply to all refugee groups in equal proportions. Boyd & Nowak describe the Canadian media's attitudes toward Mexican refugees. Canadians find it difficult to comprehend that a democratic country such as Mexico, with which Canada maintains economic and political ties, would produce refugees. Similarly, European states did not define Portuguese and US citizens as refugees, as Walaardt discusses. Women from Islamic countries more fully embody the victim-refugee image than do Mexican Catholic women subject to domestic violence. Mexico is not defined as a failed state. Yet, a state may provide protection to some of its citizens, but not to all of them. It is precisely this type of failure that shaped the 1951 Refugee Convention. In Canada there is little awareness that the situation for migrant men and women from Mexico might differ, as Boyd & Nowak describe. The current media refugee script focuses on refugee management and reduction, rather than on refugee protection and welcome. The economic costs of accepting what is portrayed as increasing numbers of Mexican refugees or asylum seekers have taken centre stage in public discussions, pushing aside any discussions of political benefits. With potential benefits, the Canadian image of the 'true' refugee also shifted.

Oxford, in this volume, adds to the literature by focusing on homosexual and transgender refugees. Homosexuals have claimed refugee status in the USA, based on their membership in a persecuted social group, using arguments similar to those used by battered women seeking refuge. Fourteen countries have granted homosexuals political asylum as members of 'a particular social group', a key phrase from the 1951 Convention (Austria, Australia, Belgium, Canada, Denmark, Finland, Germany, Ireland, the Netherlands, New Zealand, Norway, Sweden, the UK and the USA). The United Nations High Commissioner for Refugees has decreed that its policy is to consider those homosexuals who are persecuted for their sexual orientation as refugees. For at least a decade, gay advocacy groups have made immigration one of the fronts on which they fight for their agenda. They adopted the rhetoric of the civil rights movement (compare McKeown 2008, who shows how the anti-slavery discourse – as an early form of human rights discourse – played a major role in shaping exclusionary US labour migration policies in the 19th century). As observed earlier, people travel between countries, and migrants move between categories, but concepts and discourses travel as well (Forsdick 2001). Strategies that proved to be successful in one context, were copied, adapted and applied in other contexts. We see similarities between social movements. Refugee war resisters of the 1970s were important to the anti-Vietnam or anti-'colonial' war movement. Abused migrant women were important to the women's liberation movement in the 1980s (Schrover 2009). Gay asylum seekers were important to the LGBT (lesbian, gay, bisexual and transgendered) movement of the 1990s, as Oxford shows in this volume. Over time campaigns became increasingly personalised: personal stories and gruelling details were drawn on to strengthen a case. Advocacy groups instructed asylum claimants so that they could make a successful appeal, as they had done with Armenians in 1917.

In 2009, some officials in the UK argued that homosexual asylum seekers might be able to live safely in their country of origin as long as they were 'discreet' about their sexual identities. That perspective shared similarities with the highly controversial US military 'Don't Ask, Don't Tell' policy. The argument was clearly inspired by fears of large numbers of homosexuals seeking refuge in Western countries. If they were discreet, officials argued, there would be no well-founded fear of persecution. In a 2009 court case this became known as the 'Anne Frank' principle. Requiring discretion from homosexuals would be the same as claiming that Anne Frank would have been safe as long as she remained in her annex (Gower 2010). According to Walaardt, in this volume, references to the Second World War and the Holocaust are strong arguments in refugee claims. In July 2010, a court overturned the argument that homosexuals would be safe if they remained discreet. Asylum was granted to homosexuals under the Refugee Convention in order to prevent an individual from suffering persecution. Persecution was understood to mean treatment resulting in death, torture or imprisonment, sponsored or condoned by the state. Simple discriminatory treatment on the grounds of sexual orientation, or the risk of family or societal disapproval, did not amount to persecution, a court ruled.

As Oxford highlights in this volume, differences at both ends of the scale are clear, but most cases fall into a grey, middle ground. Migrants must convince immigration officials that they either face persecution or fear persecution based on their sexual or gender identity. Immigrants are required to prove that they are part of the social group of homosexuals. It is not necessary that applicants were open about their sexuality or experienced persecution in their countries of origin, but it is essential that applicants clearly describe their homosexual identity, and particularly their well-founded fear of persecution because of that identity. Homosexuality is constructed very differently in various countries. Asylum seekers may have had (occasional) same-sex partners, but need not necessarily identify as homosexuals, or be identified by others as such. However, acknowledging one's sexual identity is a necessary component of gaining asylum.

Schacher, Walaardt, Boyd & Nowak, and Oxford, in this volume, offer a new perspective on this topic through their analysis of advocates' organising and executing campaigns on behalf of refugees and asylum seekers, and the consequences of those campaigns. Overall, asylum regimes place a strong emphasis on exceptionalism. As detailed above, all countries fear establishing precedents. As a result, refugee claims are more successful when presented as exceptions, and when campaigns are highly personalised. Furthermore, there has been a strong tendency towards victimisation narratives. Victimisation has been a successful strategy for claiming rights. The price of this success, however, is that migrants came to be seen as vulnerable and in need of protection by the state. Their victimisation played a role in the construction of a counter identity of the 'Western' advocates, who formed the support groups. It explains and shapes the link with the rights movements (women's rights, gay rights). This othering worked as a disadvantage in the long term.

## State of the art and contributions to the literature: Defining family

When options for labour migration diminished in Western countries, beginning in the 1970s, family migration became more important. The shift to more restrictive labour migration regimes eventually cumulated in debates about what constitutes a family and who are family members. Family migration is usually discussed in relation to labour migration. This is surprising since it is also relevant for other categories of migrants, such as refugees and asylum seekers. Family discourse was rooted in human rights discourse, like in the case of refugees. The debates were furthermore influenced by decolonisation and adoptive practices under colonialism. In the first half of the 20th century, in many Asian colonies domestic and international adoptions were a widespread but mostly informal practice. The motives of the mothers of Asian adoptees were not always altruistic. In the 1930s and again the 1950s there were intense debates (mostly within the context of the League of Nations or United Nations) about the extent to which adopting mothers exploited their adopted children, selling them into slavery and prostitution. Colonial authorities fought these practices, legitimising their authority on the basis of these efforts (Pedersen 2001).

In the 1960s, babies from Korea were adopted in the USA, and shortly after, also in Europe. The discourse on these adoptions intertwined familial love, child rescuing, anti-communism and US paternalist responsibility. Adoptions became part of the justification for US intervention in the region. Adopting Korean babies became the US domestic equivalent of fighting communism in Asia. Korea profited financially from what became a well-organised adoption industry. Between 1953 and 2004, 156,000 to 200,000 international adoptions took place in Korea. Some 100,000 children went to the USA and about 5,000 to Canada, Australia and New Zealand. Europeans adopted almost 50,000 Korean children (Kim & Carroll 1975; Sarri, Baik & Bombyk 1998; Oh 2005; Kim 2009; Hübinette & Arvanitakis 2012). This migration was unprecedented in nature and scale. Soon other Asian countries started to 'export' children. Currently China is the largest supplier of children for adoption. Between 1991 and 2007, American parents adopted almost 60,000 Chinese children, 95% of them girls (Cheng 2007). In the literature on these adoptions, there are no references the Chinese adoption cases of the 1930s.

The current adoption practices are widely accepted. This contrasts starkly with the distrust that migrant families encounter in Europe when they try to bring adopted children or foster children to their new country of residence. Both literatures – that on adoption and that on family migration (for more references, see Kraler et al. 2011; see also Van Walsum, Jones & Legêne in this volume) – are large, but they are seldom combined. Migrant families are regarded with suspicion, and have to prove that children are biologically theirs. The issue is complicated by the fact that more than 20, mostly Muslim countries in Asia and Africa (including Algeria, Egypt, Mauritania, Morocco, Afghanistan, Bahrain, Iran, Iraq, Jordan, Kuwait, Oman, Pakistan, Qatar, Saudi Arabia, United Arab Emirates and Yemen) do not recognise the institution of adoption (Indonesia, Tunisia and Turkey do recognise it) (United Nations 2009). Migrants from countries in which adoption has not been formalised cannot bring as family members those children who have been placed in their care.

Within the framework of migration, the family is usually defined as a nuclear family. In the early days of European guest-worker migration, there was some debate about the right of men to bring more than one wife, although very few migrant men were actually involved in polygamous marriages (Bonjour 2010). Members of the extended family (grandparents for instance) were denied the right to migrate within the framework of family reunification, thereby depriving many families of existing care arrangements (Grillo 2008). Migrant families also found that leaving their biological children behind in the care of others for long periods of time led to debates about so-called 'broken bonds'. In some cases the idea that ties had ceased to exist after years of being apart resulted in the loss of the rights for children to join their families (Benhabib & Resnik 2009: 235; Schrover 2009b).

In the 1980s and 1990s, several Strasbourg international court cases revolved around the right to family life (Schrover 2009b). Article 8 of the Convention for the Protection of Human Rights and Fundamental Freedoms (adopted by the Council of Europe in 1950) states that children have the right to grow up with their families. What was disputed in these court cases was the right of children to join their families; the parents, it was suggested, had the choice of leaving in order to reunite with their children.

Closely related to these debates were cases in which children were brought to the country of origin of one parent (mostly the father), against the wishes of the other parent (mostly the mother). Betty Mahmoody's book, on which the 1991 film 'Not Without My Daughter' was based, is emblematic of both the type of stories and the media coverage. Mahmoody's book, and several others like hers, presented Western women who had married non-Western men as victims, but also as survivors who stood up for themselves and their children against alien (mostly Islamic) cultures of oppression (De Hart 2001). The parenthood rights of women, especially if they were Western, trumped those of men, especially if non-Western.

Such situations, as discussed by the authors mentioned above, suggest that the West tried and succeeded in imposing on others its dominant ideas about family, via the regulation of family migration. This is only partly true. Van Walsum, Jones & Legêne in this volume show that ideas developed in a colonial setting travelled back to the former mother country. In the Dutch colony of Suriname, Dutch authorities allowed plurality in family formation and marriage. This arose in part from the period of slavery, when slaves were not allowed to marry, where a child born from an enslaved woman was legally classified as a slave (regardless of its paternity), and enslaved parents could not recognise a child as theirs. It was also in part the result of later migrations of indentured labourers from Asia, who were encouraged to hold to their own rules regarding marriage and family formation. The ruling white and Creole elite upheld the 'nuclear' family (husband-wife-children) model, with spouses who married in accordance with civil law. Groups that attained or aspired to middle-class status appropri-

ated this model. Other family systems were allowed to exist alongside
the nuclear model. Those included Hindu and Islam marriage models,
the dual marriage structure and the extended family. In some of these
family systems, the husband-wife-children model was absent. In the
Creole working-class matrifocal family, for example, mother-child and
sibling relationships formed the durable and dependable network. They
could function as the locus for *matiwerk* relationships: socio-economic
support networks between women, in which 'same-sex' relations could
occur. Before Suriname's 1975 independence, 'parallel' family systems
had been enacted in law, for example, in the case of marriage in accordance with Hinduism or Islam. Laws recognised the authority of women
over their biological children (which is of particular importance for
matrifocal families), along with the rights of foster children and concubinage.

In debates leading to Suriname's independence, Dutch authorities
sought to foster a smooth transition to independence (unlike the transition of the Dutch East Indies to independent Indonesia, which was
far from smooth). This, along with the leniency that Dutch authorities
had demonstrated towards mixing and plurality in the colonial context,
led to the inclusion of a remarkable article in the final text of the treaty
between Suriname and the Netherlands. That treaty addressed the
admission of their respective citizens, effective on 25 November 1975.
Article 5 allowed for admission of the person with whom a citizen of
one of the State Parties, legally resident on the territory of the other, 'has
a long lasting and exclusive personal relationship'. This rule also applied
to same-sex relationships. It was the first statutory ruling in Dutch law
in which persons involved in non-marital relationships were granted
the same rights as married couples, and it allowed for the migration of
people involved in same-sex relations. According to Van Walsum, Jones
& Legêne, in contrast with the assumptions of earlier studies, definitions of family can travel both ways in the migration process. This is
surprising, since in the colonial context marriages, especially when they
were regarded as mixed – were looked upon with suspicion, or met with
disapproval. Rather paradoxically, the disapproval continued, despite
the redefinition of family, as Van Walsum, Jones & Legêne show.

Earlier literature has emphasised that family migration is frequently
suspected as being a cover for labour migration, especially when the
migrating partner is a non-Western man (Grillo 2010). In the UK, official policy discriminated mainly against Asian men between the late
1960s and 1985, when the European Court terminated it. Asian men
were suspected of seeking entrance to the UK through marriages of convenience. The Home Office assumed that men were coming for work

and were abusing the arranged marriage system (Lutz 1997b; Kofman 1999). Current discussions equate marriage migration with arranged and forced marriages. Governments have increasingly introduced age and income bars to restrict marital migration. Through income requirements, family migration is collapsed into economic migration, with an emphasis on fraud and misuse, moving it away from debates about (human) rights.

Migrating men are often suspected of having economic motives for marriage, rather than migrating for love. That is especially the case when they come from poor countries, are low skilled and marry non-migrant women. Thus, ethnicity, class and gender intersect. Denmark, the Netherlands and Germany screen prospective marriages with non-EU spouses in an attempt to discover fictitious marriages, using criteria that have been disputed in court (De Hart 2006; Kontos, Haferburg & Sacaliuc 2006). Authorities examine age differences between partners and their ability to communicate and try to establish how well partners know each other. Denmark, Germany, Austria, France, the Netherlands and the UK have introduced age restrictions (with minimum ages of 18 to 24), housing and income requirements, and tests to be taken before migration. Yet, migrants who are well educated, highly skilled and wealthy can circumvent the increasingly complicated restrictions on family migration.

Recently, the concept of 'love exiles' has appeared in debates. That term refers to people who migrate to a country where they can marry, often because they are prevented from marriage in their country of residence (Wieringa 2011). This typically applies to marriages between same-sex partners. Differences in laws between neighbouring countries lead to another type of love exiles as well. Migrants, who cannot marry in the Netherlands, move to Belgium, take up temporary residence, marry and after a while move back to the Netherlands. This is called the Belgium route. Similarly there is Irish route, which some UK migrants use, and a so-called Swedish model, which is used by migrants in Denmark. In recent discussions of this type of migration the emphasis has shifted from understanding family migration as a spin-off of labour migration, to portraying family migration in terms of exile, adopting the language of refugee migration.[1] The Love Exile Foundation in the USA writes, 'Love Exiles is giving attention to the hidden group of refugees because of lawlessness at home elsewhere "in exile" life'.[2] And:

> US immigration law effectively forces the couple to leave the country, to become 'love exiles' and seek refuge abroad. ... We can choose to leave the US and seek refuge elsewhere. Sadly, many of us have done

this, taking our property and skills to benefit the countries where our families are recognized. We are the Love Exiles.[3]

By using refugee rhetoric, rather than terms associated with labour migration, the organisations and advocates seek to reinforce their plea.

Raissiguier, in this volume, adds to this literature by examining how family life became contested in France. She illustrates that the family was defined within racialised paradigms. French national culture, not race, was central to debates about French identity. For decades the dominant notion was that being French was something that could be learned. French peasants had learned to become French in the past, and immigrants could do so as well. This 'open' national identity did not mean that subcultures were respected, or accepted, as was the case within a multicultural model (Beriss 2000). Recent changes are striking because for decades France has prided itself on its 'French model' of socialising and assimilating via schools, the military, employment and workers' unions. However, as Raissiguier points out, the old French model had elements of exclusion, based on ethnicity and gender, within its relatively generous and liberal understanding of nation and nationality. These exclusionary elements were de-emphasised when 'the French model' was contrasted with the German one and found 'generous' in comparison.

Current discussions in France about who is allowed to enter and stay are influenced not only by ideas of belonging, but also by changing possibilities in exercising control (compare to Schrover 2008). Biomedical techniques have become important tools for regulating migration. Age determination and other technical procedures offer an aura of objectiveness, and simultaneously call into question the trustworthiness of migrants and the governments in their countries of origin, as well as ideas about, for example, adoption. In the case of contesting family ties, discussions are influenced by the new possibilities of genetic testing. The 2007 French immigration law introduced DNA testing, and thus reinscribes 'blood' and 'bloodlines', into discussions of national belonging. Genetic tests target African immigrants, who are required to prove that kin are related by blood. Immigrants in France are expected to prove that they are the biological parents of the children they seek to bring into the country. That policy denies the fact that 3% to 10% of children – migrant and non-migrant alike – are not the biological offspring of one or both of their parents (as a result of adoption, in vitro fertilisation or adultery). The law that established the DNA testing policy was combined with a discursive denationalisation of migrants and their children who were, according to some, only 'French by law', according to Raissiguier. Because of these changes, a social unit that is essentially private – family – has become very public and a subject of state concern.

In France, 'family' has, for migrants, been re-labelled and narrowed down to an exclusively biological definition. That redefinition was made possible partly by DNA testing. Recently, in Norway technical possibility and distrust have led to DNA testing of spouses who are believed actually to be siblings (UDI 2012). Suspicion leads to testing, and testing to more suspicion.

The authors in this volume make a vital contribution to the literature by showing how, when and why 'family' has been redefined. The concept is not as static as policymakers would like it to be or as previous authors have believed it to be. Postcolonial trauma led to a surprising widening of the concept of family, as Van Walsum, Jones & Legêne describe, and new techniques for narrowing it, as Raissiguier points out, while in all cases distinctions are made according to class, gender, ethnicity, religion and skill level.

## State of the art and contributions to the literature: Defining difference

Beginning in the 1960s, in numerous countries, including the UK, Sweden, Germany, Australia, the Netherlands, the USA and Canada, multiculturalism emerged as an ideology and a policy for managing the cultural diversity that had resulted from migration. There is a large literature on this (see, e.g., Runblom 1994; Volpp 1996; Moller Okin 1999; Shachar 2001-2002; McGoldrick 2005; McKerl 2007: 204-205; Joppke 2007). Originally, multiculturalism held that there could be equality, despite difference. Later, this was largely replaced by the idea that equality could occur only without difference (Coleman 1996; Kurien 2004). In all countries, debates about migrant women played a crucial role when policies shifted. In this volume, Cederberg, Andreassen, and Schrover address changes in policy and in debates, which were similar in the three countries described by the respective authors (Sweden, the Netherlands and Denmark). Those changes are explained in the current literature mostly from a country-specific perspective.

Multiculturalism was introduced as a policy to facilitate integration, but in practice it often had the reverse effect (Kurien 2004; Leiken 2005; Engelen 2006: 72). It granted groups the right to make claims for (financial) support from the state, based on a conception of groups as homogenous, and having unique and innate characteristics (Parkinson

1994; Phillips 2003: 517; Uitermark, Rossi & Van Houtum 2005: 624; Salaff & Chan 2007: 126; Bhabha 2009: 57). Multiculturalism was morally and politically acceptable because ethnic minorities were seen as actual groups with inherent characteristics (Verkuyten & Brug 2004). It demanded the construction of a *public* ethnic identity (as opposed to a private one), and group formation on the basis of perceived cultural similarity (Kurien 2004). The struggle for recognition spurred ethnic formation, organisation and mobilisation. Crucial to multiculturalism is that integration was seen as a group process, which implied subsidies for immigrant organisations.

In the 1970s, Sweden was generous, relative to other countries, in granting rights to foreign citizens. As Cederberg in this volume describes, Sweden's social democratic ideology, the country's corporatist structure and the strong position of trade unions explain this. Unions and social democratic governments were concerned about workers' rights and wage-dumping. Therefore, the Swedish government granted immigrants rights in the form of employment, social welfare and political participation. Immigrant organisations were considered important and were given state support. Consequently, immigrants pursued their cultural and political interests; they also acquired the attitudes and skills needed to do so. Multiculturalism in Sweden (as elsewhere) implied collective rights for migrants and collective identities. Gender roles and family relations, which were labelled traditional and unequal, were nonetheless seen as 'authentic' elements of these collective identities. Rather paradoxically, Swedes pride themselves on gender equality, and that attitude constitutes an important element of Swedish identity. In the early days of multiculturalism, differences were introduced, maintained and subsidised. They were problematised only decades later.

In the 1980s and 1990s, the Swedish labour market was liberalised and the welfare state dismantled. When unemployment rose – among immigrants and non-immigrants alike – retaining minority culture came to be seen as hampering migrants' incorporation into majority society, and the cause of problems such as unemployment. Demands on immigrants increased, in terms of language and adaptation to Swedish norms and values, as was true in other countries. The Swedish 'value dialogue' targeted patriarchal and oppressive gender relations in 'other' – mostly Muslim – communities. Oppression of women within Islam emerged as a major issue in Sweden, according to Cederberg (this volume). It also became important in other countries (Penninx, Münstermann & Entzinger 1998; Kofman 1999). This problematisation built on ideas about protectionism and Orientalism that were formulated in the 19th century within a colonial context. That view portrayed the superior Christian societies as the rescuers and liberators of Muslim women from Muslim men (Said 1978; Stabile & Kumar 2005). These ideas were integrated into a perspective in which European women serve as the standard against which women from elsewhere were measured (Lutz 1997b). Muslim women are currently viewed, in a number of North-Western European countries, as the prototype of migrant women. They are perceived as exploited victims, handicapped by their cultures of origin. Islam and Western values are presented as incompatible (Korteweg & Yurdakul 2009). Issues such as the wearing of headscarves hold centre stage in current integration debates (Molokotos Liederman 2000; McGoldrick 2006; Brems 2006). The debates are characterised by gross overestimates of the number of women wearing headscarves. This discourse – to which some Western feminists and right-wing politicians contribute – uses well-worn stereotypes about non-Western women as religious, family-oriented, traditional and backward (Mohanty 1988).

After the headscarf debates dissipated (and after new laws had been introduced in several European countries), attention moved to the wearing of face-covering veils or niqabs. This practice was presented as the next step away from European values. The niqab was seen as a refusal to integrate, and a security risk, linked to radical Islam and terrorism (Herrera & Moors 2003). Andreassen, in this volume, describes the problematisation of veiling in Denmark. Crucial in this debate is that niqabs are frequently referred to as burqas. A burqa is the traditional Afghani garment that covers face and body. In contrast, niqabs cover the face, except for the eyes. The use of the inaccurate term is not simply a result of ignorance. By using the term burqa, an association is made between the wearing of veils and the highly subjugated position of Afghani women and other problems plaguing that country. In Denmark – and in Europe as a whole – very few women wear burqas, though some wear niqabs. Their numbers are grossly overestimated and do not warrant widespread political and public controversy, as Andreassen shows.

Danish lawmakers' efforts to ban certain head coverings arose from perceptions that Muslim women were oppressed, that Danish law could liberate them and that Muslim traditions threatened Danish values. The Danish debates present ethnic minority women as victims of a patriarchal culture, while ethnically Danish women are presented as liberated within an emancipated culture. In Denmark the Conservative Party wanted to introduce a 'burqa ban', but suggested it without first determining – as is customary – whether such a ban would violate the constitution. The Conservative Party realised that the proposal was unlikely to pass, but sought to benefit politically from suggesting the legislation. In the end the Conservative Party did not propose the ban in parliament, but the right-wing populist Danish People's Party planned to. It is notable that this party, and others like it elsewhere, argue for such bans by claiming that they favour equality and women's rights. However, these parties have in the past not voted in favour of laws or proposals aimed at limiting the oppression of women or increasing gender equality. They advocate women's rights and feminism only when it can be used as an anti-Muslim tool. In the veiling debates, 'being Danish' became synonymous with practicing gender equality, despite the fact that gender discrimination in Denmark continues to exist. By arguing that others are not practicing gender equality because of veiling, anti-veiling policies become a tool for excluding Muslims, especially women, from participating equally in Danish society.

Schrover, in this volume, describes developments similar to those in Denmark and Sweden. In the Netherlands multiculturalism in part builds on older Dutch ideas about 'living apart together'. This rendered multiculturalism acceptable to Dutch society, but also made it blind to differences between the older forms of separatism and those related to migrants. Within Dutch multicultural policy, immigrant organisations were subsidised, as was common in many countries. Subsidies were granted to a Turkish women's organisation in the Netherlands as well. When ideas about multiculturalism and policies regarding subsidies changed, and many of the subsidies were cut or disappeared, the Turkish women's organisation continued to be subsidised because the women were believed to be 'triple disadvantaged': as women, as migrants and as Muslims. Because the Turkish woman's organisation was one of the few organisations still subsidised, it became the object of a hostile takeover. In the case of the Turkish women's organisation, perceptions of a coherent and unified entity and the belief in an underlying essence, along with the search for 'authentic' cultural differences and public ethnic identities, denied differences within groups and increased competition between groups.

In the Netherlands, multiculturalism backfired. It created and emphasised differences and led to the problematisation of the position of migrants and ethnic minorities, who were believed to be unable to adapt because they were fundamentally different. This idea was fortified by several cases, which received widespread media attention. In the first place there were campaigns for Turkish women who had a dependent residence status and were to be deported to Turkey after their husbands left them. Turkey was presented as different and backward. Secondly, there were cases related to so-called 'honour killings'. From the mid-1970s onwards, crimes of passion among Turks were discussed in very different terms than those among non-Turks. Again, the emphasis was on fundamental differences, which very much fitted ideas about multiculturalism.

Cederberg, Andreassen, and Schrover describe aspects of those debates as country specific, but others are shared, despite differences between the three countries described. In all of the countries, the debate about multiculturalism eventually became a debate about Islam. Discussions about how migrants were different, or how different they should be allowed to be, progressed from subsidies for immigrant organisations (which enabled migrants to maintain 'their culture') to discussions about Swedishness, Dutchness and Danishness. Static ideas about migrants' culture led to static ideas about the dominant culture. In all of these countries, gender equality was seen as key to the dominant culture, and as lacking in the immigrants' own culture. In all three countries right-wing parties that had in the past opposed or ignored women's rights came out in support of gender equality when it concerned Muslim migrants.

## Final remarks

A concluding chapter at the end of this volume summarises what this review and the various chapters that follow it contribute to theory. This volume moves away from taking stock of differences, towards examining the functionality of those differences. We analyse debates, rather than describe migrants. Furthermore, we move away from the private sphere, and its highly personalised and dramatised stories, towards the public sphere, where boundaries are redrawn. We show how the personalised and dramatised stories, which are part of the private sphere, are used in the public sphere. We also analyse how strategies, concepts and debates travel across time, between countries, and across and between categories. Finally, we move away from the over-studied sectors of domestic work and prostitution, and the stress on victimisation, feminisation and problematisation. Instead, we analyse why differences are emphasised. Much of the academic literature on gender and migration, as well as much of the other literature on migration, closely ties in with political or policy debates. It takes a strong moral stance, which we try to avoid. Many publications present the migration of women as new, as well as their alleged problems. By taking a long-term perspective, we demonstrate that many current debates are rooted in historical trends.

## Notes

1   See www.loveexiles.org/home.htm (accessed 3 September 2012).
2   See http://madikazemi.blogspot.nl/2004/05/launch-of-love-exiles-group.html
     (accessed 3 September 2012).
3   See http://loveexiles.wordpress.com/tag/uafa/ (accessed 3 September 2012).

## References

Abu-Lughod, L. (2002), 'Do Muslim women really need saving? Anthropological reflections on cultural relativism and its others', *American Anthropologist* 104 (3): 783-790.
Accampo, E. (1993), 'Gender relations in the city: A response', *French Historical Studies* 18 (1): 50-56.
Ackers, L. (1996), 'Citizenship, gender, and dependence in the European Union: Women and internal migration', *Social Politics* 3 (2 & 3): 316-330.
Agustín, L. (2007), *Sex at the margins: Migration, labour markets and the rescue industry*. London: Zed Books.
Agustín, L. (2005), 'Migrants in the mistress's house: Other voices in the "trafficking" debate', *Social Politics: International Studies in Gender, State and Society* 12 (1): 96-117.
Agustín, L. (2003), 'A migrant world of services', *Social Politics: International Studies in Gender, State and Society* 10 (3): 377-396.
Alcalá, M.J. (2006), UNFPA *state of the world population: A passage to hope. Women and international migration*. New York: United Nations Population Fund.
Alwang, J., P.B. Siegel & S.L. Jørgensen (2001), *Vulnerability: A view from different disciplines*. Washington: Social Protection Discussion Paper Series, Social Protection Unit, Human Development Network, World Bank, no. 0115.
Anderson, B. (2000), *Doing the dirty work? The global politics of domestic labour*. London: Zed Books.
Anthias, F. & N. Yuval-Davis (1992), *Racialized boundaries: Race, nation, gender, colour and class and the anti-racist struggle*. London: Routledge.
Anthias, F.C. & G. Lazaridis (eds) (2000), *Gender and migration in Southern Europe: Women on the move*. Oxford and New York: Berg.
Bader, V.M. (1999), 'Citizenship of the European Union: Human rights, rights of citizens of the Union and of member states', *Ratio Juris* 12 (2): 153-181.
Bal, M. (2002), *Travelling concepts in the humanities: A rough guide*. London: University of Toronto Press.
Beck, U. (1992), *Risk society: Towards a new modernity*. London: Sage.
Benhabib, S. & J. Resnik (2009), *Migrations and mobilities: Citizenship, borders, and gender*. New York: New York University Press.
Berghahn, S. & P. Rostock (eds) (2009), *Der Stoff, aus dem die Konflikte sind. Debatten um das Kopftuch in Deutschland, Österreich und der Schweiz*. Bielefeld: Transcript Verlag.

Beriss, D. (2000), 'Culture-as-race or culture-as-culture: Caribbean ethnicity and the ambiguity of cultural identity in French society', *French Politics, Culture and Society* 18 (3): 18-47.

Berman, J. (2003), '(Un)popular strangers and crises (un)bounded: Discourses of sex-trafficking, the European political community and the panicked state of the modern state', *European Journal of International Relations* 9 (1): 37-86.

Bertaux-Wiame, I. (1979), 'The life history approach to the study of internal migration', *Oral History* 7 (1): 26-32.

Bhabha, F. (2009), 'Between exclusion and assimilation: Experimentalizing multiculturalism', *McGill Law Journal* 54 (1): 5445-5490.

Biemann, U. (2002), 'Remotely sensed: A topography of the global sex trade', *Feminist Review* 70 (1): 75-88.

Blanchette, T.G. & A.P. da Silva (2012), 'On bullshit and the trafficking of women: Moral entrepreneurs and the invention of trafficking of persons in Brazil', *Dialectical Anthropology* 36 (1 & 2): 107-125.

Bonjour, S. (2010), *Gezin en grens: Beleidsvorming inzake gezinsmigratie in Nederland, 1955-2005.* Amsterdam: Aksant.

Boris, E. (2005), 'On the importance of naming: Gender, race and the writing of policy history', *The Journal of Policy History* 17 (1): 72-92.

Boris, E. (1995), 'The racialized gendered state: Constructions of citizenship in the United States', *Social Politics* 2 (2): 160-181.

Bourdieu, P. (1994), 'Rethinking the state: Genesis and structure of the bureaucratic field', *Sociological Theory* 12 (1): 1-18.

Bourdieu, P. (1980), 'L'identité et la representation', *Actes de la Recherché en Sciences Sociaux* 35: 63-72.

Boyd, M. (1989), 'Family and personal networks in international migration: Recent developments and new agendas', *International Migration Review* 23 (3): 638-670.

Boyd, R, & P.J. Richerson (1987), 'The evolution of ethnic markers', *Cultural Anthropology* 2 (1987): 65-79.

Bredbenner, C.L. (1998), *A nationality of her own: Women, marriage, and the law of citizenship.* Berkeley and London: University of California Press.

Breger, R. & R. Hill (1998), 'Preface', in R. Breger & R. Hill (eds), *Cross-cultural marriage: Identity and choice*, pp. 1-32. Oxford and New York: Berg.

Brems, E. (2006), 'Above children's heads: The headscarf controversy in European schools from the perspective of children's rights', *The International Journal of Children's Rights* 14 (2): 119-136.

Brennan, D. (2008), 'Competing claims of victimhood? Foreign and domestic victims of trafficking in the United States', *Sexuality Research & Social Policy* 5 (4): 45-61.

Brennan, D. (2004), 'Women work, men sponge, and everyone gossips', *Anthropological Quarterly* 77 (7): 705-733.

Brettell, C.B. (1986), *Men who migrate, women who wait: Population and history in a Portuguese parish.* Princeton: Princeton University Press.

Brown, W. (1995), *States of injury: Power and freedom in late modernity.* Princeton: Princeton University Press.

Browne, J. (2007), 'Introduction', in J. Browne (ed.), *The future of gender*, pp. 1-15. Cambridge: Cambridge University Press.

Brubaker, R., M. Loveman & P. Stamatov (2004), 'Ethnicity as cognition', *Theory and Society* 33 (1): 31-64.

Brysk, A. (2011) 'Sex as slavery? Understanding private wrongs', *Human Rights Review* 12 (3): 259-270.

Burchell, G., C. Gordon & P. Miller (eds) (1991), *The Foucault elect: Studies in governmentality.* Chicago: University of Chicago Press.

Bush, G.W. (2010), *Decision points.* New York: Crown Publishing.

Bustamante, J.A. (2002), 'Immigrants' vulnerability as subjects of human rights', *International Migration Review* 36 (2): 333-354.

Calavita, K. (2006), 'Gender, migration, and law: Crossing borders and bridging disciplines', *International Migration Review* 40 (1): 104-132.

Carruthers, S.L. (2005), 'Between camps: Eastern Bloc "escapees" and Cold War borderlands', *American Quarterly. Special issue: Legal borderlands law and the construction of American borders* 57 (3): 911-942.

Castles S. & M.J. Miller (2003), *The age of migration: International population movements in the modern world.* Basingstoke and New York: Guilford Press.

Cheng, E. (2007), 'Sentimental journey: Transnational adoption from China and post-World War II US liberalism'. PhD dissertation, University of California, San Diego.

Coleman, D.L. (1996), 'Individualizing justice through multiculturalism: The liberals' dilemma', *Columbia Law Review* 96 (5): 1093-1167.

Connell, P. (1997), 'Understanding victimization and agency: Considerations of race, class and gender', *Political and Legal Anthropology Review* 20 (2): 116-143.

Connell, R.W. (1993), 'The big picture: Masculinities in recent world history', *Theory and Society* 22 (5) *Special Issue: Masculinities:* 597-623.

Connell, R.W. (1990), 'The state, gender, and sexual politics: Theory and appraisal', *Theory and Society* 19 (5): 507-544.

Constable, N. (1997), *Maid to order in Hong Kong: Stories of Filipina workers.* Ithaca: Cornell University Press.

Côté, A., M. Kérisit & M. Côté (2001), *Sponsorship ... for better or for worse: The impact of sponsorship on the equality rights of immigrant women.* Ottawa: Status of Women Canada.

Crenshaw, K. (1989), 'Demarginalizing the intersection of race and sex: A black feminist critique of antidiscrimination doctrine, feminist theory, and antiracist politics', *University of Chicago Legal Forum:* 139-167.

Curran, S.R. (2012), *Shifting boundaries, transforming lives: Globalization, gender and family dynamics in Thailand.* Princeton: Princeton University Press.

Curran, S.R. & A.C. Saguy (2001), 'Migration and cultural change: A role for gender and social networks?' *Journal of International Women's Studies* 2 (3): 54-77.

Dannecker, P. (2005), 'Transnational migration and the transformation of gender relations: The case of Bangladeshi labour migrants', *Current Sociology* 53 (4): 655-674.

DaVanzo, J. (1978), 'Does unemployment affect migration? Evidence from micro data', *Review of Economics and Statistics* 60 (4): 504-514.

Davis, B. & P. Winters (2001), 'Gender, networks and Mexico-US migration', *Journal of Development Studies* 28 (2): 1-26.

Davis, K. (2008), 'Intersectionality as buzzword: A sociology of science perspective on what makes a feminist theory successful', *Feminist Theory* 9 (1): 67-85.

De Haas, H. (2007), *The myth of invasion: Irregular migration from West Africa to the Maghreb and the European Union*. Oxford: International Migration Institute.

De Haas, H. & A. van Rooij (2010), 'Migration as emancipation? The impact of internal and international migration on the position of women left behind in rural Morocco', *Oxford Development Studies* 38 (1): 43-62.

De Hart, B. (2006), 'The morality of Maria Toet: Gender, citizenship and the construction of the nation state', *Journal of Ethnic and Migration Studies* 32 (1): 49-68.

De Hart, B. (2001), 'Not without my daughter: On parental abduction, orientalism and maternal melodrama', *European Journal of Women's Studies* 8: 51-65.

De Jong, G., K. Richter & P. Isarabhakdi (1995), 'Gender, values, and intentions to move in rural Thailand', *International Migration Review* 30 (3): 748-770.

Deane, T. (2010), 'Cross-border trafficking in Nepal and India: Violating women's rights', *Human Rights Review* 11 (4): 491-513.

Dodson, B. (2008), 'Gender, migration and livelihood: Migrant women in Southern Africa', in N. Piper (ed.), *New perspectives on gender and migration: Livelihood, rights and entitlements*, pp. 137-158. London: Routledge.

Doezema, J. (2005), 'Now you see her, now you don't: Sex workers at the UN trafficking protocol negotiations', *Social Legal Studies* 14 (1): 61-89.

Doezema, J. (2001), 'Ouch! Western feminists' "wounded attachment" to the "third world prostitute"', *Feminist Review* 67 (1): 16-38.

Donato, K.M., J.T. Alexander, D.R. Gabaccia & J. Leinonen (2011), 'Variations in the gender composition of immigrant populations: How they matter', *International Migration Review* 45 (3): 495-526.

Donato, K.M., D.R. Gabaccia, J. Holdaway, M. Manalansan & P.R. Pessar (2006), 'A glass half full? Gender in migration studies', *International Migration Review* 40 (1): 3-26.

Ehrenreich, B. & A.R. Hochschild (eds) (2002), *Global woman: Nannies, maids and sex workers in the new economy*. New York: Holt.

El-Cherkeh, T., E. Stirbu, S. Lazaroiu & D. Radu (2004), *EU enlargement, migration and the trafficking of women: The case of South Eastern Europe*. Hamburg: Hamburg Institute of International Economics, HWWA Report 247.

Engelen, E. (2006), 'Towards an explanation of the performance differences of Turks in the Netherlands and Germany: The case for a comparative political economy of integration', *Tijdschrift voor Economische en Sociale Geografie* 97 (1): 69-79.

España-Maram, L. (2006), *Creating masculinity in Los Angeles's little Manila: Working-class Filipinos and popular culture 1920s-1950s*. New York: Columbia University Press.

Fanon, F. (1965), *A dying colonialism*. New York: Grove Press.

Fehér, L. (2000), 'International efforts against trafficking in human beings', *Acta Juridica Hungarica* 41 (3 & 4): 181-198.

Fincher, R. & P. Saunders (eds) (2001), *Creating unequal futures? Rethinking poverty, inequality and disadvantage*. Sydney: Allen & Unwin.

Forsdick, C. (2001), 'Travelling concepts: Postcolonial approaches to exoticism', *Paragraph* 24 (3): 12-29.

Foucault, M. (1991), 'Governmentality', in G. Burchell, C. Gordon and P. Miller (eds), *The Foucault effect: Studies in governmentality*, pp. 87-104. Chicago: University of Chicago Press.

Foucault, M. (1988), 'Politics and reason', in L. Kritzman (ed.), *Politics, philosophy, culture: Interviews and other writings, 1977-1984*, pp. 57-85. New York: Routledge.

Foucault, M. (1980), *Power/knowledge: Selected interviews and other writings, 1972-1977.* 1st ed. New York: Pantheon Books.

George, S.M. (2005), *When women come first: Gender and class in transnational migration*. Berkeley: University of California Press.

Gökariksel, B. & K. Mitchell (2005), 'Veiling, secularism, and the neoliberal subject: National narratives and supranational desires in Turkey and France.' *Global Networks: A Journal of Transnational Affairs* 5 (2): 147-165.

Gould, C. (2010), 'The problem of trafficking', in I.E. Palmary, K. Burman, P. Chantler & P. Kiguwa (eds), *Gender and migration: Feminist interventions*, pp. 31-49. London: Zed Books.

Gower, M. (2010), 'Asylum: Claims based on sexual identity', Standard Note SN/HA/5618, 9 July, Home Affairs Section, Library House of Commons (UK).

Grahl-Madsen, A. (1966), 'The European tradition of asylum and the development of refugee law', *Journal of Peace Research* 3 (3): 278-289.

Grahl-Madsen, A. (1983), 'Identifying the world's refugees', *Annals of the American Academy of Political and Social Science* 467 (1): 11-23.

Grahl-Madsen, A. (1982-1983a), 'The League of Nations and the refugees', *AWR-Bulletin* 20-21: 86-96.

Grahl-Madsen, A. (1982-1983b), 'The special regime of refugees', *AWR-Bulletin* 20-21: 159-167.

Granovetter, M.S. (1973), 'The strength of weak ties', *American Journal of Sociology* 78 (6): 1360-1380

Grasmuck S. & P. Pessar (1991), *Two islands: Dominican international migration*, Berkeley: University of California Press.

Gray, B. (2006) 'Migrant integration policy: A nationalist fantasy of management and control?', *Translocations* 13 (1): 121-141.

Grillo, R. (2010), 'The family at issue: The forced marriage debate in the UK', in A. Kraler, E. Kofman, M. Kohli & C. Schmoll (eds), *Gender, generations and the family in international migration*, pp. 59-74. Amsterdam: Amsterdam University Press.

Grillo, R. (ed.) (2008), *The family in question: Immigrant and ethnic minorities in multicultural Europe*. Amsterdam: Amsterdam University Press.

Habermas, J. (1989), *The structural transformation of the public sphere: An inquiry into a category of bourgeois society*. Cambridge: MIT Press.

Hacker, H.M. (1951), 'Women as a minority group', *Social Forces* 30 (1): 60-69.

Haig, D. (2004), 'The inexorable rise of gender and the decline of sex: Social change in academic titles, 1945-2001', *Archives of Sexual Behavior* 33 (2): 87-96.

Hansen, P. (2008), 'Circumcising migration: Gendering return migration among Somalilanders', *Journal of Ethnic and Migration Studies* 34 (7): 1109-1125.

Haynes, D.F. (2004), 'Used, abused, arrested and deported: Extending immigration benefits to protect the victims of trafficking and to secure the prosecution of traffickers', *Human Rights Quarterly* 26 (2): 221-272.

Henshall Momsen, J. (ed.) (1999), *Gender, migration and domestic service*. London: Routledge.

Herrera L. & A. Moors (2003), 'Banning face veiling: The boundaries of liberal education', *ISIM Newsletter* 13 (December): 16-17.

Hoerder, D. (2002), *Cultures in contact: World migrations in the second millennium*. Durham: Duke University Press.

Hogan, D.J. & E. Marandola (2005), 'Towards an interdisciplinary conceptualisation of vulnerability', *Population, Space and Place* 11: 455-471.

Holborn, L.W. (1975), *Refugees: A problem of our time. The work of the United Nations High Commissioner for Refugees, 1951-1972*. Metuchen: Scarecrow Press.

Hollingshead, A.B. (1952) 'Trends in social stratification: A case study', *American Sociological Review* 17 (6): 679-686.

Hondagneu-Sotelo, P. (2000), 'Feminism and migration', *Annals of the American Academy of Political and Social Science* 57 (1): 107-120.

Hübinette, T. & J. Arvanitakis (2012), 'Transracial adoption: The fantasy of the global family', in N. Falkof & O. Cashman-Brown (eds), *On whiteness*, Critical Issues Series 190, pp. 221-233, Oxford: Inter-Disciplinary Press.

Human Rights Watch (2005), *Maid to order: Ending abuses against migrant domestic workers in Singapore*. New York: Human Rights Watch.

Jennissen, R. (2004), *Macro-economic determinants of international migration in Europe*. Groningen: University of Groningen Press.

Jones-Correa, M. (1998), 'Different paths: Gender, immigration and political participation', *Immigration Migration Review* 32 (2): 326-349.

Joppke, C. (2007), 'State neutrality and Islamic headscarf laws in France and Germany', *Theory and Society* 36 (4): 313-342.

Kamp, M. (2008), *The new woman in Uzbekistan: Islam, modernity, and unveiling under communism*. Seattle: University of Washington Press.

Kapur, R. (2005), *Erotic justice: Law and the new politics of postcolonialism*. London: Glass House.

Kawar, M. (2004), 'Gender and migration: Why are women more vulnerable?', in *Femmes et mouvement: genre, migrations et nouvelle division internationale du travail*, pp. 71-87. Geneva: Colloquium Graduate Institute of Development Studies.

Kempadoo, K. & J. Doezema (eds) (1998), *Global sex workers*. New York and London: Taylor & Francis.

Kennedy, J.C. (2005), *De deugden van een gidsland: Burgerschap en democratie in Nederland*. Amsterdam: Bert Bakker.

Kim, C. & T.G. Carroll (1975), 'Intercountry adoption of South Korean orphans: A lawyer's guide', *Journal of Family Law* 14 (2): 223-253.

Kim, E. (2009), *The origins of Korean adoption: Cold war geopolitics and intimate diplomacy*. US-Korea Institute Working Paper Series WP 09-09. Washington, DC: US-Korea Institute.

King, R. & E. Zontini (2000), 'The role of gender in the South European immigration model', *Papers* 60: 35-52.

Knörr, J. & B. Meier (2000), *Women and migration: Anthropological perspectives*. New York: St. Martin's Press.

Kofman, E. (1999), 'Female "birds of passage" a decade later: Gender and immigration in the European Union', *International Migration Review* 33 (2): 269-299.

Kofman, E., A. Phizacklea, P. Raghuram & R. Sales (2000), *Gender and international migration in Europe: Employment, welfare and politics*. London: Routledge.

Kontos, M., U. Haferbur & A.V. Sacaliuc (2006), *Mapping of policies affecting female migrants and policy analysis: The German case*. Working paper no. 1 – WP1. Frankfurt: Institut für Sozialforschung an der J.W. Goethe Universität Frankfurt. www.femipol.uni-frankfurt.de/docs/working_papers/wp1/Germany.pdf.

Korteweg, A. & G. Yurdakul (2009), 'Islam, gender, and immigrant integration: Boundary drawing in discourses on honour killing in the Netherlands and Germany', *Ethnic and Racial Studies* 32 (2): 218-238.

Kraler, A., E. Kofman, M. Kohli & C. Schmoll (eds) (2011), *Gender, generations and the family in international migration*. Amsterdam: Amsterdam University Press.

Kurien, P. (2004), 'Multiculturalism, immigrant religion, and diasporic nationalism: The development of an American Hinduism', *Social Problems* 51 (3): 362-385.

Labadie-Jackson, G. (2008), 'Reflections on domestic work and the feminization of migration', *Campbell Law Review* 31 (1): 67-90.

Laclau, E. & C. Mouffe (1985), *Hegemony and socialist strategy: Towards a radical democratic practice*. London: Verso.

Leiken, R.S. (2005), 'Europe's angry Muslims', *Foreign Affairs*, 120-135.

Lenz, I., H. Lutz, M. Morokvasic, C. Schöng-Kalender & H. Schwenken (eds) (2002), *Crossing borders and shifting boundaries, vol. ii: Gender, identities and networks*. Opladen: Carfax Publishing.

Lepp, A. (2002), 'Trafficking in women and the feminization of migration: The Canadian context', *Canadian Woman Studies* 21/22 (4): 90-99.

Lettinga, D.N. (2011), *Framing the hijab: The governance of intersecting religious, ethnic and gender differences in France, the Netherlands and Germany*. Amsterdam: VU University Press.

Lister, R., F. Williams, A. Anttonen, J. Bussenmaker, U. Gerhard, J. Heinen, S. Johansson, A. Leira, B. Siim & C. Tobio (2007), *Gendering citizenship in Western Europe: New challenges for citizenship research in a cross-national context*. Bristol: Policy Press.

Loescher, G. (1993), *Beyond charity: International cooperation and the global refugee crisis*. New York: Oxford University Press.

Lutz, H. (1997a), 'The limits of European-ness: Immigrant women in fortress Europe', *Feminist Review* 57: 93-111.

Lutz, H. (1997b), 'Cherchez la femme perdue: Kritsche aantekeningen vanuit een genderperspectief', *Migrantenstudies* 2: 90-96.

Lutz, H., A. Phoenix & N. Yuval-Davis (eds) (1995), *Crossfires: Nationalism, racism and gender in Europe*. London: Pluto Press.

MacLeod, M. & E. Saraga (1988), 'Challenging orthodoxy: Towards a feminist theory and practice', *Feminist Review* 28: 16-55.

Mahler, S.J. & P.R. Pessar (2006), 'Gender matters: Ethnographers bring gender from the periphery toward the core of migration studies', *International Migration Review* 40 (1): 27-63.

Mahler, S.J. & P.R. Pessar (2001), 'Gendered geographies of power: Analyzing gender across transnational spaces', *Identities: Global Studies in Culture and Power* 7 (4): 441-459.

Marshall, T.H. (1950), *Citizenship and social class and other essays.* Cambridge: University of Cambridge Press.

Massey, D.S. (1990), 'Social structure, household strategies, and the cumulative causation of migration', *Population Index* 56 (1): 3-26.

McCall, L. (2005), 'The complexity of intersectionality', *Signs: Journal of Women in Culture and Society* 30 (3): 1771-1800.

McGoldrick, D. (2006), *Human rights and religion: The Islamic headscarf debate in Europe.* Oxford: Oxford University Press.

McGoldrick, D. (2005), 'Multiculturalism and its discontents', *Human Rights Law Review* 5 (1): 27-56.

McKay, S.C. (2007), 'Filipino sea men: Constructing masculinities in an ethnic labour niche', *Journal of Ethnic and Migration Studies* 33 (4): 617-633.

McKeown, A. (2008), *Melancholy order: Asian immigration and the globalization of borders.* New York: Columbia University Press.

McKerl, M. (2007), 'Multiculturalism, gender and violence', *Culture and Religion* 8 (2): 187-217.

Minnis, M.S. (1953), 'Cleavage in women's organizations: A reflection of the social structure of a city', *American Sociological Review* 18 (1): 47-53.

Moch, L.P. (2003a), *Moving Europeans: Migration in Western Europe since 1650.* Bloomington: Indiana University Press.

Moch, L.P. (2003b), 'Networks among Bretons? The evidence for Paris, 1875-1925', *Continuity and Change* 18 (3): 431-455.

Moch, L.P. & R.G. Fuchs (1993), 'Getting along: Poor women's networks in nineteenth-century Paris', *French Historical Studies* 18 (1): 34-49.

Mohanty, C. (1988), 'Under Western eyes: Feminist scholarship and colonial discourses', *Feminist Review* 30: 61-88.

Moller Okin, S. (1999), 'Is multiculturalism bad for women?', in J. Cohen, M. Howard & M. Nussbaum (eds), *Is multiculturalism bad for women*, pp. 9-24. Princeton: Princeton University Press.

Molokotos Liederman, L. (2000), 'Religious diversity in schools: The Muslim headscarf controversy and beyond', *Social Compass* 47 (3): 367-382.

Moloney, D.M. (2012), *National insecurities: Immigrants and US deportation policy since 1882.* Chapel Hill: University of North Carolina.

Money, J. (1955), 'Hermaphroditism, gender and precocity in hypera-drenocorticism: Psychologic findings', *Bulletin of the Johns Hopkins Hospital* 96: 253-264.

Mongaya Hoegsholm, F. (ed.) (2007), *In de olde worlde: Views of Filipino migrants in Europe.* Quezon City: Philippine Social Science Council.

Morokvasic, M., U. Erel & K. Shinozaki (eds) (2003), *Gender on the move, crossing borders and shifting boundaries,* Vol. 1. Opladen: Carfax Publishers.

Moser, C.O.N. (1998), The asset vulnerability framework: Reassessing urban poverty reduction strategies. *World Development* 26 (1): 1-19.

Moya, J.M. (2007), 'Domestic service in a global perspective: Gender, migration and ethnic niches', *Journal of Ethnic and Migration Studies* 33 (4): 559-579.

Nobil Ahmad, A. (2011), *Masculinity, sexuality and illegal migration: Human smuggling from Pakistan to Europe*. Aldershot: Ashgate.

Nobil Ahmad, A. (2008), 'The romantic appeal of illegal migration: Gender masculinity and human smuggling from Pakistan', in M. Schrover, J. van der Leun, L. Lucassen & C. Quispel (eds), *Illegal migration and gender in a global and historical perspective*, pp. 127-150. IMISCOE Research. Amsterdam: Amsterdam University Press.

Oh, A. (2005), 'A new kind of missionary work: Christians, Christian Americanists, and the adoption of Korean GI babies, 1955-1961', *Women's Studies Quarterly* 33 (3 & 4): 161-188.

Oishi, N. (2005), *Women in motion: Globalization, state policies, and labor migration in Asia*. Stanford: Stanford University Press.

Orbeta, A.C., Jr. & M.R.M. Abrigo (2009), 'Philippine International Labor Migration in the Past 30 Years: Trends and Prospects', *Discussion Papers* DP 2009-33, Philippine Institute for Development Studies.

Oso Casas, L. & J.P. Garson (2005), *The feminisation of international migration: Migrant women and labour market diversity and challenges*. Brussels: OECD and European Commission Seminar.

Oude Breuil, B.C. & D. Siegel, P. van Reenen, A. Beijer & L. Roos (2011), 'Human trafficking revisited: Legal, enforcement and ethnographic narratives on sex trafficking to Western Europe', *Trends in Organized Crime* 14: 30-46.

Outshoorn, J. (2005), 'The political debates on prostitution and trafficking of women', *Social Politics: International Studies in Gender, State and Society* 12 (1): 141-155.

Oxford, C.G. (2005), 'Protectors and victims in the gender regime of asylum', *National Women's Studies Association (NWSA) Journal* 17 (3): 18-38.

Pajnik, M. & V. Bajt (2012), 'Migrant women's transnationalism: Family patterns and policies', *International Migration* 50 (5): 153-168.

Palmary, I., E. Burman, K. Chantler & P. Kiguwa (2010), *Gender and migration: Feminist interventions*. London: Zed Books.

Parkinson, P. (1994), 'Taking multiculturalism seriously: Marriage law and the rights of minorities', *Sydney Law Review* 36 (16-4): 473-505.

Pawley, L. (2008), 'Cultural citizenship', *Sociology Compass* 2 (2): 594-608.

Pedersen, S. (2001), 'The maternalist moment in British colonial policy: The controversy over "child slavery" in Hong Kong 1917-1941', *Past & Present* 171 (1): 161-202.

Penninx, R., H. Münstermann & H. Entzinger (eds) (1998), *Etnische minderheden en de multiculturele samenleving*. Groningen: Wolters-Noordhoff.

Pessar, P.R. & S.J. Mahler (2003), 'Transnational migration: Bringing gender in', *International Migration Review* 37 (3): 812-846.

Phillips, A. (2003), 'When culture means gender: Issues of cultural defence in the English courts', *The Modern Law Review* 66 (4): 510-531.

Phizacklea, A. (2003), 'Transnationalism, gender and global workers', in M. Morokva-sic-Müller, U. Erel & K. Shinokazi (eds), *Crossing borders and shifting boundaries. Vol. 1: Gender on the move*, pp. 79-101 Opladen: Leske + Budrich.

Phizacklea, A. (1998), 'Migration and globalization: A feminist perspective', in K. Koser & H. Lutz (eds), *The new migration in Europe: Social constructions and social realities*, pp. 21-38. New York: Macmillan.

Phoenix, A. & P. Pattynama (2006), 'Intersectionality', *European Journal of Women's Studies* 13 (3): 187-192.

Piper, N. (ed.) (2007), *New perspectives on gender and migration: Livelihood, rights and entitlements*. London: Routledge.

Piper, N. (2003), 'Feminization of labor migration as violence against women: International, regional, and local nongovernmental organization responses in Asia', *Violence Against Women* 9 (6): 723-745.

Portes, A. & R. Bach (1985), *Latin journey: Cuban and Mexican immigrants in the United States*. Berkeley: University of California Press.

Portes, A. & J. Sensenbrenner (1993), 'Embeddedness and immigration: Notes on the social determinants of economic action', *American Journal of Sociology* 98 (6): 1320-1350.

Roggeband, C. & M. Verloo (2007), 'Dutch women are liberated, migrant women are a problem: The evolution of policy frames on gender and migration in the Netherlands, 1995-2005', *Social Policy & Administration* 41 (3): 271-288.

Rosas, A.E. (2011), 'Breaking the silence: Mexican children and women's confrontation of Bracero family separation, 1942-64', *Gender & History* 23 (2): 382-400.

Rosenberger, S. & B. Sauer (2012), *Politics, religion, and gender: Framing and regulating the veil*. Abington: Routledge.

Ross, E. (1983), 'Survival networks: Women's neighbourhood sharing in London before World War One', *History Workshop* 15 (1): 4-26.

Runblom, H. (1994), 'Swedish multiculturalism in a comparative European perspective', *Sociological Forum* 9 (4): 623-640.

Ryan, J. (2002), 'Chinese women as transnational migrants: Gender and class in global migration narratives', *International Migration* 40 (2): 93-116.

Ryan, L. & W. Webster (2008), *Gendering migration: Masculinity, femininity and ethnicity in post-war Britain*. Aldershot: Ashgate.

Rygiel, P. (2011), *Politique et administration du genre en migration, Mondes atlantiques, xixe-xxe siècles*. Paris: Publibook.

Said, E. (1982), 'Traveling theory', *Raritan, A Quarterly Review* 1 (3): 41-67.

Said, E. (1978), *Orientalism*. New York: Vintage Books.

Salaff J. & P. Chan (2007), 'Competing interests: Toronto's Chinese immigrant associations and the politics of multiculturalism', *Population, Space and Place* 13 (2): 125-140.

Salomon, K. (1991), *Refugees in the Cold War: Toward a new international refugee regime in the early postwar era*. Lund: Lund University Press.

Sarri, R.C., Y. Baik & M. Bombyk (1998), 'Goal displacement and dependency in South Korean-United States intercountry adoption', *Children and Youth Services Review* 20 (1-2): 87-114.

Sassen, S. (2006), 'The repositioning of citizenship and alienage: Emergent subjects and spaces for politics' in Y.M. Bodemann & G. Yurdakul (eds), *Migration, citizenship, ethnos: Incorporation regimes in Germany, Western Europe and North America*, pp. 13-34. New York: Palgrave Macmillan.

Sassen, S. (2003), 'The feminization of survival: Alternative global circuits', in M. Morokvasic-Müller, U. Erel & K. Shinokazi (eds), *Crossing borders and shifting boundaries. Vol. 1: Gender on the move*, pp. 59-78. Opladen: Leske + Budrich.

Schinkel, W. (2008), 'The moralisation of citizenship in Dutch integration discourse', *Amsterdam Law Forum* 1 (1) http://ojs.ubvu.vu.nl/alf/rt/printerFriendly/56/77 (Accessed July 2012).

Schrover, M. (2013), 'Feminization and problematization of migration: Europe in the nineteenth and twentieth centuries', in D. Hoerder & A. Kaur (eds), *Proletarian and gendered mass migrations: A global perspective on continuities and discontinuities from the 19th to the 21st centuries*, pp. 103-131. Leiden: Brill.

Schrover, M. (2009a), 'Differences that make all the difference: Gender, migration and vulnerability', in M. Orly, G. Brunet, V. Barusse De Luca & D. Gauvreau (eds), *A female demography: Migration, work, fertility, family*, pp. 143-168. Bern: Peter Lang.

Schrover, M. (2009b), 'Family in Dutch migration policy, 1945-2005', *The History of the Family* 14 (2): 191-202.

Schrover, M. (2008), 'Verschillen die verschil maken: Inleiding op het themanummer over gender, migratie en overheidsbeleid in Nederland en België in de periode 1945-2005', *Tijdschrift voor Sociale en Economische Geschiedenis* 5 (1): 3-22.

Schrover, M. (2003), 'Living together, working together: Concentrations amongst German immigrants in the Netherlands in the nineteenth century', *Continuity and Change* 18 (2): 263-285.

Schrover, M., J. van der Leun, L. Lucassen, & C. Quispel (eds) (2008), *Illegal migration and gender in a global and historical perspective.* IMISCOE Research. Amsterdam: Amsterdam University Press.

Schrover, M., J. van der Leun & C. Quispel, (2007), 'Niches, labour market segregation, ethnicity and gender', *Journal of Ethnicity and Migration Studies* 33 (4): 529-540.

Schrover, M. & E.J. Yeo (2010a), 'Introduction: Moving the focus to the public sphere', in M. Schrover & E.J. Yeo (eds), *Gender, migration and the public sphere, 1850-2005*, pp. 1-13. New York: Routledge.

Schrover, M. & Yeo, E. (eds) (2010b), *Gender, migration and the public sphere in interdisciplinary perspective 1850-2005.* New York: Routledge.

Scott, J.C. (1998), *Seeing like a state: How certain schemes to improve the human condition have failed.* New Haven: Yale University Press.

Scott, J.W. (1988), *Gender and the politics of history.* New York: Columbia University Press.

Scott, J.W. (1986), 'Gender: A useful category of historical analysis', *American Historical Review* 91 (5): 1053-1075.

Shachar, A. (2001-2002), 'Two critiques of multiculturalism', *Cardozo Law Review* 23 (1): 253-297.

Sharpe P. (ed.) (200l), *Women, gender and labour migration: Historical and global perspectives*. London: Routledge.

Sinha, M. (2006), 'Gender and nation', in S. Morgan (ed.), *The feminist history reader*, pp. 323-338. Abington: Routledge.

Sinke, S. (2006), 'Gender and migration: Historical perspectives', *International Migration Review* 40 (1): 82-103.

Sjaastad, L.A. (1962), 'The costs and returns of human migration', *Journal of Political Economy* 70 (5): 80-93.

Soderlund, G. (2005), 'Running from the rescuers: New US crusaders against sex trafficking and the rhetoric of abolition', *National Women's Studies Association (NWSA) Journal* 17 (3): 64-87.

Soysal, Y.N. (1994), *Limits of citizenship: Migrants and postnational membership in Europe*. Chicago: University of Chicago Press.

Spijkerboer, T. (2000), *Gender and refugee status*. Aldershot: Ashgate.

Stabile, C.A. & D. Kumar (2005), 'Unveiling imperialism: Media, gender and the war on Afghanistan', *Media Culture and Society* 27 (5): 765-782.

Stark, O. (1991), *The Migration of Labor*. Oxford: Blackwell.

Sterett, S. (1997), 'Domestic violence and immigration in Britain', *Polar* 20 (2): 63-69.

Stewart, E. (2005), 'Exploring the vulnerability of asylum seekers in the UK', *Population, Space and Place* 11 (9): 499-512.

Stoler, A.L. (1995), *Race and the education of desire: Foucault's history of sexuality and the colonial order of things*. Durham: Duke University Press.

Stoler, A.L. (1992), 'Sexual affronts and racial frontiers: European identities and the cultural politics of exclusion in colonial Southeast Asia', *Comparative Studies in Society and History* 34: 540-551.

Studer, B. (2001), 'Citizenship as contingent national belonging: Married women foreigners in twentieth-century Switzerland', *Gender and History* 13 (3): 622-654.

Tacoli, C. (1995), 'Gender and international survival strategies: A research agenda with reference to Filipina labour migrants in Italy', *TWPR* 17 (2): 199-212.

Takkenberg, A. & C.C. Tahbaz (eds) (1989), *The collected travaux préparatoires of the 1951 Geneva Convention Relating to the Status of Refugees*. Volumes I, II and III (2nd edition). Amsterdam: Dutch Refugee Council.

Tilly, C. (1998), *Durable inequality*. Berkeley: University of California Press.

UDI (2012), *Misuse of the right to family reunification: Marriages of convenience and false declarations of parenthood. Report to the European Migration Network from the Norwegian Contact Point*. Oslo: Norwegian Directorate of Immigration.

Uitermark, J., U. Rossi & H. van Houtum (2005), 'Reinventing multiculturalism: Urban citizenship and the negotiation of ethnic diversity in Amsterdam', *International Journal of Urban and Regional Research* 29 (3): 622-640.

United Nations (2009), *Child adoption: Trends and policies*. New York: Department of Economic and Social Affairs Population Division, United Nations ST/ESA/SER.A/292.

Utas, M. (2005), 'West-African warscapes. Victimcy, girlfriending, soldiering: Tactic agency in a young woman's social navigation of the Liberian war zone', *Anthropological Quarterly* 78 (2): 403-430.

Van Walsum, S.K. & T. Spijkerboer (2007), *Women and immigration law: New variations on classical feminist themes*. Abington: Routledge.

Verkuyten, M. & P. Brug (2004), 'Multiculturalism and group status: The role of ethnic identification, group essentialism and Protestant ethic', *European Journal of Social Psychology* 34: 647-661.

Volpp, L. (2006), 'Divesting citizenship: On Asian American history and the loss of citizenship through marriage', *Immigrant and Nationality Law Review* 52: 397-476.

Volpp, L. (1996), 'Talking "culture": Gender, race, nation, and the politics of multiculturalism', *Columbia Law Review* 96 (6): 1573-1617.

Waddington, H., & R. Sabates-Wheeler (2003), *How does poverty affect migration choice? A Review of Literature*. Sussex: Working Paper T3 Institute of Development Studies.

Weitzer, R. (2010), 'The mythology of prostitution: Advocacy research and public Policy', *Sexuality Research and Social Policy* 7 (1): 15-29.

Wiebel, J.C. (2010), *Beyond the border: On rhetoric, US immigration and governmentality*, PhD thesis, University of Iowa, http://ir.uiowa.edu/etd/906 (Accessed 18 May 2013).

Wieringa, S.E. (2011), 'Portrait of a women's marriage: Navigating between Lesbophobia and Islamophobia', *Signs* 36 (4): 785-793.

Wihtol de Wenden, C. (1998), 'Young Muslim women in France: Cultural and psychological adjustments', *Political Psychology* 19 (1): 133-146.

Winter, B. (2008), *Hijab and the Republic: Uncovering the French headscarf debate*. Syracuse: Syracuse University Press.

Winter, B. (2006), 'Religion, culture and women's human rights: Some general political and theoretical considerations', *Women's Studies International Forum* 29 (4): 381-393.

Wooditch, A.C., M.A. DuPont-Morales & D. Hummer (2009), 'Traffick jam: A policy review of the United States' Trafficking Victims Protection Act of 2000', *Trends in Organized Crime* 12 (3): 235-250.

Yamanaka, K. & N. Piper (2005), 'Feminized migration in East and Southeast Asia: Policies, actions and empowerment', Geneva, United Nations Research Institute for Social Development Occasional Paper 11.

Yeates, N. (2004), 'A dialogue with "global care chain" analysis: Nurse migration in the Irish context', *Feminist Review* 77 (1): 79-95.

Zlotnik, H. (1998), 'International migration, 1965-1996: An overview', *Population and Development Review* 24 (3): 429-468.

Zolberg, A. (2006), *A nation by design: Immigration policy in the fashioning of America*. Cambridge: Harvard University Press.

# 2 Refugees and restrictionism

## Armenian women immigrants to the USA in the post-World War I era

*Yael Schacher*

## Introduction

Most scholarship on US refugee and asylum policy focuses on the period after the Second World War, though some works briefly mention that the 1917 immigration law exempted from the literacy test those fleeing from religious persecution. One scholar has claimed this early provision was 'stillborn', given the passage of increasingly restrictionist quota laws in 1921 and 1924 that guaranteed no slots for refugees (Bon Tempo 2008: 15). Another scholar categorises the literacy test exemption as part of a liberal tradition of asylum, which developed in the USA as a defence against exclusion and deportation (Price 2009: 52-58). But there has been no investigation into what actually happened to a population that was supposed to benefit from the literacy test exemption – Armenian immigrants – to assess how the binary of realities and ideals structured the provision of refuge.[1]

## Material and methods

This chapter attempts to provide this 'on the ground' story. Its main source comprises all discoverable Immigration Bureau cases involving Armenian immigrants who raised the issue of persecution between 1917 and 1924. The annual reports of the Commissioner General of Immigration do not report the number or persecution claims made, but only the number of literacy test exemptions officially granted for this reason. Thus, the statistics hide the extensive discussions about persecution carried on during admission hearings and between officials, though these are evident in the case files. Most of these case files involve Armenian women who, after the genocide, for the first time outnumbered Armenian male immigrants. Armenian women, too, were much more likely to have difficulty passing the literacy test. More than 55%

of the approximately 25,000 Armenian immigrants in the 1920s were women.[2] In order to follow Armenian women after their arrival and to analyse the perspectives of the social workers who handled their cases, this chapter also draws on some 150 case files from the international institutes of the Young Women's Christian Association (YWCA) from the 1920s, the vast majority of which are from the Boston International Institute.[3]

Examining case files helps to fill in gaps in the scholarship on the Armenian genocide and responses to it by focusing on gender and migration. Historians have illuminated the divergent and varied wartime experiences of able-bodied Armenian men and women, the former conscripted, placed in labour battalions, imprisoned and killed and the latter deported, raped, converted and taken into Muslim homes as servants or wives (Sansarian 1989; Sarafian 2001; Derderian 2005; Bjornlund 2009). Scholars have noted the importance of US missionaries in supplying graphic reports of massacres and deportations to both consuls and the press (*Turkish Atrocities* 1998; Moranian 2003). Studies have explored the significance of the Orientalist and gendered portrayals of 'ravished' and 'tragic' Armenia as a victim of Muslim barbarism and a martyred nation (Torchin 2006; Laycock 2009). Scholars are beginning to write about efforts to recover and care for Armenian women by the allied armies, Armenian volunteers in the French legion, the League of Nations, and ethnic and relief organisations (such as the American Red Cross, Near East Relief, the Armenian General Benevolent Union, and the Armenian National Union) (Shemmassian 2003, 2006; Watenpaugh 2010). Few have looked carefully, however, at the relationship between these 'rescuers' and migration. This is partly because, in a time of nationalism and restrictionism, the organisations saw themselves as engaged in projects of ethnic reconstruction and were quick to disavow emigration. Indeed, Vartan Malcolm, counsel for the Armenian National Union in Washington, DC, wrote that Armenians in America should 'go back to Armenia' after the war (Vartan Malcolm 1919: 141). Publicity materials for relief organisations hid some of the realities of the post-war situation for Armenian women that made their migration difficult, especially the prevalence of venereal disease. For instance, a promotional June 1919 American Committee for Armenian and Syrian Relief *News Bulletin* features a picture of a 'victim of Turkish cruelty' in the Near East Relief hospital in Aleppo. In the original print of this picture, the sign above the woman's head identifies her and the reason she is in the hospital: 'Aroosiag Mutafian, syphilis'. Yet this is not visible in the published version.[4] Furthermore publicity materials tried to hide the refusal to abandon children born to them in Muslim homes, children frequently rejected by fellow Armenians as 'the executioners' progeny' and disdained by relief workers as 'half casts' (Tachjian 2009: 75). 'Recounting the experience of enslavement, kidnapping, rape, and sequestration has tended to evoke a series of responses ranging from shame to outright denial in the Armenian diaspora', a historian recently noted, adding that 'rescued women ... were caught between two patriarchal systems' and abstracted into 'empty vessels into which anxieties about ... national honor ... could be poured' (Watenpaugh 2010: 1, 337). As a result, there is a 'lack of information' on what happened to those Armenian women who lived with Muslims during the genocide and then 'took refuge in Armenian communities outside of Turkey' (Peroomian 2009: 14).[5] One scholar of the Armenian diaspora wrote insightfully on the benefits and drawbacks of picture bride arrangements in facilitating transatlantic migration (Kaprielian-Churchill 1993), but few documented the various migration strategies and experiences, many of which involved co-ethnic brokers or commercial middlemen and difficult compromises, of Armenian women migrants to the USA. Historians have described the obsession of US immigration authorities with discovering incidents of trafficking and prostitution (Feldman 1967; Donovan 2006). However, none have looked at the way the wartime experiences of Armenian women – many of whom were victims of trafficking and turned to prostitution – subjected them to increased scrutiny on arrival to the USA. Historians of Armenian-Americans have written about the ethnic community's response to nativism by insisting on its whiteness, an image that relied in part on disavowing 'intermingling' between Armenians and Turks and insisting on the respectability of Armenian women and their treatment as equals by their menfolk (Craver 2009: 46). How did this stance influence the reception of Armenian women and the handling of intra-ethnic relationships that did not conform to these types in the 1920s?

A brief example, by way of introduction, will suffice to show how the case files not only deepen our understanding of the legacy of the war on the experiences of Armenian women migrants, but also fill in what was left out of media depictions that highlighted victimisation and redemption.

Perhaps the most famous Armenian woman in the USA after the war was Aurora Mardiganian. Her account of the deportations was widely read as a book and adapted into a film to publicise and raise money for the American organisation Near East Relief. The account, *Ravished Armenia*, sensationalised Turkish sexual violence against Armenian women (Mardiganian 1918).[6] Its narrative, like much of the newspaper coverage of the massacres, associates religious persecution with sexual degradation by presenting conversion to Islam and entrance into a harem as the only alternative to death for Armenian women. It also contrasts this with the religious liberty and security found in the USA, where there was 'so little of tragedy ... [and] suffering' (ibid.: 103-104). But despite its graphic details, the narrative emphasises Aurora's evasions, never detailing her rape or apostasy, allowing her to retain an image of pious purity. In the last chapter of the book, she provides a rushed account of her trip through Russia to the USA, leaving the details of her passport and fare arrangements vague, implying the support of the American relief organisation and embassy. She rejoiced at the welcome and safety symbolised by the Statue of Liberty; the support of 'kindly Americans' made her 'as happy as ever I can be' (ibid.: 201). This image of grateful rescued Armenian women migrants was echoed in press stories. *The Atlanta Constitution* (24 January 1920: 7B) ran the headline: 'Her thumb bears red tattoo mark of Moslem slave: Broken in health, Armenian girl reaches home of wealthy New York brother – Thinks she is in heaven'.[7]

But Aurora's official case file reveals a more complicated picture of her migration and reception. Five years after she arrived, immigration authorities learned that Aurora had gained entry into USA as the daughter of a naturalised Armenian named Ingian, an arrangement made by an Armenian general who paid her passage. Learning of this fraud, immigration authorities began to investigate 'lurid' allegations that Aurora lived out of wedlock with Armenian soldiers after she ran away from her Turkish captor, 'misconduct' that they believed in part because investigators had suspected she was pregnant when she first arrived, and she told them she had sexual relations with the Turk before she could escape. In investigating her case anew, an inspector questioned her closely about the arrangements made to bring her to the United States: 'You were not asked or did not promise to do anything for Mr. Ingian or anyone else – to marry someone or to live with someone or to do anything with them or for them?' In the course of their investigation, inspectors also learned that Aurora's mother had died a natural death in 1905, which contradicted the story of the mother's martyrdom recounted in *Ravished Armenia*. In pleading her case, Aurora's attorney noted that she was in the midst of a lawsuit against the makers of the film to recover salary owed her. In the end, the authorities decided not to attempt to arrest and deport Aurora for 'moral turpitude', believing that the deportation would be a 'grave hardship'. As we shall see, this kind of concession was the best refuge many Armenian survivors could obtain.[8]

## Persecution, gender, and discretion

During the congressional debates over the literacy test, it was assumed that most illiterate women would come as dependents and qualify for a general exemption for mothers, wives and daughters. There was little acknowledgement of the possibility that women refugees, who had lost husbands, parents and children during the war, would migrate alone. Moreover, inspectors were given little guidance on how to assess religious persecution claims. Immigration service rules stipulated only that 'clear and convincing proof of claims of exemption' be obtained by inspectors.[9] Thus, the persecution claims by Armenian *feme sole*, who began arriving in increasing numbers in 1920 and 1921, were unforeseen and handled on a case by case basis. The case files for those years reveal that immigration officials generally refused to acknowledge persecution claims of Armenian women, which would set a precedent and preclude the collection of fines from steamship companies. Instead, they used their discretion to parole or admit women temporarily to relatives, friends or fiancés, as cases of 'extreme hardship'.[10] By doing this, the authorities avoided challenges to their rulings in court and in response to media exposure, public pressure and letters from advocates and members of congress.

The questions asked claimants by inspectors reflect several influences. First, inspectors were influenced by the exemption's attachment to the literacy test to ask about educational opportunities to determine persecution. Typically, however, inspectors dismissed claims by attributing lack of schooling to factors other than official religious discrimination. Sometimes they attributed it to 'personal factors', especially if women told of having parents who kept them at home. An inspector followed up one such claim with the question, 'Can you explain why some Armenians living in the places where you lived were permitted to go to school?'[11] Evidence of gender discrimination in educational opportunity also facilitated rejection. One woman claimed that the Turkish authorities prevented schooling in her village, but allowed the boys to go to school for a few weeks in the wintertime. 'What prevented the girls from going to school with the boys?', the inspector asked. She answered, '[T]he school was so poor it could only take the boys.'[12] Inspectors tended to see gender discrimination and religious discrimination as mutually exclusive, rather than to view the former as compounding the latter.

Graphic claims that invoked the Orientalist redemption narrative (popularised by Aurora's tale) were a double-edged sword. The power of this narrative meant that if advocates told tales of *potential* sex-

ual risk at the hands of the Turks, illiterate women could sometimes
gain admission even when they themselves told inspectors that they
had not suffered religious persecution. In one such case, a deposition
attesting that a woman 'alone and an orphan and a Christian' would
'almost certain[ly] … be taken as a white slave by men of other religious
beliefs' in her home town convinced Louis Post, Assistant Secretary of
Labour, that she should be admitted as 'a religious refugee' in April
1920.[13] In another case, a woman's brother petitioned administrators,
arguing that her initial denial of persecution was a product of feminine
shame. One of the rehearing examiners believed that 'her statements
are borne out by the general knowledge that comes to us through the
press of the attitude of the Mohammedan toward the Turkish Christians.'[14] On the other hand, when a woman actually told a detailed
account of the 'indignities' of forced conversion and of 'violation' by
a Turk, inspectors were sceptical of the woman's innocence, especially
since she was coming to the USA to meet a fiancé she had never seen
and who paid her passage.[15] The prevalence of the Orientalist narrative of persecuted Christianity and harem slaves also meant that more
restrictionist administrators could dismiss graphic persecution claims
as scripted, or what they called the 'stock exemption' among illiterate
women coming from the Near East.[16] In one case, officials dismissed
a detailed testimony of beatings and theft as a 'subterfuge'.[17] In another
case, when an illiterate former 'inmate of a harem' was threatened with
exclusion, protests from women's clubs, politicians and church leaders horrified at the possibility of sending her back into danger led to
her admission.[18] Without advocates like these, indications of customs
considered backward and Eastern could lead to exclusion. In one such
case, an illiterate Armenian woman who arrived with a 15-year-old girl
she intended as her son's wife was rebuked by an inspector who told her
'under the laws of the United States a child of that age cannot be legally
married'.[19] Arranged marriages were increasingly looked upon as sus-
piciously pragmatic and coercive, and therefore as un-American (Haag
1999). The inspectors believed that the case of an 18-year-old Armenian
girl coming from Constantinople to marry a man who paid her uncle
to bring her over, was testament to the fact that 'the bringing of girls of
certain races to the United States for matrimonial and other purposes
has become a matter of the most sordid commercialism'.[20]

Immigration authorities also justified their decisions by referring to
the geopolitical situation in the Near East. When persecution claims
by illiterate Armenian immigrants became frequent in 1920, the immigration authorities sought guidance from the State Department, which
provided what it admitted was a 'not very responsive' reply:

The persecution of Christians ... was notoriously frequent in the former Ottoman Empire ... one important aim of the readjustments now
in progress in the Near East is to put an end to these outbreaks. It is
to be feared, however, that the present era of transition is peculiarly
favorable to such manifestations throughout the entire region ... The
French are now in military occupation ... and it is to be expected that
as conditions grow more settled under their authority, outbreaks of
fanaticism will decrease in frequency.[21]

Left to their own devices, immigration authorities consistently dismissed persecution claims by asserting that, despite what happened
during the deportations, Armenian women had not been persecuted
if they departed from areas under British or French occupation.[22] They
relied on the language of the 1917 law that exempted from the literacy test those coming 'to avoid religious persecution in the country of
their last permanent residence, whether such persecution be evidenced
by overt act or by laws or governmental regulations that discriminate
against the alien or the race to which he belongs because of his religious
faith.[23] As the French withdrew from Cilicia in late 1921 and attacks on
Armenians were reported to the State Department and in the newspapers, immigration authorities insisted that an excluded family from
Aintab had nothing to fear, arguing that 'Turkish violence [against
Armenians who cooperated with the French] will probably not take
place until some months have elapsed, for the reason that it is thought
that the Turks will not wish to bring any political complications until
they have settled into full control of the territory.[24] By the following
year, there was a disconnect between requests for refuge by Armenian
women who claimed that they had suffered and lost everything between
1915 and 1917 and evaluations of these claims by immigration authorities focused on the feasibility of sending them back in 1922. The dynamics of the Greco-Turkish war seemed to colour the way officials interpreted the very different dynamics of earlier events.[25] When an illiterate
Armenian woman arrived in July 1922, an immigration inspector asked
her if she 'at any time' suffered persecution on account of religion. She
replied that she had been deported, stripped of all of her clothing and
feared for her life in 1915. The authorities decided that the 'persecution
she claims to have suffered was the result of conditions of war.[26]
In another case that month, an illiterate Armenian woman told
immigration authorities that she fled for her life when Turks killed her
mother and brother and spent the next several years in a British-run
refugee camp.[27] The woman was excluded not only for illiteracy, but
also because she exceeded the quota for immigrants coming from Tur-

key. Indeed, the quota law that went into effect in mid-1921 drastically reduced the number of Armenians allowed admission. Single Armenian women who arrived with children had already been tainted by suspicions of 'illegitimacy'. The persecution claim of Bayzan Zilfian and her daughter Siranouche, 'that their relatives and friends have been killed by the Turks and the aliens have suffered much during the deportation by the Turks', was 'not believed' to 'represent the correct facts' by the immigration authorities. A March 1921 letter from an Ellis Island assistant commissioner insinuating that Siranouche was born out of wedlock influenced this view.[28] After the passage of the quota law, such women were scrutinised even more closely, both by consuls issuing scarce visas overseas and by immigration authorities evaluating migrants upon arrival. For example, the consul in Aleppo had to use his discretion in divvying out visas to one in four Armenians who had relatives in the USA and who were, therefore, in the preferred quota class. He decided to reject Satenig Aghajamian for having lived with a Turk.[29] Immigration authorities in the USA looked more askance at the use of picture bride arrangements by illiterates, preferring intended husbands to go overseas to pick up their brides and then return with them.[30] The new law and policies led to both an increase in fraudulent marriages and suspicions of them. The cases of Almas Najarian and Vartanouche Eremian are revealing in this regard. Almas' husband had died while serving in the Ottoman army and her children died during the deportations in 1915. During these deportations a Turkish soldier forced Vartanouche to live with him. After the war, Armenian soldiers serving in the French army demanded her release. She was pregnant at the time. Hearing that she would have trouble entering the USA with a newborn illegitimate child, she paid an Armenian man to play her husband. An Armenian 'fixer' at an emigrant hotel suggested to Vartanouche that she exchange passports with Almas, who was illiterate and would be barred from entering the US. Almas posed for a new passport picture with the Armenian man and with Vartanouche's child as her own. The plan was for Vartanouche to travel alone and for Almas to claim exemption from the literacy test because she was coming to join this photo-husband. Upon arrival, inspectors denied that Almas legally qualified for a persecution exemption to the literacy test based on her claim: 'my foster-father did not care to send me to school but wanted me to do all the heavy work … the only reason that they deported us was because we were Christians and there was no chance of going to school or church'. Suspicious of her travelling with a child to join a soldier who left her, one of the inspectors asked Almas if she was pregnant and, though she denied it, put her through a 'special medical test' after the passport scheme was discovered. As for Vartanouche, given 'the amount of falsification indulged in', the authorities refused to use their discretion to let her in temporarily on bond to her relatives. They asked her if, in addition to paying the picture husband, she also had 'immoral relations' with him. Inspectors also asked whether the Turk who compelled Vartanouche to live with him during the war had many other women, if he 'outraged' Vartanouche's younger sister, and whether Vartanouche tried to run away. Vartanouche's answers seemed to disappoint them. Vartanouche said she was the only woman the Turk selected and that he supported her and her sister. This sister testified that Vartanouche had to leave behind an older child she bore him because the Armenian soldiers 'did not want to take the child away from him'.[31]

A family connection could help an illiterate Armenian woman avoid exclusion in the early 1920s, but admission on this basis typically implied a position of dependency rather than recognition of past persecution or a guarantee of future rights. When Harotune Selvian, a rancher from outside of Fresno, was convicted of violating the immigration law for bringing over and selling wives to his neighbours, the authorities allowed these wives to stay in the USA, claiming they engaged in 'merely passive deception'.[32] Having denied the persecution claim of an illiterate Armenian widow, the authorities could 'think of no other way' to legalise her admission than to have her adopt her nephew as her son, thereby exempting her from the literacy test as an aged parent of a US resident.[33] In congressional discussion about Armenian refugees, saving womenfolk overshadowed concern for statelessness. Here is an exchange between Charles Vickrey, General Secretary of Near East Relief, and Congressman John Kleczka, Republican representative from Wisconsin:

> Kleczka: Do you not think that ... if any relief is accorded, it ought to be accorded to those who have no government at all to protect them? ... [D]o you not think that those who have no government and nobody to care for them should receive first attention?

> Vickrey: I should say so. All through this law there is the supposition that the person to whom the applicant [i.e., the refugee overseas] would primarily look is the son or the brother who has come to America, established his citizenship, perhaps acquired a fortune, and who would like to give a home to his mothers and sisters.[34]

Later in the decade, immigration officials refused to adjust to permanent admission status a woman they let in temporarily outside of the

quota, even though she could no longer be deported, having lived in
the USA for more than five years and being unable to secure a passport
from Turkish authorities, who did not permit the return of Armenians.
Thus, despite the appeals of YWCA social workers, Agniv Kurdian, who
had been living in the USA since late 1922, remained, in 1927, unable to
naturalise or to reunite with her husband in Istanbul.[35]

## Ethnicity, respectability and refuge

YWCA social workers began their work with Armenian women in Turkey, where they made an exception to their usual policy of not working
with 'fallen girls' by establishing rescue homes and a migration service.
One worker explained that, without guidance, those Armenian women
who had been taken by the Turks would remain morally tainted, 'discouraged with life' and 'hardened in their ways and low in their ideals'.
They might, because prices were high in comparison with wages, 'get
in with powder and paint' and turn to prostitution.[36] At a home run in
collaboration with Near East Relief in Harput, YWCA workers worried
about the 'Turk babies' their wards brought with them and instituted a
policy of keeping women a month before giving them material for new
clothes because 'some tried to run away after a few days to return to
the Turks'.[37] Work and marriage to Armenians seemed the best way to
save such women. At one rescue home, Armenian women learned how
to weave and sew and helped one girl, about to be married, prepare
her trousseau.[38] Frequently, marriages were to men in the diaspora and
involved migration. In its migration work, the YWCA believed itself to
be responsible, among other things, for warning migrants about un-
scrupulous brokers and ticket agents as well as the risk of exclusion.[39]
In early 1922, the State Department turned to YWCA representatives in
Constantinople to help track down Armenians who had been rejected
by the immigration authorities.[40] The YWCA's report on these returned
immigrants helped discount as 'false propaganda' the claims that persecution awaited excluded Armenians.[41] Collaboration with this investigation hinted at the overseas YWCA's future attempts to professionalise
its international migration service and to promote restored US relations
with Turkey. This led to some conflict with the YWCA's US-based division, which worked primarily with Armenian immigrants.

By the 1920s, the YWCA's Department of Immigration and Foreign
Communities had established international institutes in various US cities. These institutes employed Armenian-American social workers or
'nationality workers' to help locate refugee relatives abroad and help

them 'adjust' on arrival. The institutes saw themselves as serving not just women, but the entire ethnic community, and relied on male religious and business leaders in the communities for support. International institutes emphasised the importance of nationality, which in its celebratory form fostered folk festivals and cultural appreciation, but it also resonated with the ethnic essentialism of the 1920s and the basis of the immigration quotas.[42] An emphasis on nationality as a positive source of sociological and psychological cohesiveness[43] also led workers to attribute economic and family problems to mixed marriages, rather than to gender discrimination.[44] The Armenian-American social workers were well-educated, middle-class women, and many were single. This did not translate into support for the dissolution of arranged marriages or the pursuit of professional ambition by their female immigrant clients. In one case, a client was discouraged from defying 'the customs and conventions of the nationality group' and from attempting to 'accomplish things practically outside of her means'.[45] This condescension was sometimes mirrored by clients, who referred to social workers as unfortunate 'eksik etek' (which literally translates as 'short skirt' and idiomatically disparaged intellectual, unmarried women) and turned to male co-ethnics – frequently, lawyers, steamship agents, or church and benevolent society leaders – for help with remittances and migration arrangements.[46]

Armenian-American social workers strove to portray Armenian families in the best possible light, which was not always easy. Because many Armenian women married men they barely knew in order to get into the country, problems inevitably arose. Though frequently called upon, international institute social workers tried not to serve as witnesses in divorce cases, so as not to seem to take sides between man and wife, rather than representing the ethnic community as a whole.[47] The social workers also worked closely with the immigration authorities, mostly helping to facilitate admission and to legalise the status of their clients or as interpreters. It was the general policy of the YWCA not to 'take any action which might be interpreted as ... trying to influence the government to set aside the laws on behalf of migrants'. Aghavnie Yeghenian and Olympia Yeranian, Armenian-American YWCA social workers, helped to secure entry for their friends and siblings and acted as advocates in their personal capacities in some cases. But they consistently condemned outright fraud, like the use of false names and the claiming of false familial relationships.[48] This was sometimes a hard balancing act. In one case, immigration authorities treated three newly arrived Armenian girls poorly on the assumption that they were lying about their supposed father. According to the immigration commis-

sioner, Armenians were 'very affectionate and devoted to their children'
and the man claiming to be the father had not visited the detention
centre often enough. The fact that he could not do so without risking
his job was not the commissioner's concern. Yeranian and Yeghenian
wanted to help the girls, who had suffered through deportations, servi-
tude in a Turkish home and years in several Near East Relief orphanages
before coming to the USA. They said the girls behaved like 'real ladies
and never did anything they should not do' while in detention. But the
two social workers agreed that they could not help if the man was in
fact the uncle and not the father of the girls.[49] Cases involving Armenian women who were not as compliant and modest as these were even
more challenging for the social workers because they had little support
from the ethnic community. One such Armenian woman, though pit-
ied because she was orphaned during the war, was deemed a disgrace
because she lived an 'indecent' life. Though the woman shunned contact with Yeranian, Armenian community leaders expected her to take
responsibility for marrying the woman off, sending her to a school of
correction or getting her out of town.[50]

For Armenian-American social workers, ethnic allegiances com-
pounded already mixed motives towards rescue, objectivity and social
control.[51] Yeghenian and Yeranian were positioned between the world
of their clients and that of US social welfare professionals with missionary backgrounds. Educated in US schools in the Ottoman Empire,
they left there in response to the war. By the late 1920s, Yeghenian had
become head of the YWCA's Department of Immigration and began to
see the reclamation difficulties of the Armenian community as a product of restrictive immigration laws that prevented family unification
among the foreign born more generally.[52] Yet throughout the decade,
Yeghenian remained the point person for Armenian migration cases
handled by the various international institutes. Cases that involved
women who had been living in Turkish homes since the war put Yeghenian in touch with the Armenian prelacy, relief organisations, missionaries and consuls and forced her to make difficult accommodations. In
one case, restrictive Turkish emigration and US immigration laws and a
daughter's attachment to her Turkish life (especially her Muslim faith),
made uniting her with her mother in the US impossible.[53] In another
case, Yeghenian helped a woman obtain a divorce because she had been
forced to live with a Turk and felt that the three children she had borne
him would not be accepted by her husband in the USA.[54]

The allegiances and values of social workers were put to the test
when one of their clients, Yeranouhie Ananian, was threatened with
deportation from the USA. Yeranouhie spent the war years in a German

orphanage in Harput. After the war, she moved to a US-funded Near East Relief orphanage in Beirut until it closed down and she was sent to live in Marseilles. Prevented by the quota law from coming directly to the USA, Yeranouhie travelled to Mexico and then Cuba. A man named Maroukian, a US citizen, travelled from Providence, Rhode Island to Cuba and he and Yeranouhie married. The couple came to the USA, and Yeranouhie filed for divorce. Immigration authorities learned that Maroukian had been paid by a non-naturalised Armenian, the brother of Yeranouhie's old friend, to bring Yeranouhie into the country, as only the wives of citizens were exempt from the quota. The authorities also learned that she was pregnant. To deport Yeranouhie on the grounds that she had entered the country for an immoral purpose, the immigration authorities needed evidence that she had sexual relations with both men. They subpoenaed an Armenian-American social worker from the Rhode Island international institute who reluctantly testified that Yeranouhie told her that the baby she was carrying was her friend's brother's. 'As an Armenian woman', the social worker wrote Yeranian:

> I have interest in Mrs. Maroukian to help her any way we can, but ... I believe that anything you could do for her would reflect more against your work with the Armenian community then it could help her. The Armenian community feels that the whole case has done the Armenians generally so much harm ... if the immigration authorities had not acted so strict on this case perhaps others would try the same thing.

Maroukian told Yeranian that she only consented to marry under false pretences because she had such a miserable life during the war in Turkey and that she had decided to do anything to get out of the orphanage and into the USA.

After Yeranouhie's son John, was born, she 'begged' to leave him in the USA, but the immigration authorities 'advised' her that she should not be separated from her child. While she and John were on their way to Ellis Island for deportation, Yeranian wrote to Yeghenian that she felt 'very sorry for the poor woman, who has to bear the burden of her sin, as well as that of two men who are really responsible for her misfortune'. Yeghenian was concerned too, but focused more on professionalism and advocacy. She wrote to Yeranian that this case provided 'invaluable experience in cases of this kind ... of help to other Institutes' and was 'illustrative of the terrible human tangles involved in our restrictive law'. Indeed, Yeranouhie's deportation proved complicated. Because Turkish authorities would not allow the return of Armenians, she was sent to Cuba, but the Cuban authorities refused to admit unaccompanied married women without their husband's consent and anyone who had a passport indicating that they were deported for 'immoral purposes' since that implied involvement with prostitution.

While Maroukian was in detention in Cuba, the secretary of the Anglo-American Association there forwarded to Yeghenian a copy of a strongly worded letter of protest he sent to the US immigration authorities. The letter pointed out that while the authorities treated the 'white slavers' like barely tainted orphan rescuers, they had turned Yeranouhie into a refugee once more, she having no country to return to, and they had pushed for the deportation of her US-born child, ignoring his citizenship rights. Yeghenian found this protest 'splendid' because, she admitted, 'the sordid circumstances of the case were so appalling' that 'it did not occur' to her to try and prevent the deportation. Thus, the problem of statelessness had been overshadowed by other concerns. Yerahounie eventually managed to get a transit visa through France, where she had a hard time. 'Dear sister', Yerahounie wrote to Yeranian from Marseilles, 'We neither have a bed to sleep in nor dishes and spoon to eat food … Our people have changed a lot … they do not even want the baby in the house, nor me either.' After some difficulties, Yeranouhie obtained an identification card so that she could stay in France. In order to work to support herself, she had to put John in an orphanage not so different from the one that she had grown up in.[55]

Yeranouhie Maroukian's deportation was indeed a test case in that it affected the way international institute social workers handled other cases. In 1928, an Armenian woman came to the international institute seeking protection from the man she was living with. He was an Armenian she had taken up with during the war, after the death of her parents, to avoid being given in marriage to a Turk. The couple were never officially married, though they claimed to be when they entered the USA, so Yeghenian and Yeranian were worried that if the woman brought her case to court, the immigration authorities might issue a warrant for her deportation.[56] Another case involved a woman whose pregnancy seemed to precede her marriage in Cuba; she had been shunned by her husband but kept shut-in by her husband's family since her arrival in the USA. Yeranian advised against any court action because of the threat of deportation or any publicity because of the 'bad effect it would have on the standing of the Armenians in the community'.[57]

Yeranian thought it best to keep Yeranouhie Maroukian's 'whole story' out of the public eye 12 years after her deportation. By that time, this strategy did not primarily preserve the good image of Armenian immigrants, but rather shored up the image of the USA as a generous nation of refuge. On 30 January 1940, the *New York Herald Tribune* ran a glowing story on John Maroukian, '12 Years Away, Boy, 13, Returns to Be American'. It is worth quoting the story at length to understand how myths are made:

> John Maroukian, a native of Boston, arrived Wednesday on the liner Siboney … He was one of the many repatriates from France aboard the vessel … His first stroke of good fortune after the ship docked was in meeting Miss Olympia Yeranian … Immigration officials notified Miss Yeranian that the boy was aboard the ship. His name was famil-iar to her, and she recalled that last September the State Department had asked her to testify to the boy's American citizenship. Somehow the State Department had learned that thirteen years ago Miss Yera-nian, then a social worker in Boston, had helped the boy's mother fight against poverty and desertion. John's father, an American citizen of Armenian birth, died soon after the baby was born. Mrs. Marouk-ian was married again, this time to Simeon Moussouyan. They went to France, taking John along and making their home at Marseilles. Moussouyan, an Armenian, served in the French army against the Nazis … When John's mother heard that the State Department was re-patriating Americans in France she agreed that her boy should come here if he wanted to. A boy scout, John arrived with a blanket slung across his shoulders and his few belongings packed neatly in a small satchel and a paper parcel … With Miss Yeranian as interpreter, he said yesterday he did not have enough to eat in France … He brought ration cards along, thinking they would be necessary somewhere along the line … Visitors yesterday found John a sociable boy, ready to smile or play checkers. He is thin, his cheeks are pale, but given a few more dinners of corned beef and cabbage, such as he had yesterday, there is every reason to believe, Miss Yeranian said, that eventually he will realize his ambition of being able to send for his family.

## Conclusion

This chapter analysed the motives and methods of Armenian migrants, social workers and government authorities as revealed in cases found in the archives of the US Immigration and Naturalization Service and the international institutes of the YWCA. We paid particular attention to examinations at ports of entry and to practices of control. In doing so, we documented the significance of gender in the ideological under-pinnings of refugee advocacy, while narrating a history that prefigures contemporary gendered disparities and discourses in asylum cases.

Discretion and deportation have only recently gained the attention
of historians of immigration to the USA (Kanstroom 2007, 2010). This
chapter demonstrated gender to be crucial in order to understand the
experience of Armenians who came to the United States after World
War I. As we saw, Armenian women immigrants achieved a kind of
de facto refugee status, not unlike that in the Netherlands discussed
by Walaardt in this volume. The case files of the international institute
highlight the relationship between the state, ethnicity and advocacy,
which continues to shape the refugee experience – as also underscored
by Connie Oxford's chapter in this volume. Armenian-American social
workers, who were eager to promote the respectability of the Armenian community, opposed the harsh impact of immigration laws but
accommodated them in practice. Immigration authorities and social
workers responded to realities they shunned – to sexual violence and
gender discrimination, illegitimacy and statelessness, desperation and
deception – with a restrictionism and exceptionalism, which underlie
American refugee policy.

## Notes

1   For evidence that Armenians were one of the populations that legislators intended
    to exempt with this provision, see *Congressional Record* 31 July 1914, 51: 2704; 31
    December 1914, 52: 785; 24 March 1916, 53: 4799; 25 March 1916, 53: 4869; and 13
    December 1916, 54: 267.
2   For data on Armenian men and women admitted and taking the literacy test, see
    tables 3 and 15 in Minasian (1961).
3   The author thanks Elizabeth Haven Hawley and Dan Necas at the Immigration
    History Research Centre, University of Minnesota, for permission to use Interna-
    tional Institute files. Thanks to Marian Smith and Zack Wilske at the US Citizen-
    ship and Immigration Services history office for help in locating case files in the
    Immigration and Naturalization Service (INS) records at the National Archives.
    The names of clients in the closed case files of the International Institute have
    been disguised.
4   The original print is number 204 in the Near East Relief Collection, Aga Kahn
    Division, Fine Arts Library, Harvard University. On the prevalence of venereal
    disease, see Richards (1923): 21.
5   Jackson (2010) noted similar silences about the experiences of women in accounts
    of Sudanese displacement in the late 20th century.
6   This is reprinted, along with stills and other materials from the film, in *Ravished
    Armenia and the Story of Aurora Mardriganian*, compiled by Anthony Slide.
7   See also '"Y" Envoy adopts waif: Armenian boy, found beside track, to have
    American home,' *New York Tribune*, 30 May 1921, 16.

8    INS case files 55227/244 and 54290/493, RG 85, Entry 9, National Archives and Record Administration, Washington, DC. All INS case files hereafter cited come from this record group at the National Archives.

9    *Immigration laws: Rules of May 1, 1917* (Washington, DC: Government Printing Office, 1917), 40.

10   See, for example, INS case files 55190/ 561 and 55375/518.

11   INS file 55190/561.

12   INS file 55866/172.

13   INS file 54766-627.

14   INS file 54766/974.

15   INS file 54766/777.

16   INS file 54766/952.

17   INS case 54766/966.

18   INS case 54766/777.

19   INS case 54999/363.

20   INS case 55180/434.

21   Letter of Bainbridge Colby to Secretary of Labor, 2 September 1920, 150.676/37, Visa Division, Correspondence Related to Immigration, 1910-39, General Records of the Department of State, RG 59, NARA.

22   INS case files 54766/771, 55018/351, 55190/572.

23   Section 3 of 39 Stat. 877.

24   INS case file 55021/24. For State Department reports, see file 860J.4016 in Records of the Department of State Relating to Internal Affairs of Armenia, 1910-1929, microfilm T1192, NARA.

25   According to Bloxham (2006: 31), 'The Armenian genocide was a one-sided destruction of a largely defenceless community ... the dynamics were slightly different in many of the events of 1917-1923, and markedly so in the Greco-Turkish war. The latter episodes, in all their bloody complexity, would ... be a vital factor in retrospectively shaping external perceptions of the 1915-1916 genocide.'

26   INS case 55255/210.

27   INS case 55255/350.

28   INS case 54999/166.

29   Correspondence of the American Consulate in Aleppo, Syria, Class 811.1, 1923, Volume 93, RG 84, NARA.

30   See opposition to admitting illiterate women to intended husbands in case 55175/735 (September 1921), and case 55236/45 (November 1922).

31   INS cases 55018/371 and 55018/392.

32   INS case 55063/51.

33   INS case 54866/638.

34   Hearings on H. R. 13269, Admission of Near East Refugees, 67th Congress, 4th session, 15, 16, and 19 December 1922, 86.

35   INS case 55301/361.

36   Letter from Margaret White to Sarah Lyon, 15 April 1919, folder 4, reel 63, YWCA of the U.S.A. Records, Sophia Smith Collection, Smith College, Northampton, Mass (hereafter, YWCA Smith).

37  Report of the Oversees Committee of War Work Council, 149-50, folder 5, box 707, YWCA Smith.

38  Report of Margaret White for October 1919, folder 4, reel 63, YWCA Smith.

39  The migration service in Constantinople published a pamphlet entitled 'Take Thought Before Migrating to the USA' to inform migrants of the quota laws. Folder on Migration Work, reel 64, YWCA Smith.

40  Relevant correspondence between the chair of the House Committee on Immigration, the State Department, and Consular and YWCA personnel in Turkey can be found in file 860J.4016/113-158, Records of the Department of State Relating to Internal Affairs of Armenia, 1910-1929, T1192, reel 5, National Records and Archives Service, General Services Administration, 1975.

41  Letter from Ruth Larned to Mary Hurlbutt, 2 February 1922, folder 2, Migration Work, reel 64, YWCA Smith.

42  'The International Institute's approach is on the basis of a respect for, and a recognition of, natural social cohesiveness of the nationality consciousness.' December 1929 report, Folder: Reports 1910-1934, Immigration, reel 100, YWCA Smith.

43  'We believe that the nationality sense is naturally a dominant factor for any foreigner... Work for the individual is inseparable from an interest in and cultivation of the nationality community that circumscribes her life. A foreign community is a psychological unity.' Edith Terry Bremer, International Institute: Re-Analysis of our Foundations, in Confidential Proceedings of the Conference of International Institutes, Washington, DC, 14-16 May 1924, folder 6, Reel 100, YWCA Smith.

44  Derm. case, International Institute of Boston, Closed Case files, box 1, Immigration History Research Center, University of Minnesota (hereafter IHRC).

45  Arz. case, International Institute of Boston, Closed Case files, box 1, IHRC.

46  Case 699, International Institute of Boston, Closed Case files, box 16, IHRC.

47  Bohh. case, International Institute of Boston, Closed Case files, box 1, IHRC.

48  In INS case 55270/565 Yeghenian appealed to the authorities to admit her sister; in case 617, box 15, International Institute Boston, IHRC, Yeranian acted in her capacity as a 'private individual', but then closed the case when she found out the client used a false name.

49  Case 216, International Institute Boston, Closed Case files, box 12, IHRC.

50  Case 503, International Institute Boston, Closed Case files, box 14, IHRC.

51  For insight into the mixed motives of social workers in the 1920s, see D. Walkowitz (1990) and R. Kunzel (1993).

52  In April 1927, Yeghenian authored a YWCA report on the family of the foreign born under restrictive immigration that highlighted 100 cases of separated families from the records of different International Institutes. Twenty-three of the cases involved Armenian families and the rest involved families of other nationalities.

53  Case 502, International Institute of Boston, Closed Case files, box 14, IHRC.

54  Ku. case, International Institute of Connecticut, Closed Case files, box 5, IHRC.

55  Case File 576, box 15, International Institute of Boston, IHRC and INS case 55611/376.

56  Case 750, box 16, International Institute Boston, IHRC.

57  Case 732, box 16, International Institute Boston, IHRC.

## References

Bloxham, D. (2006), 'Roots of American genocide denial: Near Eastern geopolitics and the interwar Armenian question', *Journal of Genocide Research* 8 (1): 27-49.

Bon Tempo, C.J. (2008), *Americans at the gate: The United States and refugees during the Cold War*. Princeton: Princeton University Press.

Bjornlund, M. (2009), '"A fate worse than dying": Sexual violence during the Armenian genocide', in D. Herzog (ed.), *Brutality and desire: War and sexuality in Europe's twentieth century*, pp. 16-58. New York: Palgrave Macmillan.

Craver, E. (2009), 'On the boundary of white: The Cartozian naturalization case and the Armenians, 1923-1925', *Journal of American Ethnic History* 28 (2) (Winter): 30-56.

Derderian, K. (2005), 'Common fate, different experience: Gender-specific aspects of the Armenian genocide, 1915-1917', *Holocaust and Genocide Studies* 19 (1): 1-25.

Donovan, B. (2006), *White slave crusades: Race, gender and anti-vice activism, 1887-1917*. Urbana: University of Illinois Press.

Feldman, E. (1967), 'Prostitution and the alien woman and the progressive imagination, 1910-1915', *American Quarterly* 19 (2) (Summer): 192-206.

Haag, P. (1999), *Consent: Sexual rights and the transformation of American liberalism*. Ithaca and London: Cornell University Press.

Jackson, L. (2010), 'Where are the girls? War displacement and the notion of home among Sudanese refugee children', in M. Schrover & E.J. Yeo (eds), *Gender, migration and the public sphere in interdisciplinary perspective 1850-2005*, pp. 160-178. New York: Taylor and Francis/Routledge.

Kanstroom. D. (2010), 'Loving humanity while accepting real people', in D. Hollenbach (ed.), *Driven from home: Protecting the rights of forced migrants*, pp. 115-145. Washington, DC: Georgetown University Press.

Kanstroom, D. (2007), *Deportation nation: Outsiders in American history*. Cambridge: Harvard University Press.

Kaprielian-Churchill, I. (1993), 'Armenian refugee women: The picture brides, 1920-1930', *Journal of American Ethnic History* 12 (3) (Spring): 3-29.

Kunzel, R.G. (1993), *Fallen women, problem girls: Unmarried mothers and the professionalization of social work, 1890-1945*. New Haven and London: Yale University Press.

Laycock, J. (2009), *Imagining Armenia: Orientalism, ambiguity, and intervention*. New York and Manchester: Manchester University Press.

Mardiganian, A. (1918), *Ravished Armenia: the story of Aurora Mardiganian, the Christian girl, who lived through the great massacres*. New York: Kingfield Press.

Minasian, E. (1961), 'They came from Ararat: The exodus of the Armenian people to the United States'. PhD thesis, University of California, Berkeley.

Moranian, S.E. (2003), 'Armenian genocide and American missionary relief efforts', in J. Winter (ed.), *America and the Armenian genocide of 1915*, pp. 185-213. Cambridge: Cambridge University Press.

Peroomian, R. (2009), 'Women and the Armenian genocide: The victim, the living martyr', in S. Totten (ed.), *Plight and fate of women during and following genocide*, pp. 7-24. New Brunswick: Transaction.

Price, M. (2009), *Rethinking asylum: History, purpose, and limits*. Cambridge and New York: Cambridge University Press.

Richards, G.L. (1923), *Medicalwork of the Near East Relief*. New York: Near East Relief.

Sarafian, A. (2001), 'The absorption of Armenian women and children into Muslim households as a structural component of the Armenian genocide', in O. Bartov & P. Mack (eds), *In God's name: Genocide and religion in the twentieth century*, pp. 209-221. New York and Oxford: Berghahn Books.

Sansarian, E. (1989), 'Gender distinction in the genocide process: A preliminary study of the Armenian case', *Holocaust and Genocide Studies* 4 (4): 449-461.

Shemmassian, V.L. (2003), 'The League of Nations and the reclamation of Armenian genocide survivors', in R. Hovannisian (ed.), *Looking backward, moving forward*, pp. 81-112. New Brunswick: Transaction.

Shemmassian, V.L. (2006), 'The reclamation of captive Armenian genocide survivors in Syria and Lebanon at the end of World War I', *Journal for the Society of Armenian Studies* 15: 113-140.

Tachjian, V. (2009), 'Gender, nationalism, exclusion: The reintegration process of female survivors of the Armenian genocide', *Nations and Nationalism* 15 (1): 60-80.

*Turkish Atrocities: Statements of American missionaries on the destruction of Christian communities in Ottoman Turkey, 1915-1917* (1998), compiled by J. Barton. Ann Arbor: Gomidas Institute.

Torchin, L. (2006), 'Ravished Armenia: Visual media, humanitarian advocacy, and the formation of witnessing publics', *American Anthropologist* 108 (1) (March): 214-220.

Walkowitz, D. (1990), 'The making of a feminine professional identity: Social workers in the 1920s', *American Historical Review* 95 (4) 1051-1075.

Watenpaugh, K.D. (2010), 'The League of Nations' rescue of Armenian genocide survivors and the making of modern humanitarianism, 1920-1927', *American Historical Review* 115 (5) (December): 1315-1339.

# 3 New refugees?

## Manly war resisters prevent an asylum crisis in the Netherlands, 1968-1973

### Tycho Walaardt

### Introduction: Two types of heroes

In the late 1960s and early 1970s, a few hundred Portuguese war resisters and an American deserter sought refuge in the Netherlands.
These 'New Refugees' (Cohen & Joly 1989: 6) were the first substantial
group of asylum seekers to flee from non-communist countries to the
Netherlands since the beginning of the post-Second World War era.
Their arrival was part of a broader phenomenon: after the late 1960s the
number of asylum applicants increased, and their countries of origin
and their reasons for fleeing diversified (Paludan 1981: 69; Hoeksma
1987: 98; Gallagher 1989; Bronkhorst 1990: 44). This chapter describes
the responses of Dutch authorities and powerful lobby groups to their
arrival. Large numbers of people applied for asylum, but their social
backgrounds, countries of origin, as well as their motives, had shifted.
This, in turn, might have led to a moral panic in Dutch society and subsequent changes in refugee policy. In reality it did not.

According to some scholars, the arrival of the New Refugees led to
departures from earlier post-war refugee asylum policies (Van Esterik
1998: 120). These New Refugees were less successful than the anticommunists had been in Western asylum procedures (Bronkhorst 1990:
140; Van Esterik 1998: 120). Authorities viewed the New Refugees with
suspicion, because they were not the 'enemies of our enemies', as the
anticommunists had been (Zolberg 2006: 18). Portuguese war resisters were rarely granted refugee status, but they were seldom forced to
leave the Netherlands. Fewer than 3% of the Portuguese refugees were
denied residence permits from 1968 to 1973. This number contradicts
the image of a restrictive policy. Dutch authorities chose a pragmatic
solution: New Refugees were granted residence permits, but denied
refugee status.

Before 1970, most asylum seekers were characterised as anticommunists. The 1950s refugee was depicted as a heroic male figure fight-

ing against the terrors of communism (Carruthers 2005). A political activist, he was a member of his country's intelligentsia, and an asset to Western society. Defectors played a crucial role in anticommunist propaganda. Anticommunists did not arrive in large numbers, except following the 1956 Hungarian Uprising and the 1968 Prague Spring. But those who managed to cross the Iron Curtain are believed to have been warmly welcomed. In reality, their welcome was not particularly friendly (Walaardt 2009, 2012). Poles were suspected of espionage and interned in the Netherlands for months. Those who had, prior to their arrival in the Netherlands, lived in Belgium or Germany were deported there. Many Eastern European communists were granted residence permits rather than refugee status.

The war resisters' profile contrasted with the image of the Cold War refugee. This chapter illustrates how the popular image of a refugee changed when the New Refugees replaced the Cold War refugees. Both groups consisted mainly of men. The anticommunists were replaced by men who had stood up against the brutalities of colonial wars. New Refugees were not fleeing left-wing dictatorships, but rather escaping from right-wing regimes. These young men fled because they refused to fight in Africa or Vietnam. This 'entirely new category of asylum seekers' posed challenges to Western European states (Loescher 2001: 179). Although their numbers were not large, they appeared prominently in public and political discussions.

In the 1960s, thousands of young Portuguese men were shipped to Africa to fight colonial wars in Angola and Mozambique. Some tried to avoid conscription, while others fled the battlefront. In April 1974, 80,000 Portuguese men trying to avoid the draft lived abroad, mainly in France (Van Krieken 1976: 265). In a number of European countries, student support groups were established to assist these Portuguese war resisters. In Sweden, for instance, Portuguese deserters' committees were formed in Lund, Stockholm and Uppsala (Sellström 2002: 84). This was an era of mass protest and of the rise of leftist youth movements in many countries, including the Netherlands (Jansse de Jonge, Prakken & De Roos 1983: 113) Activist groups used the New Refugees to attract publicity to their protests against the brutalities of the Portuguese army in Africa. During this period left-wing political parties were part of the opposition and used the war resisters to show disapproval of the conservative – mainly Christian – government.

In this period, economic growth in the Netherlands slowed to a standstill. As a result, the recruitment of guest workers, including the Portuguese, ended. In 1971, 3,400 Portuguese men remained in the Netherlands (Lindo 1988: 20). The reception of the Portuguese war resisters was influenced by the earlier recruitment of Portuguese guest workers. If the war resisters failed to obtain refugee status, they switched roles and were categorised as guest workers. Ministry of Justice officials acknowledged that there were two categories, but found it hard to distinguish between them.[1]


## Asylum crisis, gender and masculinity

Scholars of refugee policy have argued that changes in asylum policy are caused by changes in the identities and composition of asylum seekers (Freeman 1992: 1162; Alink 2006). As a result, authorities panic and react by issuing new policies, because the newcomers constitute unprecedented challenges to the legal machinery. In many European countries, asylum processes evolved from relative stability in the mid to late 1980s, into a phase of institutional crisis (Alink, Boin & 't Hart 2001: 287). Freeman argues that beginning in the late 1980s authorities became more focused on 'tough talk than tough action' (Freeman 1992: 1161-1162). When scholars discuss 'the asylum crisis', they refer to different periods. Some date the crisis to the 1970s, while others point to the mid-1980s and others still to 2000 (Cohen & Joly 1989: 6; Boswell 2000: 559; Alink, Boin & 't Hart 2001: 291). Most scholars, however, situate the asylum crisis as one that began between the fall of the Berlin Wall and the liberation of Eastern Europe (Freeman 1992: 1155). According to Boswell (2000: 559) an asylum crisis was caused by a combination of three factors: a large number of asylum seekers, an economic downturn, and the impact of globalisation on identity and state legitimacy. Another factor that contributed to the crisis was that the New Refugees were culturally and ethnically different from their hosts. Newcomers lacked kin and potential support groups in the country where they applied for asylum (Stein 1981: 330). Finally, asylum seekers had higher profiles, both because of their larger numbers and because the media and governments placed them in the spotlight (Cohen & Joly 1989: 8). For example, in 2002 asylum seekers were 'viewed almost exclusively in crisis terms within UK (and European) media' (White 2002: 1056).

All of these elements to some degree existed before the arrival of the New Refugees. Clearly, one might anticipate that an asylum crisis would occur in the early 1970s, but that situation did not materialise. The absence of crisis can be explained by gender aspects and the social connection that the New Refugees shared with Dutch society. While a large body of literature on gender and asylum exists, there is relatively little historical research on differences between men and women in

asylum cases. Most of that literature assumes that the starting position
of men and women in Western asylum procedures differs (Van Baalen
1997; Bhabha 2004; Van Wetten et al. 2001; Valji, De la Hunt & Moffett
2003; Mascini & Van Bochove 2007). Authors state that women are less
likely to be recognised as refugees, because they are less involved in visible political activities (Spijkerboer 1994: 5; Valji, De la Hunt & Moffett
2003: 61; Leiss & Boesjes 2004; Montgomery & Foldspang 2005: 454-
467). Women's activities occur in the private sphere and are therefore
regarded as non-political (Crawley 2000). The 1951 Refugee Convention is cited as the reason behind their deprived position in Western
asylum procedures, because it implicitly assumes refugees to be men
(Greatbatch 1989: 518; Kelly 1993; Macklin 1999; Bhabha 2004; Bloch,
Galvin & Harrell-Bond 2000; Kneebone 2005; Oxford 2005; Calavita
2006).

Scholars have analysed the effects of ideologies about women's roles
on migration and integration, but there is little research on masculinity
(but see McKay 2007; Nobil Ahmad 2008). In the literature on masculinity, a distinction is made between violent masculinity and heroic
masculinity; the latter is characterised by political struggle, rather than
by the physical violence that typifies the former (Unterhalter 2000).
Both Cold War refugees and war resisters were ascribed heroic masculinity. This is less surprising in the first case than in the second. War
resisters were negatively portrayed by their opponents as 'fools' and
'faggots' – labels which implied that their manhood was in question
(Thorne 1975: 183). If it were true that the army made boys into men, as
many believed, war resisters were stuck in permanent boyhood. The US
war-resister movement countered this image by emphasising the masculinity of the war resisters. The war-resistance mystique they created
served to minimise the passive ('feminine') connotations of non-vio-
lence by shifting the focus to activism and collective agency (Ziemann
2008). This made it possible to construct the war resisters as vulnerable
and in need of support,[2] while maintaining and bolstering the masculine interpretation of a refugee (Connell 1993: 601).

In the Netherlands, war resisters were portrayed as young intellectu-
als and idealists belonging to the middle and higher echelons of Portuguese society. They were welcomed. That dynamic was also true for US
war resisters in Canada (Churchill 2004). The sudden arrival of the new
asylum seekers might have caused an asylum crisis, but their reputation
for manly heroism worked in their favour. The masculine image of the
1950s refugee was reinforced by the New Refugees. Those factors, and
their connection to Dutch leftist youth groups, prevented an asylum
crisis.

## The Dutch asylum procedure

People who arrived in the Netherlands as refugees were required to report to a local Dutch police station and request asylum and residence
permits. If a refugee claim was seen as potentially successful, the police
referred the case to the Ministry of Justice. The Geneva Convention was
incorporated into the Dutch Aliens Act. Refugees were those with a
well-founded fear of persecution because of their political opinion, nationality, race or religion, or because they belonged to a particular social group, who physically located outside their countries of origin and
could not re-avail themselves of the protection of their home countries.
The 1967 Protocol of New York extended the cut-off date of the Refugee
Convention. Individuals fleeing persecution after 1951 were now also
eligible for refugee status.

In 1970, the Dutch government issued special guidelines to address
the situation of Portuguese war resisters.[3] When a Portuguese applicant
fulfilled three conditions, an ordinary residence permit was issued, but
refugee status was not granted. The applicant needed to have political
motives for his draft evasion and must have arrived in the Netherlands
within one month after leaving Portugal. Portuguese citizens who had
stayed in a safe country after they left Portugal were not admitted, otherwise 'we'll get all the Portuguese staying in France', one civil servant said.[4] Thirdly, a Portuguese asylum seeker had to find housing and
needed to submit an employment contract. Six months after the issuance of the permit, the case of the Portuguese citizen was evaluated.
Only in case of gross misconduct was the permit not renewed. In sum,
the Dutch authorities acknowledged that the Portuguese had valid reasons not to return to their country, but felt that they did not meet the
definition of a refugee. The permit could be compared to a de facto refugee status (Paludan 1981: 71). Desertion was not accepted as grounds
for refugee status, but the non-refoulement principle was observed, as
the Geneva Convention forbade repatriation to a country where persecution could be possible.

With the residence permit a Portuguese citizen could apply for a
mandate declaration from the United Nations High Commissioner for
Refugees (UNHCR). A UNHCR representative issued such declarations
to individuals who fulfilled the criteria of the Refugee Convention. The
representative conducted eligibility assessments with asylum seekers.
Draft evasion was not sufficient. The UNHCR issued mandate declarations only to those Portuguese who were involved in oppositional activities. A residence permit was a prerequisite for obtaining a mandate
declaration. The Ministry of Justice also had to approve the issuance of

a mandate declaration (Van Krieken 1976: 126). The Ministry of Foreign Affairs opposed issuing these declarations to Portuguese, so as not to offend the authorities in Portugal – a NATO ally.

Very few asylum seekers were granted refugee status. Between 1967 and 1972 more than 2,100 people requested asylum, but just three individuals were admitted as refugees based on the Dutch aliens' law, whilst more than 1,200 asylum seekers obtained a mandate declaration.[5] The authorities were reluctant to issue asylum seekers refugee status, because they feared that an unbreakable tie with the Netherlands would thus be created. It was almost impossible to deport persons with refugee status. Only those who had stayed for years in the Netherlands, and proved that they had adjusted and assimilated, were admitted as refugees. Mandate declarations were less problematic, because no ties with the Netherlands were created, just with the UNHCR (Duynstee 1972: 49).

In the late 1960s and early 1970s, the number of asylum seekers was low, especially compared to the 1990s, but it did rise. Between June 1968 and June 1970, 1,203 people applied for asylum. Most of them (938) came from Czechoslovakia and all were admitted on a prima facie basis following the Prague Spring. The others came from Portugal (97), Poland (49), Hungary (32), Yugoslavia (18), Romania (13), Nigeria (10), Greece (6), South Africa (4), East Germany (4), Russia (3) and other countries (25). Of those, 995 were accepted, 68 migrated to another country, 13 left or disappeared, 10 cases were still pending in 1970 and only 21 (2%) were rejected.[6] Between 1968 and 1974, 600 to 800 Portuguese war deserters came to the Netherlands (Bronkhorst 1990: 44).[7] While all applied for residence permits and refugee status, only 17 were granted a mandate declaration.[8] Just three were deported. This figure exemplifies perfectly the intended outcome of asylum requests.

Three groups of actors influenced the outcomes of asylum requests. First, there was the decision-making body. Employees of local aliens' offices received asylum seekers and interviewed them. They sent their interview notes, including a recommendation, to the Ministry of Justice. The Minister of Justice and civil servants from the Aliens Department and Border Protection assessed the asylum seekers' cases. The Minister of Foreign Affairs collected data on the countries of origin and approved or denied the claim of each application. The Minister of Social Affairs protected the labour market.

Lobby groups formed the second group of actors. The Angola Committee was the most influential of these, and had provided legal counsel to Portuguese since 1968. According to the Ministry of Justice, this Committee recruited Portuguese in Paris with the prospect of higher wages. A civil servant grumbled that members of this Committee had stronger political opinions than the Portuguese themselves. They looked after their clients 'like fathers'.[9] The Committee accused other refugee organisations of being traditional in assisting only asylum seekers from behind the Iron Curtain. A director of a left-wing group stated that the older groups were staffed by those who were afraid of the long-haired Portuguese.[10]

The third group consisted of people who became involved in the lives of the Portuguese. Friends, relatives, employers and concerned Dutch citizens challenged the outcomes of New Refugee asylum requests. Particularly important were leftist parliamentarians and senators, who frequently asked questions in parliament.

## Materials and methods

This chapter analyses who influenced the asylum procedure, how they influenced the outcomes of asylum requests and how Dutch authorities dealt with the arrival of the New Refugees. It discusses at length the case of the most famous asylum seeker in the Netherlands: the American Ralph Waver.

The main source for this research is Ministry of Justice archives. The analysis is based on 23 individual case files of asylum seekers. Case files document who were involved in the asylum procedure (the actors), and why they believed the Netherlands should or should not offer asylum, in other words, their arguments. Case files contain policy documents, internal memos and letters from refugee support groups and others. In addition, 45 policy documents from the ministries of Foreign Affairs and Justice were used. Analysis of policy files traces policy changes and debates between the officials and their departments, and with external actors. The analysis also draws on newspaper articles.

The arguments used in letters and memos are analysed according to the principles of frame-analysis. 'Frames' are a series of claims tied together in a more or less coherent way. Frames are used to define and diagnose problems, to present moral judgements, and sometimes to offer solutions (Entman 1993: 52). The function of framing is to select, highlight or obscure repeating elements in pleas. Frames shows who or what was defined as a problem, by whom and why (Schrover 2009: 192). Recently, scholars have used frame analysis to look for the social construction of asylum seekers in media coverage and political debates (D'Haenens & De Lange 2001; Van Gorp 2002; Lynn & Lea 2003; Nickels 2007: 41-48). In the asylum procedure, seven types of arguments were used. Table 3.1 lists the seven types and the solutions that logically followed from them.

**TABLE 3.1**  *The seven frames actors used in the Dutch asylum procedure*

| Frame | Argument | Solution |
|---|---|---|
| 1. Persecution | Asylum seeker feared persecution | Clear persecution → admitted |
| 2. Criticising the asylum procedure | Right to fair treatment | Absence of fair treatment → admitted |
| | Principles of equality or precedent | Fear of precedent → rejected<br>Unequal treatment → admitted |
| | Stay in a safe country | Stay in safe third country → rejected |
| | Asylum policies of other countries | Keep pace with other countries → admitted or rejected |
| | Duration of asylum procedure | Longer stay → admitted |
| 3. Credibility | Credibility issues | Credible claim → admitted<br>Incredible claim → rejected |
| 4. Humanitarian | Solidarity, humanity & Christian traditions | Admitted |
| | Tradition of hospitality | Admitted |
| 5. Politics | Condemnation country of origin | Condemning policy of country of origin → Admitted or rejected |
| | Diplomatic relations | Maintaining diplomatic relations → rejected |
| 6. Benefits and threats | Issues of the Dutch society | High unemployment, overpopulation, reduced economic growth → rejected |
| | Fear of public unrest | Strong support within Dutch society → admitted |
| | Images and vulnerability of group | Vulnerable image of the group → admitted<br>Negative image of the group → rejected |
| 7. Individual characteristics | Working capabilities | Useful on the labour market → admitted |
| | Character of individual | Sympathetic → admitted |
| | Family situation | Single → admitted |

## Persecution frame

The key phrase of the 1951 Refugee Convention is a *well-founded fear of persecution*. Those who pleaded in favour of admission argued that the New Refugees feared persecution, while those who opposed admission denied this. Actors defined fear of persecution in various ways. The Minister of Justice argued that the Portuguese fled due to a feeling of uneasiness and therefore did not meet the definition of a convention refugee.[11] He claimed that Portuguese war resisters faced severe consequences, but that their experiences differed from those of Cold War refugees. Fear of persecution was a 'serious controversy between a person and his government, followed by intimidation and repression'. A Ministry of Foreign Affairs official added that in order to meet the definition of refugee, an applicant had to actively oppose the Portuguese regime.[12] Refugee support groups argued that desertion was a political deed. Deserters opposed a colonial regime and feared persecution due to their political opinions.[13]

Officials of the Ministry of Justice, the UNHCR and the Ministry of Foreign Affairs discussed in a meeting whether a Portuguese man, known as P., was a refugee. The first two agencies argued that he was, because he had an objective fear of persecution.[14] According to the UNHCR, P. feared persecution because he rejected the Portuguese regime. He was not an adventurer. Fear of persecution does not require literally 'feeling a bayonet in the back'. Fear might result from having a deviating political opinion, according to the UNHCR. A Ministry of Justice official added that P., the son of a wealthy businessman, might have paid his way out of military service. That P. did not leave for economic reasons made him more credible. The Ministry of Foreign Affairs representative argued that P. would be prosecuted, but not persecuted, in Portugal. P. would be penalised for desertion, but not for his political opinions. Interestingly, Foreign Affairs won the argument and P. received a residence permit. The arguments in this frame show that actors disputed whether or not the New Refugees feared persecution. It was almost impossible for Portuguese asylum seekers to be recognised as refugees.

## Criticising-the-asylum-procedure frame

Refugee support groups criticised the Dutch asylum procedure. UNHCR, for example, argued that it was too lengthy, that police work was poor and that interviews were incomplete.[15] They complained that interviewers paid attention solely to the labour market. Some actors accused local aliens' services officials of deterring Portuguese from requesting asylum by encouraging them to settle for a residence permit.[16] Apparently, the Portuguese were told that their situation was not bad, and that Dutch young men also had to serve.[17]

A frequent complaint was the absence of an independent appeals process.[18] Aliens had the right to appeal at the Aliens Advice Committee (ACV), but this committee was limited to a consultative role and was composed of former civil servants. The Minister of Justice responded to this criticism by arguing that he followed the committee's advice, even when unfavourable to him. Not everybody was admitted, but an 'awful lot' were, he said.[19]

Parliamentarians, refugee support groups and journalists often compared the New Refugees with Cold War refugees. They concluded that the first group had fewer chances than the latter, and their pleas stressed the similarities. Actors explained that both groups had fled from totalitarian regimes and were in need of asylum. Some socialist politicians claimed that Portuguese motives were unjustly regarded as non-political, while those of Czechoslovakians were regarded as political.[20] They questioned whether the dictatorial regime in Portugal was less dangerous than a communist one. The Minister of Justice responded that when a Czech citizen applied for asylum, all appearances were in his favour, while the odds were against a Portuguese. He denied that he favoured those fleeing communism, arguing that Portuguese were admitted, albeit not as refugees. The Minister of Justice added that he had no reason to believe that Portuguese or Czechs were nicer people.

Civil servants said that the New Refugees and anticommunists were not equal. Ministry of Justice officials feared creating a precedent, just as immigration officials did in the 1920s (see Schacher in this volume). In one case file, a civil servant noted that if this Portuguese man were granted refugee status, it would serve as an open invitation to every Portuguese. If this man was granted refugee status, he added, strict secrecy was needed.[21] Another civil servant warned that more tolerant asylum policies would lead to more asylum seekers.[22] One editorial stated that the Netherlands' admission policies should be similar to those of nearby countries.[23]

Actors criticised the Ministry of Justice for threatening to deport those Portuguese who had spent more than a month in France before arriving in the Netherlands. This was the case for three Portuguese men. They claimed that French authorities were deporting many young Portuguese following a treaty agreement between France and Portugal. They added that the Portuguese secret service (the PIDE) was active in France, so that those asylum applications should not have been denied.[24]

Refugee support groups stressed that the New Refugees deserved to stay, because authorities took too long to assess their cases. The Minister of Justice yielded to the pressure to issue permits to 20 Portuguese who had endured a long bureaucratic delay.[25] A civil servant blamed that on understaffing.[26] The Minister agreed that the procedure was too long, but argued that that 'lots of time' was needed to determine whether the applicant was serious and trustworthy.[27] Deporting a rejected asylum seeker became more complicated, according to the UNHCR, in cases where applicants had established personal ties in the Netherlands.[28]

## Credibility frame

According to Kagan (2003: 384-386) credibility issues were the most common reason for rejection of asylum requests. The UNHCR stressed that in a short and serious procedure the asylum requests of 'nine or ten out of ten' New Refugees had to be rejected.[29] That guideline shows the obstacles faced by Portuguese asylum seekers.

Credibility issues arose in many cases. In one case a Portuguese claimed to be a member of the resistance, while research showed that he was not.[30] One civil servant argued that many Portuguese migrated to the Netherlands for economic reasons. He believed that they sought to profit from the Dutch welfare system, noting that many left Portugal prior to being drafted.[31]

Civil servants believed that the Angola Committee in the Netherlands 'imported' Portuguese from France and instructed them to claim that they could not serve for political reasons.[32] The Minister of Justice argued that it was difficult to establish whether a desertion was genuinely politically motivated.[33] In a document relating to the Portuguese 'B.', a civil servant wrote, 'his statements were all standard'.[34] B. had first claimed that he wanted to work in the Netherlands. Only after his claim was rejected did he state his strong opposition to the colonial war. But, the civil servant concluded, because of pressure from a parliamentarian, he should 'for reasons of process efficiency' be issued a residence permit. Despite credibility concerns, B. was ultimately admitted.

## Humanitarian frame

Refugee support groups urged the Minister of Justice to apply humanitarian and lenient policies to *all* asylum seekers. One refugee support group argued that there existed sufficient humanitarian grounds to admit the Portuguese A. A civil servant said that while A.'s refusal to serve and his political activities did not amount to a fear of persecution, he should still receive a residence permit on humanitarian grounds.[35]

Actors appealed to the Minister of Justice to honour the age-old Dutch tradition of hospitality to political exiles.[36] A parliamentarian referred to 'our very old views about equality and justice [which] forced us to be generous towards individuals that came from totalitarian states'.[37] The editor of one newspaper disputed this reputation of hospitality, citing the long and bureaucratic procedures that the New Refugees had to endure.[38] He stated that asylum seekers were interrogated numerous times and the secret service initiated investigations of them.

In the end, he concluded, few were granted refugee status. In 1972, during a colloquium, the question of the Dutch reputation for hospitality was discussed.[39] Participants concluded that while Dutch authorities proudly referred to their generous, humane and lenient asylum policies, such generosity was limited to the issuing of residence permits. A remarkable aspect of the hospitality argument is the frequent reference to the failed policies of the Dutch authorities toward Jewish refugees from Germany in the late 1930s. According to one editorial, the New Refugees were welcomed exactly like the Jews in the late 1930s.[40]

## Political frame

Ministry of Foreign Affairs officials worried about diplomatic relations with NATO countries. Granting refugee status to Portuguese would offend a NATO ally, they feared, by implying that Portugal persecuted its citizens (Doesschate 1993: 146). NATO countries were, by definition, democratic and therefore honoured civil rights, civil servants and politicians believed.[41] Another official wondered how the Dutch would have responded if Portuguese authorities had granted asylum to Dutch deserters during its 1940s colonial war in the Dutch East Indies.[42]

The 1967 Ministry of Justice yearbook stated that a Portuguese man had been offered asylum. The Portuguese *chargé d'affaires* was shocked at this information, asked for his name and questioned why he had been granted asylum.[43] The Dutch Minister of Foreign Affairs was also surprised that the man was granted asylum, because normally 'we are very reluctant' to grant refugee status, especially to citizens of 'our allies'. In fact, the man was not offered refugee status: the term 'asylum' had been used incorrectly. He had received a residence permit, based largely on his work record. His refusal to serve had not influenced the decision.[44]

Left-wing parliamentarians, concerned Dutch citizens and refugee support groups condemned Portugal's brutal wars in Africa. They asserted that those who opposed these wars had to be welcomed. In 1973, the Angola Committee expressed its concern when it discovered that three Portuguese men who had been repatriated by the Dutch authorities were arrested at Lisbon airport. Two of them were immediately handed over to the military police.[45] According to the Committee, by deporting Portuguese, Dutch authorities were, in essence, supporting violence against Angolans. A Dutch man expressed bitter disappointment at the treatment of the Portuguese war resisters, because Portuguese soldiers had a reputation for brutality in the colonies.[46]

Therefore, Portugal's foreign policies justified granting refugee status to all Portuguese war resisters.

## Benefits-and-threats frame

According to a senior-level civil servant, the Netherlands' 'absorption capacity' was limited because of population density, rising unemployment and housing shortages. Not all Portuguese could stay.[47] The Minister of Social Affairs favoured a strict interpretation of the Refugee Convention, arguing that granting residence permits after an asylum application had failed, jeopardised the guest-worker recruitment system.[48]

Several memos characterised Portuguese deserters as bad workers.[49] That reputation was particularly problematic, because obtaining a residence permit required an employment contract. A civil servant noted several cases of Portuguese who had asked for social security support after they had been fired due to wilful absenteeism.[50] Even worse was their association with criminality. Authorities linked the Portuguese with drug abuse and drug dealing, and therefore a threat to Dutch society. The Amsterdam police blamed them for a resurgence of pick pocketing.[51] However, research on criminality among Portuguese shows no alarming statistics. Of the 460 Portuguese who had applied for asylum only 30 had been charged, most of them with minor offences.[52]

In contrast, refugee support groups depicted the Portuguese as vulnerable. They did not speak Dutch and did not have the right contacts.[53] They were young, confused and disorientated, and therefore they deserved support.[54] One parliamentarian noted that undoubtedly some Portuguese came to work, but for most of these young 'fellows' leaving their country was a huge and emotional step.[55] Support was thus generated by stressing the vulnerability of these young men.

Public influence is evident in the case files of the New Refugees. One official explained that the 'noise made by *those groups* in the cases of Portuguese deserters was disproportional to its importance'.[56] One Portuguese man, V., was allowed to stay because of 'leftist youth' protests, another memo stated.[57] To yet another official, the Dutch asylum policies were unclear, except when the Angola Committee or parliamentarians intervened; in such cases leniency was shown.[58] One official added, the 'louder parliamentarians shouted, the more deserters were admitted'.[59] In the case of a Portuguese couple, the Minister of Justice yielded after he received telegrams with death threats and a coffin and after questions were asked in parliament.[60] These cases reveal that the Ministry of Justice relented when lobbied by the Angola Committee (see also Doesschate 1993: 202).

One case file shows that the Angola Committee helped a Portuguese man to enter the Netherlands and hid him for two months. They finally brought him to the police, escorted by journalists, a lawyer and a member of parliament. The following day his story appeared in the media.[61] An Angola Committee member claimed that this public display made it impossible for R. to return to his country. He added that if R. had approached the police immediately after his arrival, he would have been deported. The Minister of Justice told this parliamentarian that hiding a Portuguese refugee was a blemish on democratic society. A similar case concerned the arrival of two Portuguese men who had lived in France before arriving in the Netherlands. The men claimed that they faced death if they returned to France. To the authorities it was not clear what threat the men feared in France: 'Murder? Kidnapping?'[62] A civil servant said that while he was used to hearing exaggerated statements, it was insulting to think that he would be convinced by them. The Angola Committee justified its behaviour by explaining that success was guaranteed, because authorities feared negative publicity. In the end, the two were allowed to stay, despite having first gone to France. The Ministry of Justice chose to avoid public unrest, so it searched for quiet solutions, rather than imposing restrictive policies.[63]

## Individual-characteristics frame

The last frame focuses on personal characteristics of asylum seekers. The New Refugees' employment records and age influenced the outcome of their asylum applications. Critics argued that just as welders and soccer players would be granted admission, so too would drug users, if they qualified.[64] One of the three requirements for the Portuguese to obtain de facto refugee status was an employment contract. According to a civil servant, the Portuguese asylum seekers V. and S. were a fraction of all 'the aliens that stayed in the Netherlands'. The two were admitted, because they seemed to be genuine labourers and not 'quasi-intellectuals'.[65] One 53-year-old Portuguese man was denied asylum based on his age, despite his employer's support. According to the Ministry of Justice, his presence in the Netherlands was not vital.[66] This was an economic argument that had nothing to do with his asylum request.

* * *

In general, Portuguese asylum seekers benefited from the fact that they could switch roles to that of guest worker. Most were allowed to stay, albeit not as refugees. This is similar to the Armenian women's claims of persecution (Schacher in this volume). They were denied refugee status by US officials, but were allowed to stay because of 'extreme hardship'. Civil servants feared creating a precedent and offending a NATO ally. The authorities sought to minimise the influence of the media, because such attention tipped the balance in a refugee's favour. Support groups used the Portuguese in their protests against colonial wars. They made claims on traditional hospitality, used strong tropes, including comparisons to the fate of Jewish refugees in the 1930s, and emphasised the vulnerability of the asylum seekers.

## The case of Ralph Waver

Now that we have a clearer view of the strategies that actors used in the Portuguese war resisters' cases, we use frame analysis to examine the case of Ralph Waver, the American war resister. He became an anti-Vietnam protest symbol (Van Eekert, Hellema & Van Heteren 1986; Van der Maar 2007),[67] and his case influenced refugee law (Van Krieken 1976; Maarseveen 1972: 930). His case file contains many letters written by action groups and 'ordinary Dutch' who sought to influence the Ministry of Justice decision. Waver arrived in the Netherlands on 26 June 1970, when he deserted the MS Marias, a NATO fleet ship. Waver was married and had two children. He was born into a conservative family, and he proudly referred to himself as its 'black sheep'.[68] In 1967 he voluntarily joined the military, motivated by the salary and the fact that by joining the Atlantic fleet he would avoid being sent to Vietnam. From 1970, he tried to leave the army legally, but claimed that his supervisors hindered him from obtaining a military exemption (Van der Maar 2007: 151). Waver justified his desertion by pointing to the oppressive military politics of the USA. He became alienated from his country and opposed the pervasive racial discrimination on board.[69]

One month after his desertion, Waver moved to Sweden because his lawyer told him that his chances for asylum were higher there. Sweden did not belong to NATO, and was not obliged to extradite American deserters. Swedish officials had, however, handed over some deserters to American authorities. Waver decided to return to the Netherlands and apply for a residence permit. Accompanied by two socialist parliamentarians and his lawyer, he went to the Ministry of Justice. Waver learnt that he should not be too optimistic. Afterwards, a highly positioned civil servant spoke briefly to the two parliamentarians. According to them, Waver was promised a residence permit if he fulfilled five conditions: he was not to publicise his case; he was to remain outside of Amsterdam (so as not to convince other Americans to leave the military), he was to find work, he was not to request refugee status, and finally, his statements had to be found credible. According to his lawyer, Waver never intended to become a martyr, and he felt no qualms about not being granted refugee status.[70] Waver fulfilled all conditions and applied for a residence permit at the aliens' police in the town of Haarlem, where he had found work in a warehouse.

Waver's case was not ideal for an anti-war publicity campaign. He had entered the military service voluntarily and was not at risk of being sent to Vietnam. So, why did his case become so widely celebrated? First, Waver was a charismatic person, and appeared sympathetic. Secondly, Waver gave the anti-Vietnam movement a much-needed face (Van der Maar 2007: 158-159). Thirdly, his case made it possible to protest against the way the conservative Dutch government dealt with aliens. Hospitality became the centre of the discussion. Unlike the Portuguese, Waver did not obtain de facto refugee status. If he had received a residence permit nobody could argue that the Dutch authorities were slavishly obeying the USA. The main concern was that if Waver were admitted, other Americans would follow his example. Fear increased within the administration after a parliamentarian called Waver's situation a test case.

## The legal procedures

One civil servant doubted Waver's motives and felt that his flight was economically motivated.[71] His supervisor feared that the Vietnam anti-war movement would use him to attract other Americans to the anti-war cause. He decided to reject Waver's application, because he was not a genuine conscientious objector, despite the uproar a rejection would cause.[72] There was no threat that he would be sent to Vietnam, he said, adding that it was inappropriate to admit a citizen of a NATO ally.[73] Waver was asked to leave the Netherlands voluntarily. To the Minister of Justice it was 'clear that Mr. Waver did not belong in our country', but he was worried that the press would portray him as a deserter for reasons of principle.[74] In the official rejection letter, just one reason was provided for the rejection: his 'absence of ties with the Netherlands'.

Waver and his lawyer were shocked when they received the rejection.[75] They organised a well-attended press conference and told the public that the Ministry of Justice had broken its promise. The lawyer protested against the new, improvable condition: 'ties with the Netherlands'. The US authorities could not remain quiet. On 5 May 1971 they requested Waver's extradition. Shortly afterwards, Waver was arrested. At that point, popular support for Waver increased. Many local refugee support groups were formed, for example, in the small town of Soest. This group presented a petition to the authorities and organised a well-attended discussion regarding Waver's extradition.[76]

An examining judge was called upon to determine whether extradition was justified.[77] The defence argued that Waver returned to the Netherlands from Sweden not because of his desertion, but because he sought a residence permit. The defence added that Waver was no longer a member of the US military and therefore he could not be extradited. The judge argued that these arguments needed clarification and forbade Waver's extradition. During his hearing Waver asked to be granted refugee status, since he feared persecution in his country of origin due to his political opinions. The Ministry of Justice disregarded that request and decided to extradite Waver, because it argued that his stay in Sweden had not rendered him ineligible for extradition.[78] US officials maintained that Waver had not been discharged from military service. Finally, they argued, Waver was not a refugee, because the US authorities would not persecute him.

Following the decision against him, Waver's lawyer started summary proceedings. Two weeks later, the judge forbade the Dutch authorities from expelling Waver for a period of six months, stating that he was unable to decide a complicated juridical matter on such short notice.[79] The question for the judge was what should prevail: the Geneva Convention or the extradition request. In June 1971 the ACV reviewed the rejection of a residence permit and debated whether Waver met the refugee status criteria. The committee advised that Waver was not a refugee, because his penalty in the USA would be the same if he had deserted for non-political reasons.[80] The Ministry of Justice rejected his application for refugee status and a residence permit.

Waver had the right of appeal at the Council of State. Waver's lawyer argued that Waver was guilty of a civil offence, but that the penalty was inhumane because of his political opinions. The Council of State suggested that after balancing 'all subjective and objective arguments' Waver had a well-founded fear of persecution in his country.[81] This conclusion amazed the authorities, since there was no objective well-founded fear of persecution. Officials anticipated that the ruling would lead to the arrival of more deserters, and that whenever an applicant characterised his motives for flight as political, he would be granted refugee status. By extension, hijackers and bank robbers would now be eligible for refugee status.[82]

The Dutch legal system allowed the submission of a 'memorandum of objections' against the Council of State conclusion. Authorities felt that the Council of State would not deny Waver refugee status if threatened with expulsion. First, the authorities granted him a residence permit in December 1970.[83] Secondly, US authorities had to withdraw their request for extradition.[84] The Dutch ambassador in Washington, DC, informed the US authorities that deportation of Waver would cause unrest in the Netherlands and might harm the alliance.[85] US officials subsequently revoked their request.[86] They accepted the argument that if Waver were granted refugee status, future US deserters would claim refugee status as well.

In the memorandum of objections the authorities argued that Waver faced prosecution in the USA, but that he would receive his penalty in a well-functioning state. The Council of State ignored the contents of the memorandum, because the Dutch authorities ignored that 'Waver, on the one hand, had to fulfil his military obligations, but, on the other hand, was convinced that he no longer could be part of an army that, in the name of freedom and democracy, committed war crimes'.[87] The Ministry of Justice ignored the recommendation of the Council of State,[88] though it was highly unusual and controversial to do so. The rejection letter argued that country of origin information showed that Waver did not fear persecution in the USA.[89]

## Frames, results

Three archives contained a total of 63 letters, telegrams and petitions from refugee support groups and individuals. All but one opposed Waver's extradition.[90] Some letters were short, such as one that stated simply, 'Waver stay, NATO away'. Another was a four-page typed plea.[91] Table 3.2 presents the most common arguments. Some letters contained several arguments. Some British residents argued that Waver would be jailed for many years because of his political views and that his extradition violated the well-known Dutch tradition of hospitality.[92] Not surprisingly, none of the actors referred to Waver's stay in Sweden or the fear of creating a precedent.

TABLE 3.2 *Frames as used in 63 letters*

| Frame | Argument | Number of references |
|---|---|---|
| 1. Persecution | Persecution | 27 |
| 2. Asylum procedure | Right to fair procedure | 14 |
| | Stay in a safe third country | 0 |
| | Asylum policies of other countries | 0 |
| | Principles of equality | 15 |
| 3. Credibility | Credibility issues | 4 |
| 4. Morality | Duration of asylum procedure | 2 |
| | Solidarity, humanity and Christianity | 23 |
| | Tradition of hospitality | 28 |
| | Reference to what happened with the Jews in the late 1930s | 11 |
| 5. Politics | Condemnation of country of origin | 10 |
| | Diplomatic relations | 13 |
| 6. Benefits and threats to Dutch society | Issues of Dutch society | 2 |
| | Fear of public unrest | 4 |
| | Images and vulnerability of group of asylum seekers | 3 |
| 7. Individual characteristics | Working capabilities | 2 |
| | Character of individual | 13 |
| | Family situation | 2 |

Twenty-seven actors assured the Ministry of Justice that Waver would face persecution in the USA and years of imprisonment. They bolstered their claims with references to treaties. One person emphasised that Article 14 of the Universal Declaration of Human Rights stated that all persons had the right to seek and enjoy asylum.[93] A group of lawyers stressed the unlawfulness of an extradition, because Waver was a refugee under the 1951 Refugee Convention.[94] The only person who supported the authorities' position was a former parliamentarian. Extradition was justified, he believed. To avoid a sense of injustice among Dutch citizens, he suggested that Waver be allowed to migrate to a country of his choice.[95]

Fourteen actors felt that Waver did not get a fair hearing, because he had not exhausted all legal remedies and his case had not (yet) been heard in the highest court.[96] Others accused the authorities of being too bureaucratic and unable to interpret facts in a humanitarian way. Fifteen people argued that asylum seekers from NATO countries stood no chance, while Hungarians and Czechoslovakians were readily accepted. East Europeans were met with excessive friendliness and 'only had to say the word asylum and "you" [the Minister of Justice] came to their aid', one letter writer stated.

Twenty-three actors stressed that there were sufficient humanitarian considerations to block Waver's extradition.[97] Those who shared commonalities with Waver were most likely to offer that argument. More than 2,000 citizens of Haarlem – the town where Waver found refuge – submitted a petition stating that humanity should always be given primacy.[98] A group of conscientious objectors (who opposed the Dutch draft) expressed their solidarity and advocated strongly to grant him political asylum.[99] Three writers emphasised the Christian roots of Dutch society and reminded the Ministry of Justice that it would not render the Last Judgement. Some Christian members of government experienced personal attacks, accusing them of ignoring their Christian principles. A Christian government should present a Christian solution to those who struggled for peace and 'holy' justice.[100] One actor claimed he had attended school with the state secretary. He speculated that because the latter had underperformed and been bullied by classmates in his youth, he was now trying to act tough.[101]

Table 3.2 shows that most actors made reference to the Dutch tradition of hospitality and offering a safe haven to political exiles. In a newspaper advertisement, 300 Dutch celebrities urged the Dutch administration not to dispense with the tradition that had been so generously applied to Hungarians and Czechs.[102] There were 11 references to the Second World War, especially to the hostile treatment of Jews at the Dutch border in the late 1930s.[103] The Jews were true refugees – like Waver – and we must remember what happened to them, these letter writers emphasised. Many writers declared that Americans had committed war crimes, like the Germans and Japanese. Those opposing such acts should be welcomed.

Ten persons condemned the aggressive US foreign policy in Vietnam. One man claimed that he did not want to stay in a country that preferred to sacrifice the life of Waver rather than to see the angry face of Nixon.[104] He cursed those Dutch officials who placed a higher priority on US diplomatic relations than on showing a human face. One political party accused the Dutch administration of being lackeys of the US.[105] Waver was a hero, who felt that he had to desert to stop the war. Students gathered in front of the courthouse shouting and holding banners stating, 'The Ministry of Justice proposes, the Ministry of Foreign Affairs disposes' and 'NATO is a crime, desertion a blessing'.[106]

Fear of public unrest was decisive. When US officials revoked their request for extradition, they cited the controversy the case had caused in the Netherlands as the reason. Some letter writers threatened mass protest if Waver were handed over to the USA.[107] Many wondered why Waver's case was problematic, given the large numbers of migrant workers.[108] One action group hoped that Waver could change the Dutch mentality. By giving lectures, he could enlighten Dutch society about repression elsewhere in the world.[109]

Waver's personality was discussed in 13 letters. Amnesty International argued that Waver's strong personality was not sufficiently brought out during his asylum case.[110] Waver made many personal sacrifices; he had, for example, lost contact with his father, wife and children. One person argued that he was a lovely young man, who had earned respect for his struggle for human rights.[111]

Frame analysis indicates that the Dutch public believed that Waver should not be extradited because he feared persecution in the USA, based on his political views, and that the Dutch should uphold the tradition of hospitality. Again, just as in the Portuguese situation, public influence was decisive. Many actors referred to the principles of equality and objected to the obedience of the Dutch to the USA.

## The Ministry of Justice's reply

Most letter writers received standard replies from the Minister of Justice and were informed that after considering all evidence and legal arguments, Waver had to be extradited, because he could not be granted refugee status.[112] Some actors received a personal reply. A group of Quakers was told that the well-known Dutch hospitality could not be extended in this case, because the Netherlands was one of the most densely populated countries in the world and itself wrestled with issues including housing shortages and unemployment.[113] The Dutch had to realise that people were uprooted throughout the world, but that the 'absorption capacity' was limited. Students were told that Waver's extradition was not tantamount to supporting the Vietnam War because Waver served on the Atlantic fleet.[114] Another man was told that the Dutch authorities were tolerant towards many immigrants, especially towards the Portuguese.[115] Indeed, in the recent past 'we were a welcoming country, but now we need to mark time'. Dutch authorities were enraged when actors referred to what happened to German Jews. Waver's case was very different because, unlike Jews, he had access to legal support and did not fear persecution in his country.

## Conclusion

Scholars often make a distinction between the Cold War refugees, who were welcomed by the Dutch authorities, and the New Refugees of the late 1960s and early 1970s, who were not. An asylum crisis could have resulted from that difference, but it did not occur. Dutch authorities and lobbyists felt that they were encountering a new phenomenon, but the ways that Dutch authorities treated asylum seekers hardly changed. They stretched the margins of the existing system to accommodate the newcomers. While the New Refugees were not granted official refugee status, they benefited from de facto refugee status, and avoided deportation to Portugal, where they claimed to fear persecution. An asylum crisis was averted because New Refugees were portrayed in such a way that they did not differ significantly from the Old Refugees. They were not as culturally and ethnically distinct from the Dutch as the asylum seekers of the 1980s would be. The refugees remained manly heroes, like the ones who came before. The New Refugees further benefited from connections with Dutch youth. To the dismay of authorities, the Portuguese and Waver became popular figures. Early 1970s activists used the heroism of the New Refugees to protest against the wars in Africa and Vietnam. Public sentiment forced authorities to continue their old policies.

Frame analysis indicates that the Portuguese were admitted largely because of their economic qualifications, rather than their experiences in Portugal. While Dutch authorities denied that they were persecuted, they allowed them to remain because they could switch roles to those of the Portuguese guest workers. As long as they remained self-supporting, and caused no problems, they were not deported. Rejections were exceptional, as was also true during the Cold War (Walaardt 2009). The authorities yielded to the public's arguments that the Dutch should maintain the tradition of hospitability and that the Portuguese were not given the same rights as Cold War refugees. If, in an exceptional case, an asylum seeker faced deportation, public pressure almost guaranteed that a residence permit would be granted in the end.

Men fleeing communism and those fleeing from colonial wars were portrayed similarly. Both groups were portrayed as masculine, with the courage to oppose what were, from the Dutch perspective, detestable regimes. Both groups were characterised as protest heroes. The New Refugees were not as different from prior groups as was commonly believed; this defused a potential crisis. They arrived from different countries, and had new claims and lobby groups, but they were strikingly similar to past asylum seekers. Heroic images of male refugees continued to dominate the asylum discourse. In the Netherlands, it would take another decade and several other groups of New Refugees before attention shifted to female asylum seekers.

## Notes

1   The National Archive, Archive of the Immigration and Naturalization Service and its Predecessors (hereafter 'NA') 5.023.5027, inventory number (hereafter 'inv. no.') 1415, Report of meeting at the Ministry of Justice, 28 May 1970.
2   'Situatie van Portugese vluchtelingen in Nederland', *Angola Bulletin* 11 (1) (1972/1973) 8.
3   NA, 5.023.5027, inv. no. 1442, memo of permanent under-secretary of the Ministry of Justice, subject: guidelines to deal with Portuguese asylum seekers, reference: 1132 19 May 1970.
4   NA, 5.023.5027, inv. no. 1453, memo of head of Department of Aliens Cases and Border Protection of the Ministry of Justice (hereafter AC & BP), subject Portuguese deserters, no reference, 11 February 1971.
5   NA, 5.023.5027, inv. no. 1589, article of Dutch lawyer submitted for revision to the Dutch authorities 16 August 1973.
6   NA, 5.023.5027, inv. no. 1415, memo of civil servant of AC & BP, subject: asylum policies, no reference, 17 April 1970.
7   'Actie voor Portugese vluchtelingen', *Angola Bulletin* 12 (3) (1974) 5.
8   'Situatie van Portugese vluchtelingen in Nederland', *Angola Bulletin* 11 (1) (1972/1973) 8.
9   NA, 5.023.5027, inv. no. 1436, memo of head of AC & BP, subject: Portuguese, reference: AJZ 3104/E-1971 (11 February 1971).
10  'Hebben we nog een trui liggen voor de onvervalste vluchteling?', *Trouw* 12 September 1992.
11  Parliamentary proceedings, 1968-1969, statements of Minister of Justice (22 April 1969) 2666-2668.
12  Archive of the Ministry of Foreign Affairs (hereafter FA) 1965-1974, inv. no. 15016, notes in margins on letter of Department of International Affairs of Ministry of Foreign Affairs, subject: refugees, reference 141.351 (no date).
13  NA, 5.023.5027, inv. no. 1443, letter of head of University Asylum Fund, subject: admission of Portuguese asylum seekers (8 January 1973).
14  NA, 5.023.5027, inv. no. 1443, report of meeting between the Ministry of Justice, Dutch Foundation for Refugee Aid (hereafter NFV) and Foreign Affairs (12 August 1970); BZ 1965-1974, inv. no. 5016, memo of Head of Department of General Affairs of the Ministry of Foreign Affairs (hereafter GA), subject: granting of a refugee status, reference: 60/70 (12 August 1970).
15  NA, 5.023.5027, inv. no. 1443, letter of representative of the UNHCR, subject: Portuguese, reference: HO/73/10 (13 February 1973).
16  Sorber (1971), 'Nederland, Portugal en Zuidelijk Afrika: Een greep uit het werk van het Angola Comité', *Wending* 26 April, 125; 'Studiedag lost weinig vragen op: Vluchtelingenrecht is nog erg onduidelijk', *Trouw* 12 June 1972.

17  NA, 5.023.5027, inv. no. 1443, remark of a socialist parliamentarian during radio broadcast, 2 June 1973.

18  Parliamentary proceedings, 1969-1970, questions of Christian parliamentarian Wttewaall van Stoetwegen (CHU) D21-D22 (23 April 1970).

19  Parliamentary proceedings, 1969-1970, juridical commission, D22-D28 (23 April 1969).

20  NA, 5.023.5027, inv. no. 1425, petition of Socialist Party Amsterdam, no reference (8 May 1972).

21  NA, 5.023.5027, inv. no. 1425, unknown author (unknown date 1969).

22  NA, 5.023.5027, inv. no. 1455, memo of civil servant of AC & BP, subject: new asylum procedure, reference: AJZ 3104/E-1971 (17 September 1973).

23  'Hoe gastvrij is Nederland?', *Haagse Post* 20 January 1968.

24  NA, 5.023.5028.9621, memo of head of AC & BP, subject: deportation of Portuguese, reference: 59/43814 (31 August 1971).

25  NA, 5.023.5027, inv. no. 1443, report meeting between Ministries of Justice and Social Affairs (14 February 1973).

26  NA, 5.023.5027, inv. no. 1455, memo of head of AC & BP, subject: Portuguese refugees, reference: AJZ 3104/E (17 September 1973).

27  NA, 5.023.5027, inv. no. 1443, memo of head of AC & BP, subject: questions of representative of University Asylum Fund (Hereafter UAF), reference: AJZ 3104/E-1971 (15 February 1973).

28  NA, 5.023.5027, inv. no. 1443, letter of the representative of the UNHCR, subject: Portuguese, reference: HO/73/10 (13 February 1973).

29  NA, 5.023.5027, inv. no. 1443, letter of the representative of the UNHCR, subject: Portuguese, reference: HO/73/10 (13 February 1973).

30  NA, 5.023.5027, inv. no. 1443, memo of Attorney-general Amsterdam, subject: asylum requests of Portuguese, reference: 7022 1 February 1973); 'Hoe gastvrij is Nederland?', *Haagse Post* 20 January 1968.

31  NA, 5.023.5027, inv. no. 1436, memo of head of AC & BP, subject: Portuguese, reference: AJZ 3104/E-1971 (11 February 1971).

32  NA, 5.023.5027, inv. no. 1116, memo of civil servant of AC & BP, subject: Egyptian deserter S., reference: 2240/E1236 (2 December 1969).

33  NA, 5.023.5027, inv. no. 1412, reply of Minister of Justice to NFV reference: AJZ 3104/E-1971- I 19 February 1970); parliamentary proceedings, 1969-1970, D22-D28 (23 April 1969).

34  NA, 5.023.5028.9533, remarks on the memo of head of AC & BP, reference: 49/423345 (25 October 1971).

35  NA, 5.023.5028.40, memo of head of AC & BP, subject: A., reference 743.26.0002 (10 April 1974).

36  Fort example: parliamentary proceedings 1969-1970, remarks of Democratic Parliamentarian Goudsmit (D66), D25 (23 April 1969).

37  Parliamentary proceedings 1969-1970, question of Socialist Singer.

38  'Hoe gastvrij is Nederland?', *Haagse Post* 20 January 1968.

39  'Is Nederland werkelijk zo gastvrij in het opnemen van vluchtelingen?', *NRC Handelsblad* 9 June 1972.

40 I. Cornelissen, 'Ralph Waver wil in Nederland blijven: Amerikaanse deserteur loopt stuk', *Vrij Nederland* 27 March 1971.

41 FA 1965-1974, inv. no. 5016, response of Minister of Justice to Minister of Foreign Affairs, subject: costs of asylum procedure, reference: AJZ 2699/E-1627 (104/1968).

42 FA 1965-1974, inv. no. 5016, memo of civil servant of GA, subject: asylum requests, reference: 699 (2 October 1967).

43 FA 1965-1974, inv. no. 5016, memo of head of GA, subject: asylum requests, reference: 697 (26 September 1967).

44 FA 1965-1974, inv. no. 5016, memo of head of GA, subject: asylum request (5 October 1967); FA 1965-1974, inv. no. 5016, memo of head of GA, subject: asylum requests, reference: 139/67 (16 October 1967).

45 NA, 5.023.5027, inv. no. 645, letter of Angola Committee, no reference (3 July 1973).

46 NA, 5.023.5027, inv. no. 645, letter of R. (16 July 1973).

47 NA, 5.023.5027, inv. no. 1456, memo of permanent under-secretary of the Ministry of Justice to parliament (30 November 1973).

48 NA, 5.023.5028.9533, police of Amsterdam, reference: 141/71 (10 February 1971).

49 NA, 5.023.5027, inv. no. 1436, memo of Department of Special Statuses of the Ministry of Justice, reference AJZ 3104/W-1971-VI (31 October 1969); NA, 5.023.5027, inv. no. 1443, memo of AC & BP, subject: Portuguese, reference: 3104/E – 1971 (4 December 1969).

50 NA, 5.023.5027, inv. no. 1436, memo of head of AC & BP, subject: Portuguese, reference AJZ 3104/E-1971 (11 February 1971).

51 NA, 5.023.5027, inv. no. 1443, memo of attorney-general Amsterdam: subject: Portuguese, reference: 7022 (1 February 1973).

52 NA, 5.023.5027, inv. no. 1449, memo of head of AC & BP, no subject, no reference (13 February 1973.

53 Parliamentary Proceedings 1969-1970, questions of Christian parliamentarian Wttewaall van Stoetwegen D21-D22 (23 April 1970).

54 NA, 5.023.5027, inv. no. 1443, letter of representative of UAF (8 January 1973).

55 NA, 5.023.5027, inv. no. 1443, radio broadcast, 2 June 1973.

56 NA, 5.023.5027, inv. no. 1412, remarks of vice permanent under-secretary to representative of the NFV, reference: AJZ 3104/E-1971- I (19 February 1970).

57 NA, 5.023.5023.9621, remarks in margin of memo of head of AC & BP, reference: 59/438141 (7 July 1971).

58 NA, 5.023.5027, inv. no. 1415, memo of head of AC & BP, subject: Portuguese, no reference (6 October 1969).

59 FA 1965-1974, inv. no. 5016, memo of civil servant GA, subject: Angola Committee and Portuguese deserters, reference: 1002 (16 December 1969); memo of head of GA, subject: Angola Committee and Portuguese deserters, reference: 136/69 (24 December 1969).

60 NA, 5.023.5027, inv. no. 1436, memo of official of AC & BP, reference: AJZ 3104/1971-VI (10 December 1970).

61 *Trouw* 6 December 1990, remarks of vice permanent under-secretary of Ministry of Justice.

62 NA, 5.023.5027, inv. no. 1329, memo of permanent under-secretary of Ministry of Justice, subject: arrival of Portuguese, reference: 59/328314/5 (14 April 1969).

63  NA, 5.023.5027, inv. no. 1329, memo of permanent under-secretary of Ministry of Justice, subject: admission of two Portuguese (24 April 1969).

64  'Studieconferentie Utrecht', *De Volkskrant* 10 June 1972.

65  NA, 5.023.5028.9621, memo of permanent under-secretary of the Ministry of Justice, subject: Portuguese, reference: 1371 (12 October 1971).

66  NA, 5.023.5028.9543, police report, The Hague (24 March 1972).

67  Broadcasting organisation VPRO, OVT, 4 and 11 February 2007, The Case Waver.

68  VPRO, OVT, 4 February 2007. The Case Waver 1, remarks by Ralph Waver.

69  FA 1965-1974, inv. no. 15016, plea note at Council of State, reference: 7015 (1971) (1 November 1971).

70  VPRO, OVT, 11 February 2007, The Case Waver 2.

71  NA, 5.023.5027, inv. no. 643, memo of civil servant of AC & BP, subject: Waver, no reference (unknown date December 1970).

72  NA, 5.023.5027, inv. no. 643, memo of head of AC & BP, subject: Waver, reference: 59/415593 – A (10 December 1970).

73  NA, 5.023.5027, inv. no. 643, memo of permanent under-secretary of Ministry of Justice, no subject, reference: 1242 (18 January 1971) and remarks Minister of Justice.

74  NA, 5.023.5027, inv. no. 643, memo of Minister of Justice, no subject, reference: 4345 P/W (20 January 1970).

75  VPRO, OVT, 11 February 2007, The Case Waver.

76  'Ook in Soest actie tegen uitlevering Ralph Waver', *Soester Courant* 11 June 1971; 'Is Ralph Waver deserteur of politiek vluchteling?', *Soester Courant* 19 November 1971.

77  Minister of Justice, 3091, report examining judge Haarlem, reference; A – 1354/1971 (1 June 1971).

78  NA, 5.023.5027, inv. no. 643, decision of permanent under-secretary of Ministry of Justice of the Ministry of Justice, subject: extradition of Waver, reference: 325/271 (10 June 1971).

79  NA, 5.023.5027, inv. no. 643, report summary proceedings, reference: 71/212 (14 June 1971).

80  FA 1965-1974, inv. no. 15014, memo of head GA, subject: Waver, reference: 29/71 (24 June 1971).

81  FA 1965-1974, inv. no. 15016, report Council of State, subject: Waver, reference: 7015 (30 November 1971).

82  FA 1965-1974, inv. no. 15016, memo of head of GA, subject: Waver, reference: 71/71 (2 December 1971).

83  Waver still lives in the Netherlands and never returned to the US. He lost contact with all his relatives. VPRO Radio, The track back, the case Waver (11 February 2007) www.vpro.nl/programma/vrijegeluiden/afleveringen/31489819/items/33167467.

84  NA, 5.023.5027, inv. no. 643, report of meeting between the ministers of Foreign Affairs and Justice (1970).

85  FA 1965-1974, inv. no. 15016, memo of Minister of Foreign Affairs, subject: extradition request of Waver, reference: 13846 (2 December 1971).

86  FA 1965-1974, inv. no. 15016, US Embassy, The Hague, to Ministry of Foreign Affairs, confidential, number 58 (27 December 1971).

87  FA 1965-1974, inv. no. 15016, Council of State, reference 7017 (1971)/206 (5 June 1972).

88  NA, 5.023.5027, inv. no. 644, memo of permanent under-secretary of Ministry of Justice, subject: Waver, reference: AJZ 3687/c 741 (23 June 1972).

89  FA 1965-1974, inv. no. 15016, memo of head of GA, subject: Waver, reference: 90/72 (22 August 1972).

90  Letters were found in the archive of the Ministry of Justice, inventory numbers 3086 and 3088 and in the National Archive: NA, 5.023.5027, inv. no. 643.

91  Archive of Ministry of Justice, inv. no. 3086, letter of G. (no date) and letter of Z. (11/6).

92  Archive of Ministry of Justice, inv. no. 3086, letter of British residents in the Netherlands (8 June 1971).

93  Archive of the Ministry of Justice, letter of B. (13 June 1971).

94  Archive of Ministry of Justice, inv. no. 3086, telegram of lawyers and attorneys of four Dutch towns (4 June 1971).

95  Archive of Ministry of Justice, inv. no. 3086, telegram of former parliamentarian K. (12 June 1971).

96  Archive of Ministry of Justice, inv. no. 3086, letter of Dutch Youth Community (14 June 1971); letter of Humanist Society (14 June 1971).

97  Archive of Ministry of Justice, inv. no. 3088, petition of 300 students (23 November 1971).

98  Archive of Ministry of Justice, inv. no. 3088, petition of Regional Council of Churches (25 November 1971).

99  Archive of Ministry of Justice, inv. no. 3086, telegram Conscientious Objectors Eindhoven (12 June 1971).

100 Archive of Ministry of Justice, inv. no. 3086, letter of B. (13 June 1971); letter of citizens of Haarlem (13 June 1971).

101 Archive of Ministry of Justice, inv. no. 3086, letter of citizens of Bloemendaal (13 June 1971).

102 Archive of Ministry of Justice, inv. no. 3086, petition of 300 Dutch citizens (no date).

103 NA, 5.023.5027, inv. no. 643, letter of R. (21 October 1971).

104 Archive of Ministry of Justice, inv. no. 3086, letter of D. (12 June 1971).

105 Archive of Ministry of Justice, inv. no. 3086, petition of Pacifist-Socialist Party, Department The Hague (15 June 1971).

106 Archive of Ministry of Justice, inv. no. 3086, news item (11/6) 'Protest at Summary Proceedings Ralph Waver'.

107 Archive of Ministry of Justice, inv. no. 3086, letter of Z. (11 June 1971).

108 Archive of Ministry of Justice, inv. no. 3086, letter of J.-G. (12 June 1971).

109 NA, 5.023.5027, inv. no. 643, petition of Centre for Development Aid and Third World Aid Shop (October 1971).

110 Archive of Ministry of Justice, inv. no. 3086, letter of Amnesty International (14 June 1971).

111 NA, 5.023.5027, inv. no. 643, letter from K. (12 November 1971).

112 Ministry of Justice 3086, standard reply of permanent under-secretary of Ministry of Justice (11 June 1971).

113  NA, 5.023.5027, inv. no. 643, reply from the permanent under-secretary of Ministry of Justice to the Quakers (30 November 1971).

114  NA, 5.023.5027, inv. no. 643, reply from the permanent under-secretary of Ministry of Justice to petition of students (30 November 1971).

115  NA, 5.023.5027, inv. no. 643, reply from the permanent under-secretary of Ministry of Justice to R. (21 October 1971).

## References

Alink, F.B. (2006), *Crisis als kans? Over de relatie tussen crises en hervormingen in het vreemdelingenbeleid van Nederland en Duitsland.* Amsterdam: Vosius Press UVA & Amsterdam University Press.

Alink, F., A. Boin & P. 't Hart (2001), 'Institutional crises and reforms in policy sectors: The case of asylum policy in Europe', *Journal of European Public Policy* 8 (2): 286-306.

Baalen, A. van (1997), 'Asiel in wonderland: De patriarchalisering van vluchtelingen', *Tijdschrift voor vrouwenstudies* 18 (4): 418-432.

Bhabha, J. (2004), 'Demography and rights: Women, children and access to asylum', *International Journal of Refugee Law* 16 (2): 227-243.

Bloch, A., T. Galvin & B. Harrell-Bond (2000), 'Refugee women in Europe: Some aspects of the legal and policy dimensions', *International Migration* 38 (2): 169-188.

Boswell, C. (2000), 'European values and the asylum crisis', *International Affairs* 76 (3): 537-557.

Bronkhorst, D. (1990), *Een tijd van komen: De geschiedenis van vluchtelingen in Nederland.* Amsterdam: Jan Mets.

Calavita, K. (2006), 'Gender, migration, and law: Crossing borders and bridging disciplines', *International Migration Review* 40 (1): 104-132.

Carruthers, S.L. (2005), 'Between camps: Eastern Bloc 'escapees' and Cold War borderlands', *American Quarterly* 57 (3): 911-942.

Churchill, D.S. (2004), 'An ambiguous welcome: Vietnam draft resistance, the Canadian state, and Cold War containment', *Social History* 37 (73): 1-26.

Cohen, R. & D. Joly (1989), 'Introduction: The "new refugees" of Europe', in D. Joly & R. Cohen (eds), *Reluctant hosts: Europe and its refugees,* pp. 5-18. Aldershot: Avebury/Gower Publishing Group.

Connell, R.W. (1993), 'The big picture: Masculinities in recent world history', *Theory and Society* 22 (5) *Special Issue: Masculinities* (October): 597-623.

Crawley, H. (2000), 'Gender, persecution and the concept of politics in the asylum determination process', *Forced Migration Review* 9: 17-20.

D'Haenens, L. & M. de Lange (2001), 'Framing of asylum seekers in Dutch regional newspapers', *Media, Culture & Society* 23: 847-860.

Doesschate, J.W. (1993), *Asielbeleid en belangen: Het Nederlandse toelatingsbeleid ten aanzien van vluchtelingen in de jaren 1968-1982.* Hilversum: Verloren.

Duynstee, F.J.F.M. (1972), 'Het Nederlandse vreemdelingenrecht', in W. Riphagen, F.J.F.M. Duynstee & J.H. Smeets, *De vreemdeling in Nederland,* pp. 36-53. Deventer: Kluwer.

Eekert, P. van, D. Hellema & A. van Heteren (1986), *Johnson moordenaar! De kwestie Vietnam in de Nederlandse politiek, 1965-1975*. Amsterdam: Mets.

Entman, R.M. (1993), 'Framing: Toward clarification of a fractured paradigm', *Journal of Communication* 43 (4): 51-58.

Esterik, C. van (1998), *Het zout der aarde, UAF 1948-1998: Vijftig jaar hulp aan vluchteling-studenten*. Amsterdam: Bert Bakker.

Freeman, G. (1992), 'Migration policy and politics in the receiving states', *International Migration Review* 26 (4): 1144-1167.

Gallagher, D. (1989), 'The evolution of the international refugee system', *International Migration Review* 23 (3): 579-598.

Gorp, B. van (2002), 'Werken aan de werkelijkheid: Een casestudie over de Inplanting van een asielcentrum', *Tijdschrift voor Sociologie* 23 (3/4): 325-342.

Greatbatch, J. (1989), 'The gender difference: Feminist critiques of refugee discourse', *International Journal of Refugee Law* 1 (4): 518-527.

Hoeksma, J. (1987), 'Vluchtelingen in het Europa van de Burger: Asiel zoeken in Europa', *Justitiële Verkenningen* 13 (8): 98-121.

Jansse de Jonge, H., T. Prakken & T. de Roos (1983), 'Action and law in the Netherlands', *Contemporary Crises* 7 (2): 113-133.

Kagan, M. (2003), 'Is truth is the eyes of the beholder? Objective credibility assessments in refugee status determination', *Georgetown Immigration Law Journal* 17 (3): 367-415.

Kelly, N. (1993), 'Gender-related persecution: Assessing the asylum claims of women', *Cornell International Law Journal* 26: 625-674.

Kneebone, S. (2005), 'Women within the refugee construct: "Exclusionary inclusion" in policy and practice – the Australian experience', *International Journal of Refugee Law* 17 (1): 7-42.

Krieken, P.J. van (1976), *Deserteurs, dienstweigeraars en asielrecht*. Assen: Van Gorcum.

Leiss, A. & R. Boesjes (2004), 'Women, children and access to asylum', *International Journal of Refugee Law* 16 (2): 227-243.

Lindo, F. (1988), *Zuideuropeanen in Nederland (Portugezen, Spanjaarden, Italianen, Grieken en Joegoslaven)*. Rijswijk: Ministerie van Cultuur, Recreatie en Maatschappelijk Werk.

Loescher, G. (2001), *The UNHCR and world politics: A perilous path*. Oxford: Oxford University Press.

Lynn, N. & S. Lea (2003), '"A phantom menace and the new Apartheid": The social construction of asylum-seekers in the United Kingdom', *Discourse & Society* 14: 425-452.

Maar, R. van der (2007), *Welterusten, mijnheer de president: Nederland en de Vietnamoorlog 1965-1973*. Utrecht: Boom.

Maarseveen, H.Th.J.F. van (1972), 'Ralph Waver: Vreemdeling of vluchteling?', *Nederlands Juristenblad*: 33-38.

Macklin, A. (1999), 'A comparative analysis of the Canadian, US, and Australian directives on gender persecution and refugee status', in D. Indra (ed.), *Engendering forced migration: Theory and practice*, pp. 272-307. Oxford: Berghahn Books.

Mascini, P. & M. van Bochove (2007), 'Gender en asiel: "Zelfstandige" mannen en "Afhankelijke" vrouwen', *Sociologie* 3 (1): 111-130.

McKay, S.C. (2007), 'Filipino sea men: Constructing masculinities in an ethnic labour niche', *Journal of Ethnic and Migration Studies* 33 (4) (May): 617-633.

Montgomery, E. & A. Foldspang (2005), 'Predictors of the authorities' decision to grant asylum in Denmark', *Journal of Refugee Studies* 18 (4): 454-467.

Nickels, H.C. (2007), 'Framing asylum discourse in Luxembourg', *Journal of Refugee Studies* 20 (1): 37-59.

Nobil Ahmad, A. (2008), 'The romantic appeal of illegal migration: Gender masculinity and human smuggling from Pakistan', in M. Schrover, J. van der Leun, L. Lucassen & C. Quispel (eds), *Illegal migration and gender in a global and historical perspective*, pp. 127-150. Amsterdam: Amsterdam University Press.

Oxford, C.G. (2005), 'Protectors and victims in the gender regime of asylum', NWSA *Journal* 17 (3): 18-38.

Paludan, A. (1981), 'Refugees in Europe', *International Migration Review* 15 (1): 60-73.

Schrover, M. (2009), 'Family in Dutch migration policy, 1945-2005', *History of the Family* 14: 191-202.

Sellström, T. (2002), *Sweden and national liberation in Southern Africa. Vol II. Solidarity and assistance 1970-1994*. Stockholm: The Nordic Africa Institute.

Sorber, J. (1971), 'Nederland, Portugal en Zuidelijk Afrika: Een greep uit het werk van het Angola Comité', *Wending* 26 (April): 125.

Spijkerboer, T. (1994), *Asylum seekers: A comparative study concerning policy and jurisprudence in the Netherlands, Germany, France, the United Kingdom, also dealing summarily with Belgium and Canada.* Amsterdam: Dutch Refugee Council.

Stein, B.N. (1981), 'The refugee experience: Defining the parameters of a field study', *International Migration Review* 15 (1 & 2): 320-330.

Thorne, B. (1975), 'Women in the draft resistance movement: A case study of sex roles and social movements', *Sex Roles* 1 (2): 179-195.

Unterhalter, E. (2000), 'The work of the nation: Heroic masculinity in South African autobiographical writing of the anti-apartheid struggle', *The European Journal of Development Research* 12 (2): 157-178.

Valji, N., L.A. de la Hunt & J.H. Moffett (2003), 'Where are the women? Gender discrimination in refugee policies and practises', *Agenda* 55: 61-72.

Walaardt, T. (2009), 'Het paard van Troje: Het verlenen van asiel door Nederland in de periode 1945-1955', *Tijdschrift voor Sociale en Economische Geschiedenis* 6 (2): 63-93.

Walaardt, T. (2012), *Geruisloos inwilligen: Argumentatie en speelruimte in de Nederlandse asielprocedure, 1945-1994.* Hilversum: Verloren.

Wetten J. van, C.J.H. Bijleveld, F. Heide & N. Dijkhoff (2001), 'Female asylum seekers in the Netherlands', *International Migration* 39 (3): 85-98.

White, A. (2002), 'Geographies of asylum, legal knowledge and legal practices', *Political Geography* 21: 1055-1073.

Ziemann, B. (2008), 'The code of protest: Images of peace in the West German peace movements, 1945-1990', *Contemporary European History* 17 (2): 237-261.

Zolberg, A.R. (2006), *A nation by design: Immigration policy in the fashioning of America.* Cambridge: Harvard University Press.

# 4 A gender-blind approach in Canadian refugee processes

## Mexican female claimants in the new refugee narrative

*Monica Boyd and Joanne Nowak*

## Introduction

Women refugees have long faced barriers to the refugee process. However, in the 1990s a number of countries adopted a formal set of gender guidelines to assist them in taking gender issues into account in refugee adjudications. Consequently, many women successfully obtained refugee status by claiming gender-based persecution. Additionally, gender-related abuses were incorporated into the larger refugee narrative emphasising political and humanitarian concerns. Focusing on the recent influx of Mexican refugees to Canada, this chapter argues that today's refugee narrative has moved away from a gender-inclusive approach, and reverted to the traditional gender-blind perspective. Using a framing analysis of more than 100 articles in the Canadian media, this chapter traces this shift and the conditions that influenced it, as well as the implications for refugee women.

Women have long been overrepresented in refugee flows, but underrepresented in refugee claims in the industrialised countries (Foote 1996; Boyd 1999). This pattern has numerous explanations. One stresses the tendency of women to remain near their countries of origin (in neighbouring countries); a second emphasises the delayed migration of women, who follow their spouses or male relatives through family migration once the former have made refugee claims abroad (Mascini & Van Bochove 2009). This chapter moves beyond the individual level by focusing on how the migration of female refugees may be influenced by *institutional* actors, particularly the media, within countries of settlement.

During the 1990s, select states, including Canada, addressed the gendered nature of the refugee process, specifically through the development of formal gender guidelines to be used in the refugee claimant adjudication process. At the urging of the United Nations, Canada was the first country to officially adopt these guidelines in 1993. Success in addressing gendered differences is manifest in Canadian refugee data (Mawani 1993). In 1986, roughly 7,800 women refugees obtained permanent resident status, while in 2010 this number increased to nearly 12,100.[1] Numerous Immigration and Refugee Board (IRB) cases in Canada cite gender-related persecution as the main reason why claimants are allowed to remain. The strategy has been so successful that refugee scholars have described this pattern of refugee adjudication as following a 'good women, bad men' script. Where gender-related claims made by women are seen as valid reasons for asylum claimants, the claims of male refugees are often associated with economic motivations and therefore viewed as invalid or bogus (Boyd 1999; Mascini & Van Bochove 2009). Mexican female claimants have been especially successful in their use of the Canadian Gender Guidelines in gender-related persecution claims.[2] However, notwithstanding this improvement in women's status, the number of male refugee claimants, as well as the number of men granted permanent residence to Canada as refugees, has been higher than corresponding numbers for women every year for the past 25 years.[3] It seems that women's success is late in coming, and limited in its scope. The gains were also relatively short lived, as recent economic and political developments have re-scripted the refugee narrative from one that considers the needs and vulnerabilities of women, to a largely genderless story.[4]

The discussion in this chapter can be situated within the larger literature that focuses on political and economic factors that influence refugee policies and narratives, especially foreign policy interests and domestic special interest groups (Mitchell 1989; Zolberg 1999; Spijkerboer 2000; Cornelius & Rosenblum 2005) (for other examples, see the chapters in this volume by Walaardt, Schacher, and Oxford). In this chapter, we focus on the gendered aspects of the refugee narrative, examining the conditions under which a focus on gender issues recedes into the background in refugee processes. We argue that the traditional refugee story in the Canadian media has been re-scripted by new geopolitics between 'democratic' countries in the post-Cold War era, the recent large-scale influx of Mexican refugee claimants to Canada, as well as the costs of this influx to Canadian taxpayers and the refugee system. The narrative has shifted from providing protection to refugees from failed states (using a gender-inclusive approach), to managing and reducing refugees from democratic countries (using a gender-neutral approach). This shift in the narrative has the strong potential of limiting the ability of refugee women to access the refugee process and to have successful resolutions of their claims. This chapter begins by examining how and why the refugee narrative has changed. It then discusses the implications of these changes for female refugee claimants, particularly Mexican women.[5]

## Literature review: The historical development of the gendered refugee narrative

The traditional refugee narrative emerged in the 1950s within the historical and political context of the post-Second World War period. A key element of this narrative was the creation of a formal international refugee definition, put forward in Article 1 of the 1951 United Nations Convention Relating to the Status of Refugees. That convention states that a refugee is a person who 'owing to a well-founded fear of being persecuted for reasons of race, religion, nationality, membership of a particular social group or political opinion, is outside the country of his nationality and is unable, or owing to such fear, is unwilling to avail himself of the protection of that country'. This definition of a refugee draws attention to violations committed directly by the state against individuals (Connors 1997). Critics have observed that this focus on the actions of the state and the violation of civil and political rights places a disproportionate emphasis on public, rather than private, forms of persecution.

The lack of attention to persecution in private settings disproportionately impacts women, since gender roles and stratification constrain women in many societies to the private sphere, while men are the main actors in the public arena. Gender scholars and advocates note that the UN definition of refugee privileges the recognition of refugee status for men relative to women, suggesting that forms of persecution experienced by women in more private settings are less likely to be recognised as grounds for persecution. Such forms include rape, dowry-related burnings, forced marriages, female genital mutilation and domestic violence (Foote 1996; Boyd 1999). In some situations, the state could be the agent denying basic human rights, or it may fail to offer protection to certain groups, even though such protection is within its capacity (Connors 1997; Boyd 1999).

Critics also note with some concern the procedures whereby persecution is established. Assessing accounts of harmful acts involves understanding the conditions within the country or state from which the person has fled, as well as understanding the consequences should the person return. Yet country descriptions usually emphasise the public sphere, not the private sphere. Country-specific information may be genderless, rather than illuminating gender inequalities. In either case, women might find it difficult to argue that their victimisation is based on one or more grounds found in the refugee definition. Rather than being viewed as violations of human rights, their experiences may be perceived by the courts, the public and the media, as private acts inflicted by other individuals (Connors 1997; UNHCR 1997; Boyd 1999). Furthermore, Inlender (2009) argues that the likelihood of success with gender claims is complicated by the difficulty of proving that acts traditionally seen as private matters (within the family sphere) are in fact government sanctioned, whether implicitly or tacitly.

Over time, these issues have led to three modifications in the refugee narrative. First, violence against women (particularly sexual violence) emerged as a key concern (UNHCR 1995). Second, the discussion broadened to include forms of gender-based persecution, such as female genital mutilation and other harmful practices, as well as domestic violence where no community or legal state protection is provided (UNHCR 1997). Third, governments developed tools to increase adjudicators' awareness of how persecution is mediated by gender. One such tool is the Gender Guidelines, implemented in Canada in 1993. Similar procedures were adopted later by the USA and Australia. The Canadian guidelines present ways for adjudicators to be gender sensitive when considering persecution grounds and special efforts to be made in the refugee determination process, such as having female interviewers (Foote 1996). In sum, the emphasis on gender-related abuses, along with the promise of state protection by refugee adjudicators and governments in the 1990s, resulted in the creation of a more gender-inclusive refugee narrative (Mascini & Van Bochove 2009).

## The demise of the (gendered) refugee narrative

The emphasis on providing protection to female refugees which culminated in the development of the Gender Guidelines in the 1990s, is currently receding into the background – even in the very country that launched the guidelines onto the global stage. Challenges to a relatively friendly female refugee narrative existed earlier through concerns about the general costs of refugees, and the legitimacy of female refugee claimants.[6] Recently these critiques have been made on a more regular basis, leading to a noticeable shift in foci, assumptions and values promoted in the refugee narrative. Support can in fact be found for the claim that the move from the Cold War to the neo-liberal period, as well as the recent increase in the number of refugees (and in costs) to Canada, has shifted the refugee narrative. Instead of a focus on providing protection to refugees from failed states using a gender-inclusive approach (that takes gender-based persecution into account), the emphasis is increasingly on managing and reducing refugees from partner democratic countries, using a gender-blind approach. However, a gender-blind approach cannot be equated with gender neutrality in outcomes. Gender stratification and hierarchies of power in countries of origin and countries of settlement can produce immigration practices and regulations that not are gender-specific in their terms of reference, but which often have gender-specific impacts (Boyd 1989, 1995; Boyd & Pikkov 2008).

## Case study: Mexican migration to Canada

Mexican refugees have been coming to Canada for decades. However, there has been a significant increase in the number of refugee claimants from this country. In fact, there has been a fivefold increase in the past ten years. In December 2001, 3,600 refugee claimants from Mexico represented 3.2% of all claimants present in Canada. By December 2005, more than 8,000 claimants were from Mexico, with the number rising to nearly 16,000 in 2010. As a result, Mexican claimants constituted 8% and 16% of the entire refugee claimant population in 2005 and 2010, respectively.[7] Concomitantly, there was a noticeable increase in female Mexican claimants. In 2000, they represented just under 4% of the total female refugee claimant population in Canada, but in 2007 the number had risen to more than 17%.[8] While several factors could explain why women are fleeing Mexico, the level of gender-related violence in the country is an important push factor. More than 130,000 cases of domestic violence are reported in Mexico each year.[9] In terms of state protection, roughly half of the female respondents who identified themselves as victims of violence in a 2003 Mexican national study did not seek assistance, while nearly 80% of those who did seek assistance relied primarily on family and friends rather than the police.[10]

Yet Mexico continues to be described as a safe and democratic state by the Canadian media and government. In fact, the government recently took a powerful symbolic step in this regard by requiring visas from Mexicans entering Canada in a bid to separate the 'few' legitimate refugee claimants from those abusing the refugee process.[11] Consequently, the gender-related concerns of Mexican women appear to have receded into the background in the current refugee narrative. But Mexican refugees have not disappeared, and Mexican women refugee claimants currently represent the largest group of female claimants in Canada.[12] How can we explain this altered narrative, given the plight of women refugee claimants?

## Materials and methods

We answer this question using reports that appeared in major Canadian newspapers with nationwide or province-wide circulation, such as the *National Post*, the *Globe and Mail*, the *Toronto Star*, the *Ottawa Citizen* and the *Montreal Gazette*, as well as local newspapers, such as the *Edmonton Journal* and the *Windsor Star*. We also examined blogs on immigration issues. The objective of this selection was twofold. The first aim was to cover a broad spectrum of newspapers discussing refugee issues at both the national and local levels, thus providing a comprehensive picture of the Canadian press. The second aim was to acknowledge the increasing importance of the electronic media as a disseminator of news and culture.

From these newspapers and blogs, we selected articles and editorials that discussed topics related to gender and Mexican refugees, the Canadian refugee system, domestic violence, bogus (or economic) refugees, democratic states and safe states between 1990 and 2009. These general topics were developed into specific codes, and analysed in terms of the narratives and portrayals of Mexican refugee claimants to Canada, with a focus on female claimants.

Framing theory guided the analysis. Using media reports, we identified frames (or narratives) within media articles to provide an organising structure for understanding key issues, phenomena and groups (Snow et al. 1986; Olausson 2009; Seijio 2009). As Pan and Kosicki (1993) point out, identifying these media frames enables scholars to tease out the analytical and conceptual schemata provided to the public through which events, phenomena and people are given meaning (additional discussion of frame analysis appears in the chapter by Walaardt in this volume). These dominant frames are often taken for granted. Thus, to better understand the particular meanings, assumptions and values promoted by these seemingly neutral frames, we must deconstruct and critique them. Further, since the frames shape what is presented as common sense, they are intimately related to issues of power. An analysis of frames in the media therefore also considers the dominant economic, political and cultural forces at play.

Critical discourse analysis (CDA) provides a complementary technique in this analysis. It is used to identify implicit values and assumptions, taking a constructionist approach to discourses and narratives in the media and connecting these to dominant actors and forces in society (McGrath 2009).[13] CDA thus assists in uncovering the interests, values and assumptions of refugee narratives.

The objective of the research presented in this chapter is threefold. It first identifies the dominant frames that are used in the media and shape the public's views and understandings of Mexican refugee claimants. It then notes the political and economic forces behind these particular frames and examines the conditions under which shifts in refugee frames (or narratives) take place.

## Findings

The results of our analysis indicate a move away from a gender-inclusive approach that seeks to provide protection to refugees, to a gender-neutral approach that emphasises managing refugees from democratic countries. The portrayal of Mexican women refugees in the media, or rather the lack thereof, is an integral component of this shift. For instance, among more than 100 articles and editorials discussing the large influx of Mexican refugee claimants to Canada, roughly 10% refer to women or gender in the title. Mexican claimants are consistently described as a homogeneous group, as the following headlines demonstrate: 'Flood of Mexican refugees shows poor border controls'[14] and '9,000 ordinary people flee Mexican drug war'.[15] In these examples, the script takes on a gender-blind or gender-neutral tone that neglects consideration of the gender-related issues of female claimants.

In terms of content, only a minority of the articles reporting on Mexican refugees meaningfully focus on the issues faced by Mexican women, their refugee experiences or the types of claims they advance. The mismatch between the genderless refugee narratives and reality is underscored by refugee experts' descriptions of the most common types of claims: 'Over the past six years, most Mexican claims have involved threats or brutal physical attacks related to narco-traffickers, violent domestic abuse and homophobia'[16] and 'Women who flee domestic violence make up many of the claims. Amnesty International, the UN and Human Rights Watch all document the lack of protection for such women'.[17]

Thus, while gender issues remain prevalent in actual refugee claims, they have receded into the background in the media's refugee narratives. How did this shift in narrative occur? We posit three main conditions: a shift in the geopolitical relationships influencing refugee processes, a significant increase in refugee claimants from certain countries of origin, and economic decline in the countries of settlement.

## Conditions underlying the shift in the refugee narrative

### NEW GEOPOLITICAL RELATIONSHIPS IN REFUGEE PROCESSES

The attitudes of states towards refugee admissions have shifted over the past several decades, leading to a significant change in the dominant refugee narrative articulated in the media. Political interests during the Cold War played a key role in shaping refugee admissions and helping to write the larger refugee narrative. Specifically, refugees from communist countries were welcomed in the West in a bid to highlight their desire to live in a democratic, Western country rather than a communist one (Zucker & Zucker 1987; Zolberg 1999). As a bonus, the political interests of the countries of settlement and the humanitarian needs of these refugees tended to coincide. Consequently, the dominant refugee narrative emphasised during the Cold War period was one of providing protection to political and humanitarian refugees from failed (or backward) states.

Now, two decades after the end of the Cold War, geopolitical relationships have changed. The world is no longer divided into clear ideological camps, a situation in which governments stood to benefit from lenient refugee policies. Consequently, there is less willingness to become heavily involved in refugee issues. The broad emphasis has shifted from conflicts based on politico-ideological regimes, to allegiances based on economic ties and political-economic regimes.[18] More specifically, states have moved away from refugee protection towards refugee management and reduction. These changes are reflected in the refugee narrative. Media no longer discuss politico-ideological differences between countries of origin and settlement, but talk of cultivating ties between economically like-minded countries. For instance, several articles discussing Mexican refugees' attempts to cross the border emphasise Mexico's status as Canada's 'trading partner'. Labelling a trading partner as an unstable state that cannot protect its citizens is an economically risky move. The following quotations connect Canada's reluctance to welcome Mexican refugees to the political and economic ties between the party countries of the North American Free Trade Agreement (NAFTA):

> Canada's Conservative government, however, has been treading softly in their dealings with Mexico about these cases – afraid, no doubt, of the political and economic fall-out that may occur by alienating a NAFTA partner.[19]

> Many view Mexico as a tourist destination, a democratic country that is also our partner in trade with NAFTA, says Gozlan [immigration lawyer].[20]

These strong economic interests work against providing refugee protection, and they work towards refugee management from countries with whom Canada has trading ties.

As suggested elsewhere (Olausson 2009), the polity and the media are intimately connected. Thus, media frames usually reflect dominant political interests. In this case, changing geopolitical interests are shifting the refugee narrative away from protection and humanitarianism and toward refugee reduction. This cautious or reluctant approach towards refugees is even more salient when the refugee claimants are from countries deemed 'democratic'. Under such conditions, the Canadian government and the media rely on the assumption that since Mexico is a democratic country, it protects its citizens. But immigration lawyers and refugee advocates issue the following warnings:

> The principal reasoning behind these kinds of rejections is because the IRB says the claimant has to show state protection is not available to the claimant. The onus is higher on them to show that protection is not available the more democratic a country is, says Michael Tilleard, past chair of the Canadian Bar Association's immigration and citizenship section for northern Alberta. Often the IRB decisions will say Mexico is a democracy, or even a fledgling democracy, so you should have recourse to state protection if you're living in a democratic state.[21]

> Dench [Executive Director of the Canadian Council for Refugees] also warns about Kenney's position that claimants who come from so-called 'democratic' countries can't be legitimate refugees.[22]

Newspapers often describe Mexico as a democratic country and contrast it with failed states, such as Somalia, as the following quotation illustrates: 'Compare Mexico's low numbers with countries like Somalia, which last year had 74 Calgary applications and an acceptance rate of 100 per cent.'[23] Through such juxtapositions, the papers imply that refugee claimants from the former are necessarily false claimants. More specifically, these 'bogus refugees' are described as economic refugees trying to exploit Canada's labour market illegally or escape from their domestic drug violence problems, rather than remain within their own legitimate and democratic country:

> In another 'big racket', Argentines are travelling to the U.S. because they don't need a visa. They then present themselves to Canada as refugees, live in hotels and dine on welfare money. After they finish their two- or three-month Canadian holiday, he says, many simply

return home. A percentage of Mexican refugee claimants reportedly also take similar vacations here.[24]

Although there is a significant level of crime and drug violence in Mexico, the media frames democratic countries such as Mexico as safe countries that protect their citizens and do not produce refugee claimants. This democratic country narrative constructs Mexican refugees as unworthy, limiting their ability to be portrayed as legitimate refugees. This public narrative is also reflected in the longstanding 'deserving and undeserving refugee' discourse within the academic literature, the former being associated with the minority of (Mexican in this case) asylum seekers granted Convention status and the latter reserved for the majority who do not obtain this status (Sales 2002; Mascini & Van Bochove 2009).

The influence of the 'deserving versus undeserving refugee' narrative (compare Schacher and Walaardt in this volume) can be seen in the views among the Canadian public on Mexican refugees as expressed in editorials and letters to newspapers. While Mexico's poor economic conditions and drug violence conjure up some sympathy, most respondents comment that these are not valid criteria for refugee claimants and that Canada cannot be a haven for all people in need:

> A lot of Windsorites have voiced their opinion on the Mexican refugee situation, both negative and positive responses, but the bottom line doesn't change. I am all for the best for all human beings, but we cannot save everyone.[25]

> I sympathize for their economic plight but their problems are not Canada's to solve. Canada has its own poverty issues to deal with and much of it is generated by an out of control immigration system. The economic poverty of Mexicans is Mexico's responsibility.[26]

The emphasis on the democratic – and therefore safe – Mexican state is especially meaningful for women, as it contains the potential to remove gender considerations from the claimant process. Assuming that a democratic country provides protection to its citizens overlooks the possibility that such a state can be patriarchal and neglect to provide equal protection to all residents. In the case of women in Mexico, a number of organisations document a persistently high rate of domestic violence against women with little or no police protection provided.[27] According to the 2003 National Survey on Household Relationship Dynamics, roughly 10% of Mexican women report being physically abused, and nearly 37% reported emotional abuse. These numbers are likely even higher, since they only represent those women who are willing to report such violence (Frias Martinez 2009). Numerous reports document instances where Mexican women have gone to the authorities and reported domestic violence and received no protection.[28] In fact, the Mexican researcher Teresa Doring found that 80% of women killed by husbands or boyfriends had asked police for help from one to five years beforehand.[29]

According to the United Nations' definition, a convention refugee must be a person with a well-founded fear of persecution based on race, religion, nationality, political opinion or membership in a particular social group. Furthermore, that person must demonstrate that his government is unable, or unwilling, to provide protection from this persecution.[30] Writers suggest that Mexican women experiencing domestic violence meet this definition given that (1) they belong to a particular social group (i.e., women) being persecuted (i.e., abused) as a result of their membership in this group, (2) this persecution is pervasive, and (3) their government appears unable, or unwilling, to provide protection (from domestic violence). That last is evidenced by the lack of police protection and failure to prosecute perpetrators of domestic violence in Mexico (Teran 1999).[31]

Nevertheless, the Canadian media's discussion of Mexican refugees utilises a gender-blind script that emphasises drug violence and human smuggling as the main factors pushing Mexicans to seek refuge in other countries, glossing over the experiences of domestic violence that drive many women to seek asylum. Consider, for example, the following genderless narratives:

> Everything is related to the climb of violence in Mexico. Some of them have received direct threats for different reasons – because they were caught in the middle of drug cartels when they are trying to control an area, or they saw a crime or corruption, you name it [Martinez, Toronto's FCJ Refugee Centre].[32]

> Hundreds of Mexican refugee claimants are entering Canada every month due to spiralling drug cartel violence and the presence of scam artists promising refuge in Canada, experts say.[33]

In articles such as these, Mexican refugees are discussed as a monolithic, homogenous group.

These media accounts indicate that a dividing line is being drawn between democratic countries that do not (or cannot) produce refugees

on the one hand and conflict-ridden countries without functional government, such as Somalia, on the other. However, this framing of countries of origin relies on a traditional understanding of refugees based on
public persecution; that is, fleeing war or conflict or a lack of political
governance or state apparatus. It ignores the advances in the refugee
discourse of the 1990s, underscoring persecution in the private realm,
even with a functional government and general *public* safety. The framing overlooks the fact that a state can be both patriarchal and democratic – in other words, providing protection to its citizens generally –
but not meet the specific needs of women. The earlier narrative, which
focused on providing asylum for ideological purposes using a gender-
inclusive approach, has thus shifted to one that emphasises maintaining good economic and political ties with governments deemed 'democratic' using a gender-blind approach.

## Dramatic increase in refugee claimants

Another key condition influencing today's refugee narrative is the dra-
matic increase in refugee claimants to Canada from specific countries
of origin, such as the previously noted fivefold increase in the number
of Mexican refugee claimants in the past decade.[34] The perceived inten-
sity of this influx is heightened by the media's use of metaphors related
to contagion and flooding of these allegedly 'bogus' refugees (the emphasis is ours in the following):

> The NAFTA partner has been the top source country for refugee claims
> in Canada since 2005. It was also the top source country for refugee
> claims in Alberta for 2007 and 2008, *dwarfing* the number of claims
> from other top source countries such as Colombia, Somalia, and Zim-
> babwe.[35]

> A sudden flood of Mexican refugee claimants *pouring* into Windsor
> has left local officials scrambling and raised fears about how many
> more may be on their way.[36]

> Mexicans *pour* into Canada from US: Agencies brace for thousands
> more at border.[37]

> Mexicans are *flooding* into Canada and claiming refugee status. Why
> is it happening, and what can we do to stop it?[38]

This rhetorical technique has also been used in describing other refugee inflows, such as the sudden increase of Tamil asylum seekers to
the Netherlands in the 1980s (Van Dijk 1988). The result is often a portrayal of asylum seekers as a threat to the integrity of Canadian system.
Moreover, these images create a distance between the influx of new asylum seekers (as a separate Other) and Canadian society.

## Economic decline in the country of settlement

A final key condition influencing the development of the current refugee narrative is economic decline in the country of settlement. The economic costs (rather than political benefits) of accepting refugees are often centre stage in public discussions. This economic focus is prevalent
in media discussions at both the national and local levels. The former
highlights the overall costs to the Canadian taxpayer. For instance, the
National Post estimated the cost of maintaining one refugee as approximately $10,000 to $12,000 per year on taxpayers.[39] While much analysis has focused on the development of refugee narratives at the macro
level (i.e., within international institutions, national governments and
national newspapers), local actors and institutions also shape portrayals of refugees amongst the Canadian public. As the following texts illustrate, municipal newspapers and news media emphasise the costs
of Mexican refugees in local services and resources, making the issue
more personal and threatening to local residents:

> Municipal agencies dealing with the sudden influx of mainly Mexican
> refugee applicants are renting out hotel rooms and bracing for pre-
> dicted thousands more to come ... We are not able to deal with this
> potential crisis locally.[40]

> Francis [the mayor of Windsor] has written the federal and provincial
> governments asking for funding to help cover the cost of keeping the
> refugees housed while they wait for their refugee claims to be heard.
> Last week, he said it had so far cost the city $230,000, about 20 per
> cent of the annual budget for shelters. Windsor's unemployment rate
> is currently pushing 10 per cent, making the influx of jobless refugees
> the last thing its economy needed.[41]

This emphasis on the unmanageable costs created by the influx of
Mexican refugees reinforces the legitimacy of the narrative's call to
manage the growing number of refugees.[42] In the following, Mexican

female claimants are specifically discussed, but in reference to the cost of their migration and their children:

> Last week, he said it had so far put up 50 families, some with up to nine children, at four city hotels. The bills, including those for meals, are being sent to the city's social services department.[43]

> To complicate things further, one of the 200 people in Windsor recently gave birth to a child, and another woman has one on the way. Both children will have claims to Canadian citizenship, and strengthen the residency case of the mothers involved.[44]

In sum, the new refugee narrative emphasises *refugee costs rather than claims*. Although both men and women are targeted, women refugee claimants are uniquely disadvantaged; their experiences and claims risk being relegated to the background, while their costs as mothers and women are brought to the foreground. As a result, they are particularly marginalised in the refugee narrative that appears in the media.

## Discussion

The Canadian media refugee script through 2009 focused on refugee management and reduction, rather than refugee protection and welcome. In today's geopolitical situation, the economic costs of accepting (what seems to be an increasing number of) Mexican refugees have taken centre stage, pushing aside any extensive discussion of political benefits. Although the influence of international relations on asylum processes is not new (Spijkerboer 2000), this latest shift in the refugee agenda towards economics is relatively new. The shift in the refugee narrative has had a significant impact on the public legitimacy of all Mexican refugees, but its effects on women have been particularly damaging. Very few of the articles we looked at mentioned the refugee intentions or experiences of Mexican women. Instead, the dominant script portrays Mexican refugees as one homogeneous group, while downplaying the legitimacy of claimants from 'democratic' countries.

This framing of Mexican refugees, however, does not consider that states deemed democratic and safe for their general citizenry are not necessarily assessed in terms of the safety they provide to specific groups, such as women in the private sphere (Markard 2007). As Oxford notes in her chapter in this volume, the state can fail to protect its citizens in a multiplicity of ways. Second, the current gender-blind script may result in disproportionately negative legal and policy implications for Mexican women. For instance, the Federal Court of Canada recently overturned several Immigration and Refugee Board decisions involving domestic violence refugee claims by Mexican women.[45] One could therefore argue that the narrow and homogeneous portrayal of Mexican refugees in the media may be influencing refugee adjudicators' understanding of female Mexican refugee experiences. More broadly, there is a danger that today's gender-blind refugee script has (or will) become the standard among the public and officials working in the refugee system, with little regard for the diversity (and legitimacy) of claims within this large refugee group.

The Canadian government recently implemented a visa requirement for entry of Mexicans. The justification for this policy shift expressed by government officials in the media relies heavily on a new refugee narrative, which frames Mexico as a democratic country that can protect its citizens and does not produce refugees. The Canadian Minister of Citizenship and Immigration has made a number of media announcements like the following:

> Instead, he [Citizenship and Immigration Minister Jason Kenney] says he has been told of widespread abuse of the system by relatively well-off Mexicans who take one-way flights to Canada and stay in the country until they are kicked out. He said unscrupulous immigration consultants in Mexico and the U.S. are coaching people on how to make a refugee claim in Canada. 'I'm simply saying that as a matter of policy we need to do a better job of expediting the processing of false claims, as most other democratic countries do,' Kenney said in an interview Friday.

> In a speech to the Canadian Council for Refugees in Toronto in November, Mr. Kenney raised the possibility of a two-tier system where applicants from what he called 'liberal democracies' like Mexico, Britain and the Czech Republic are treated differently than those from conflict zones or totalitarian societies ... Mr. Kenney also said that a 90 per cent rejection rate of claims made by Mexicans at Canada's Immigration and Refugee Board 'would suggest wide scale and almost systematic abuse.'[46]

The implications of this policy decision on Mexican claimants' access to the refuge process are clear: there were virtually no asylum claims from Mexican nationals in the first two weeks after the imposition of the travel visas.[47] Further, five features of the application for a visitor's visa suggest that the class and gender impacts of this process may be the greatest for women seeking to quickly remove themselves from a state that cannot or will not protect them. The requirements include (1) obtaining a visa, which requires access to funds in order to pay the application fee of Can. $75 for a sole applicant seeking a single entry and $400 for a family; (2) an interview may be required, held at the Mexico City visa office; (3) a valid travel document (such as a passport) is required for the applicant and for each family member on the application; (4) two photographs of the applicant and of each accompanying family member must be included in the application, the photos must be less than six months old and they must conform to specifications regarding head poses and size; and finally (5) despite a processing rate of 90% within two days from the Canadian visa office in Mexico City, documents must be submitted and returned via mail unless the applicant can appear in person. Use of mail or courier services lengthens the time needed to obtain a visa and raises concerns that valuable documents may be stolen in transit.[48] The gender- and class-related difficulties produced by these visa procedures are readily evident when one considers the economic situation of most Mexican women compared to men (women earned roughly 22% less than men in the 1990s) (Brown, Pagan & Rodriguez-Oreggia 1999), and the fact that the need to flee quickly will seldom allow obtainment of passports, photos and pre-issued visas. Indeed, the requirement for documents risks creating a paradox: documents are needed to enter Canada but if documents are available, refugee claimant adjudicators could interpret a woman's claim as premeditated. While premeditated flight by itself is not synonymous with a fraudulent use of the claimant process, the possibility remains that having documents would be interpreted as such.

## Conclusion

This chapter outlined a significant shift in the refugee narrative articulated in the Canadian media, from one focused on providing protection to refugees from failed states (using a gender-inclusive approach), to the management and reduction of refugees from democratic countries (using a gender-neutral approach). We underlined three main conditions that have contributed to this shift narrative: changing geopolitical relationships influencing refugee processes, a significant increase in numbers of refugee claimants from certain countries of origin (in this case, Mexico), and economic slowdown in the countries of settlement (in this case, Canada). This shift is prevalent not only in North

America. Similar trends have been found by scholars studying changes in the European refugee regime, suggesting that broad shifts are taking place in the refugee narrative in a number of regions (Keely and Stanton 1994).

As a result of these shifts, the benefits that governments stand to gain from granting asylum are now less clear than in the Cold-War era. Specifically, economic (rather than political) concerns have come to dominate the refugee agenda. This shift has conceptual and practical consequences. In terms of the former, the focus on refugee management and reduction from democratic countries – rather than the provision of protection to refugees – provokes a default negative attitude towards refugee claimants. Moreover, the gender-neutral approach overlooks the possibility that a democratic country can also be patriarchal, and therefore neglect to provide equal protection to all of its citizens. This chapter acknowledges that some Mexican claimants applying for refugee status may not have valid claims. Nonetheless, the picture painted in the media overlooks the heterogeneity of those seeking refuge. Given that Mexican women continue to face high levels of domestic abuse and other gender-related exploitation, this gender-blind approach to the refugee system reverses past gains and signals a significant weakening of Canada's leadership in promoting women's rights in refugee processes.

## Notes

1 *Citizenship and Immigration Canada*, 'Facts and figures 2010'.
2 *Immigration and Refugee Board of Canada*. RPD MA-07954, 3 October 2002; CRDD VA0-01624 et al., Forsey, Clague, 8 March 2001; CRDD A95-01027, A95-01028, Blackburn, Gaboury (6 March 1997).
3 *Citizenship and Immigration Canada*, 'Facts and figures 2010'.
4 For the purposes of this chapter, the refugee narrative refers to media discussions of the following: refugees, refugee claims, the impact of refugees on countries of origin and countries of settlement, as well as refugee policies.
5 Although the authors recognise the intersections of gender, class and ethnicity in media depictions of refugees, we focus on the first in order to highlight the shift in the *gendered* aspect of the refugee narrative in particular.
6 Barbara Amiel, 'The female refugee: A fraudulent concept', *Macleans* 106: 13 (1993) 9-10; Donna Jacobs, 'Bill C-11 "deeply flawed": Ex-immigration official', *Ottawa Citizen* 1 November 2001.
7 Nicholas Keung, 'Mexican refugee requests', *Toronto Star* 5 August 2007; *Citizenship and Immigration Canada*, 'Backgrounder: The visa requirement for Mexico', 13 July 2009.
8 *Citizenship and Immigration Canada*, 'Facts and figures 2012 – immigration overview: Permanent and temporary residents', 26 February 2012, http://www.cic.

gc.ca/english/resources/statistics/facts2010/index.asp. *Citizenship and Immigration Canada*, 'Facts and figures 2007 – immigration overview: Permanent and temporary residents', 12 November 2008, http://www.cic.gc.ca/english/resources/statistics/facts2007/temporary/30.asp (accessed 27 July 2009). More recent data for 2008-2010 does not include information by sex.

9   *Immigration and Refugee Board of Canada*, 'Mexico: State protection', May 2005, http://www.fcjrefugeecentre.org/docs/Archives/State per cent 20 Protection-2.htm (accessed 4 September 2009).

10  Ibid.

11  *Citizenship and Immigration Canada*, 'News release – Canada imposes a visa on Mexico', 13 July 2009, www.cic.gc.ca/english/department/media/releases/2009/2009-07-13.asp.

12  *Citizenship and Immigration Canada*, 'Facts and figures 2007'.

13  *Citizenship and Immigration Canada*, 'Facts and figures 2007'.

14  Wayne Ewen, 'Flood of Mexican refugees shows poor border controls', *Star-Phoenix*, 2 October 2007.

15  Marina Jiménez, '9,000 ordinary people flee Mexican drug war', *Globe and Mail*, 20 October 2008.

16  Peter Showler, 'The bogus refugee myth', *Ottawa Citizen* 12 August 2009. Peter Showler is the director of the Refugee Forum at the Human Research and Education Centre, University of Ottawa.

17  Maureen Silcoff, 'Seeking refuge from Mexico', *Globe and Mail*, 7 February 2009. Silcoff is a former member of the refugee board.

18  While we highlight economic concerns as gaining ascendancy in the refugee agenda, others suggest that geopolitical and cultural axes also play a key role in shaping the credibility and portrayal of (women) asylum claimants today. For more on this, see Spijkerboer (2000).

19  John Intini, 'Guns in the sun: Escalating violence may be making Mexican vacations too risky', *Macleans*, 4 June 2007.

20  Samatha Sarra, 'New hearing for rejected Mexican', *Xtra*, 16 April 2008.

21  Alexandra Zabjek, 'Local family wins refuge from Mexico's drug wars', *Edmonton Journal*, 3 March 2009.

22  Dale Smith, 'British queer activist warns Canada of 'rigged' asylum system', *Xtra*, 5 August 2009.

23  Valerie Fortney, 'Desire for a better life lures Mexicans to Alberta', *Calgary Herald*, 24 March 2009.

24  Donna Jacobs, 'Bill C-11 "deeply flawed": Ex-immigration official', *Ottawa Citizen*, 1 November 2001.

25  Diane Renaud, 'Be compassionate but we must draw the line', *Windsor Star*, 13 October 2007.

26  *Canadian Immigration Reform Blog*, 'Mexican "refugees" strain Windsor's social services', 20 September 2007, http://canadianimmigrationreform.blogspot.com/2007/09/mexican-immigrants-strain-windsors.html.

27  *Immigration and Refugee Board of Canada*, 'Mexico: State protection'; *Amnesty International*, 'Protection law fails Mexican women', 30 January 2009, www.amnesty.org/en/news-and-updates/news/protection-law-fails-mexican-women-20090130 (accessed 6 September 2009).

28 We do not discount the possibility that some Mexican men are physically abused by their (female) partners. However, the majority of studies in this area emphasise the disproportionate number of women being abused by their male partners. We therefore focus on the latter.

29 Lesley Ciarula Taylor, 'Protest highlights plight of refugee claimants', *Toronto Star*, 3 October 2008.

30 *Citizenship and Immigration Canada*, 'Resettlement from outside Canada: Convention refugees abroad class', 31 March 2007, www.cic.gc.ca/english/refugees/outside/convention.asp (Accessed 5 September 2009).

31 Chris McGreal, 'Obama moves to grant political asylum to women who suffer domestic abuse', *Guardian*, 24 July 2009, http://www.guardian.co.uk/world/2009/jul/24/obama-women-abuse-political-asylum-us (accessed 14 February 2010).

32 'Canada ignoring refugees from Mexican violence: Advocates', *Canadian Press*, 28 March 2009.

33 Giuseppe Valiante, 'Mexican refugees seek haven in Canada', *National Post*, 25 June 2009.

34 Keung, 'Mexican refugee requests'.

35 Alexandra Zabjek, 'Local family wins refuge from Mexico's drug wars', *Edmonton Journal*, 3 March 2009.

36 Jessica Rafuse, 'Windsor braces for refugee tide', *Globe and Mail*, 22 September 2007.

37 Sarah Sacheli and Roberta Pennington, 'Mexicans pour into Canada from US: Agencies brace for thousands more at border', *Windsor Star*, 18 September 2007.

38 Chris Selley, 'Mexicans are flooding into Canada and claiming refugee status: Why is it happening, and what can we do to stop it?' *Macleans*, 4 October 2007.

39 James Bissett, 'Stop bogus refugees before they get in', *National Post*, 27 September 2007.

40 D. Schmidt, 'Refugees pose "potential crisis"', *Windsor Star*, 19 September 2007.

41 'Day promises "consequences" for illegal refugees', *CTV News*, 28 September 2007.

42 Despite the trend in the local and national newspapers to negatively describe these refugees (and their costs), there were a few articles that highlighted the potentially legitimate humanitarian claims of these refugee claimants. See Bonnie Drago, 'Treat Mexican refugees as you'd like to be treated', *Windsor Star*, 4 October 2007, p. A9. Nevertheless, articles using this tone were few and far between.

43 Adrian Humphreys, 'Illegal migrants lured to Canada', *National Post*, 20 September 2007.

44 'Mexicans invade Canada, Canadians invade the US', *Law is Cool Blog*, 22 September 2007.

45 Jiménez, '9,000 "ordinary people" flee Mexican drug war'.

46 Steven Edwards, 'Spike in Canada refugee claims shows "systemic abuse" Kenney charges', *Financial Post*, 24 March 2009.

47 Raphael Alexander, 'Jason Kenney is doing a great job', *National Post*, 30 July 2009, http://network.nationalpost.com/np/blogs/fullcomment/archive/2009/07/30/raphael-alexander-jason-kenney-is-doing-a-great-job.aspx (Accessed 4 September 2009).

48 Personal conversation with a researcher living in Mexico, 5 October 2009.

## References

Boyd, M. (1999), 'Gender, refugee status and permanent settlement', *Gender Issues* 17 (1): 5-25.

Boyd, M. (1989), *Migrant women in Canada: Profiles and policies*. Report prepared for Monitoring Panel on Migrant Women, Organization for Economic Co-operation and Development, Directorate for Social Affairs, Manpower and Education (1987). Ottawa: Employment and Immigration Canada, Public Affairs Inquiries and Distribution.

Boyd, M. & D. Pikkov (2008), 'Finding a place in stratified structures: Migrant women in North America', in N. Piper (ed.), *New perspectives on gender and migration: Livelihoods, rights, and entitlements*, pp. 19-58. London: Routledge.

Brown, C., J.A. Pagan & E. Rodriguez-Oreggia (1999), 'Occupational attainment and gender earnings differentials in Mexico', *Industrial & Labor Relations Review* 53 (1): 123-135.

Citizenship and Immigration Canada (2009a), 'Facts and figures 2008, Immigration overview: Permanent and temporary residents. Canada – permanent residents by gender and category, 1984 to 2008', 25 August 2009, www.cic.gc.ca/english/resources/statistics/facts2008/permanent/01.asp (Accessed 10 September 2009).

Citizenship and Immigration Canada (2009b), 'News release – Canada imposes a visa on Mexico', 13 July, www.cic.gc.ca/english/department/media/releases/2009/2009-07-13.asp.

Citizenship and Immigration Canada (2008), 'Facts and figures 2007, Immigration overview: Permanent and temporary residents', 12 November.

Citizenship and Immigration Canada (2007), 'Resettlement from outside Canada: convention refugees abroad class', 31 March.

Connors, J. (1997), 'Legal aspects of women as a particular social group', *International Journal of Refugee Law* 9: 159-164.

Cornelius, W. & M. Rosenblum (2005), 'Immigration and politics', *Annual Review of Political Science* 8: 99-119.

Dijk, T.A. van (1988), 'Semantics of a press panic: The Tamil "invasion"', *European Journal of Communication* 3: 167-188.

Foote, V. (1996), 'Refugee women and Canadian policy: Gaining ground?', *Canadian Woman Studies* 16 (3): 65-68.

Frias Martinez, S. (2009), Gender, the state and patriarchy: Partner violence in Mexico. PhD dissertation, University of Texas, Austin.

Inlender, T. (2009), 'Status quo or sixth ground? Adjudicating gender asylum claims', in S. Benhabib & J. Resnik (eds), *Migration and mobilities: Citizenship, borders and gender*, pp. 356-380. New York: New York University Press.

Keely, C. & S. Stanton (1994), 'Responses of industrial countries to asylum-seekers', *Journal of International Affairs* 47 (2): 399-417.

Markard, N. (2007), 'Gendered violence in "new wars"', in T. Spijkerboer & S. van Walsum (eds), *Women and immigration law: New variations on classical feminist themes*, pp. 67-85. New York: Routledge-Cavendish.

Mascini, P. & M. van Bochove (2009), 'Gender stereotyping in the Dutch asylum procedure: "Independent" men versus "dependent" women', *International Migration Review* 43 (1): 112-133.

Mawani, N. (1993), 'The factual and legal legitimacy of addressing gender issues', *Refuge* 13 (4): 7-10.

McGrath, R. (2009), 'A discourse analysis of Australian local government recreation and sport plans provision for people with disabilities', *Public Management Review* 11 (4): 477-497.

Mitchell, C. (1989), 'International migration, international relations and foreign policy', *International Migration Review* 23 (3): 681-708.

Olausson, U. (2009), 'Global warming – global responsibility? Media frames of collective action and scientific certainty', *Public Understanding of Science* 18: 421-436.

Pan, Z. & G.M. Kosicki (1993), 'Framing analysis: An approach to news discourse', *Political Communication* 10: 55-75.

Sales, R. (2002), 'The deserving and the undeserving? Refugees, asylum seekers and welfare in Britain', *Critical Social Policy* 22 (3): 456-478.

Seijio, F. (2009), 'Who framed the forest fire? State framing and peasant counter-framing of anthropogenic forest fires in Spain since 1940', *Journal of Environmental Policy & Planning* 11 (2): 103-128.

Snow, D., B. Rochford Jr., S. Worden & R. Benford (1986), 'Frame alignment processes, micromobilization, and movement participation', *American Sociological Review* 51 (4): 464-481.

Spijkerboer, T. (2000), *Gender and refugee status.* Aldershot: Ashgate.

Teran, L. (1999), 'Barriers to protection at home and abroad: Mexican victims of domestic violence and the violence against women act', *Boston University International Law Journal* 1: 1-78.

UNHCR (1995), 'Sexual violence against refugees: Guidelines on prevention and response', Geneva: Office of the United Nations High Commissioner for Refugees.

UNHCR, Executive Committee of the High Commissioner's Programme (1997), 'Progress report on refugee women and UNHCR's framework for implementation of the Beijing platform for action', Standing Committee 9th Meeting', 15 August, EC/47/SC/CRP.47.

UNHCR (1997), 'Gender-related persecution: An analysis of recent trends', *International Journal of Refugees* 9: 79-113.

Zolberg, A.R. (1999), 'Matters of state: Theorizing immigration policy', in C. Hirschman, P. Kasinitz & J. DeWind (eds), *The handbook of international migration: The American experience*, pp. 71-93. New York: Russell Sage.

Zucker, N.L. & N. Flink Zucker (1987), *The guarded gate: The reality of American refugee policy.* San Diego: Harcourt Brace Jovanovich.

# 5  Queer asylum

US policies and responses to sexual orientation
and transgendered persecution

*Connie Oxford*

## Introduction

This chapter examines US asylum laws (both legislative and case law) and policies regarding sexual orientation and transgendered persecution. It addresses the gendered nature of US asylum laws and policies towards lesbian, gay, bisexual and transgendered (LGBT) migrants, paying particular attention to the claims of gay men and transgendered women. Queer asylum seekers face particular obstacles in immigrant advocacy communities, and the current laws and policies have implications for what constitutes queer identity. Sexual and family violence has emerged as the dominant narrative in asylum declarations by gay men and transgendered women. The chapter argues that queer asylum is gendered in that laws and policies seemingly facilitate gay men and transgendered women's claims.

Scholars have only recently begun to explore the ways in which sexuality organises migration (Alexander 1994; Espín 1997; Luibhéid 2002, 2005; Rand 2005; Manalansan 2006). While migration studies have a long and rich history, their focus on the nation-state as the primary category of analysis has often ignored the gendered and sexualised bodies of those who cross borders. Sexuality studies, a comparatively newer field of inquiry, took up the task of applying its ideas about sex and gender to migration only during the last two decades.[1] This turn in migration scholarship may be explained, in part, by two significant changes: the growth of sexuality studies as a lens for understanding social phenomena and the emergence of queer subjects as legitimate mobile bodies recognised by the state. 'Legitimate mobile bodies' refers to the emergence of laws and policies that facilitate movement across national borders for a range of gendered and sexualised people.

This chapter's contribution to the emerging literature on sexuality and migration studies lies in its examination of US asylum laws and policies regarding sexual orientation and transgendered persecution.

Following the work of Martin F. Manalansan IV, it situates queer in a larger intersectional framework, one of gender and nation in particular, but it uses the term as an 'anti-normative signifier' as well (Manalansan 2006: 225). Therefore, queer refers to a range of gendered and sexual identities, such as lesbian, gay, bisexual and transgendered, that do not fit neatly into the heteronormative schema of masculinity, femininity and heterosexuality.[2]

The discussion relies on the notion of gender as a social relationship between femininity and masculinity. It entails an analysis of the ways in which gender and sexuality are constitutive of one another, rather than solely comparing the claims of 'women' and 'men', such as migration studies that reproduce heteronormative ideas about mobile bodies (see Manalansan 2006 for a critique of this literature). Although a range of gendered and sexualised bodies are discussed, the focus in particular is on asylum claims by gay men and transgendered women. I argue that these claims emerge as hegemonic narratives of queer persecution, particularly amongst legal precedent cases in the USA. This accounts for the apparent gender unevenness of the examples showcased through-out the chapter.

This chapter argues three points regarding queer asylum seekers. The first two illuminate the tension of being 'out', or open about one's sexual or gender identity. First, LGBT immigrants face obstacles specific to their status as sexual minorities because of homophobia and transphobia in their own immigrant communities. Second, the process of seeking asylum for queer immigrants requires that the applicant be open about her or his sexual or gender identity, in order to convince an immigration official that one has been persecuted or fears persecution based on that identity. Third, the dominant narrative of queer persecution for gay men and transgendered women is one of sexual and family violence, making the content of these claims similar to those of gender-based asylum claims espoused by women. Moreover, queer asylum is gendered in that the passage of laws and policies hailed as victories by immigrants and their advocates seems to facilitate gay men and transgendered women's asylum claims, rather than those of all LGBT migrants. This chapter highlights the ways in which men too are gendered (Donaldson et al. 2009). As discussed by Walaardt, in this volume, with regard to male war resisters, expectations about masculinity are embedded in immigration policies and immigrant practices.

This chapter first outlines the key pieces of legislation and judicial cases that have shaped queer immigration in the USA. It then discusses the implementation of queer asylum, drawing on ethnographic research with asylum seekers and their advocates.

## Queer immigration law in the USA

Until the end of the 20th century, US immigration laws and policies adversely affected sexual minorities. US lawmakers crafted immigration laws using language that pathologised homosexuals as mentally ill in an effort to restrict queer migrants. The term 'homosexuality' never explicitly entered the US immigration lexicon. Rather, prohibition of immigrants based on sexual orientation was disguised in language that denied entrance to queer migrants due to their lack of conformity to normative displays of gender and sexuality. The practice of formally excluding queer migrants can be traced to the 1917 Immigration Act, which made immigrants whom the state deemed 'constitutional psychopathic inferiors' as well as those with 'abnormal sexual instincts' excludable from entering or remaining in the country (Luibhéid 2002; Somerville 2005).

In 1952, the McCarran-Walter Act changed the language of exclusion only slightly to target those with 'psychopathic personalities' as a vetting technique for immigration officials. In 1950, two years prior to the passage of the McCarran-Walter Act, a Senate Committee of the Judiciary report suggested that 'classes of mental defects [who are excludable] should be enlarged to include homosexuals and other sex perverts', making explicit the intentions of who would be excluded (Luibhéid 2005: 77-78). The Immigration and Nationality Act of 1965 included the most comprehensive changes in US immigration law at the time of its passage. Yet it maintained the spirit of excluding queer migrants as the language of the Act described them as 'sexual deviants' (ibid.: 75-91).

One consequence of these laws was to give immigration officials the authority to deny entry into the USA and prevent naturalisation to US citizenry of any immigrant whom the state deemed sexually abnormal or deviant.[3] Two examples illuminate key differences in how these laws were applied to show the effects of class and race as well as gender and sexuality on whether immigrants were admitted into the USA.

In her study of the Ellis Island port of entry, Rand (2005) discusses Frank Woodhull, a Canadian citizen who, although biologically female and named Mary Johnson at birth, routinely dressed in men's clothing, went by the name Frank, and passed as a man. Upon arrival at Ellis Island on 4 October 1908, Woodhull admitted that he was a woman dressed as a man only when forced to disrobe for inspection.[4] Woodhull explained that he did so in order to do men's work that gave him a life of 'independence and freedom' (ibid.: 79). Although Woodhull was subjected to a medical examination and brief detention at Ellis Island, he was released and allowed to remain in the USA.

Luibhéid (2005) documents how the Immigration and Naturalization Service (INS), the agency charged with controlling immigrant populations, used surveillance techniques governed by heteronormative
assumptions about gender and sexuality to exclude immigrants from
entering the USA.[5] Luibhéid details the story of Sara Harb Quiroz, a
Mexican national who was detained at the El Paso, Texas, port of entry
on 6 January 1960. According to transcripts from the INS inspector,
Quiroz was stopped because she was wearing trousers and a shirt and
'her hair was cut shorter than most women's' (ibid.: xiii). While there
is no evidence that Quiroz was indeed a lesbian, she was repatriated to
Mexico.

As these examples demonstrate, immigration officials did not uniformly equate gender non-conformity with homosexuality during
exclusionary time periods. Moreover, they indicate that race and class
may have subjugated gender and sexual location for Woodhull and
Quiroz in ultimately determining admittance into the USA. Woodhull
lived as a man – a white Canadian man who possessed the economic
means to support himself. This made him less suspect as a potential
public charge by immigration officials than Quiroz, who may have been
repatriated not only for being suspected as a lesbian, but also because
she was a woman of colour.

## Two precedent-setting cases that changed immigration law

It was not until the passage of the Immigration Act of 1990 that Congress lifted the 'sexual deviants' admission criterion, formally opening
the gates of the USA to queer immigrants. After nearly a century of explicit language that prohibited the entrance of homosexual immigrants,
just three years later, in 1993, Marcelo Tenorio, a gay man from Brazil,
became the first person in the USA to be granted asylum based on sexual orientation by an immigration judge. One year later, Ariel da Silva, a
gay man from Mexico, was granted asylum by the INS (Randazzo 2005).
While these cases mark a significant milestone in US immigration history, they affected only Tenorio and Da Silva and were not precedent
cases. Precedent cases are distinct because they are models whose principles may be applied to other cases for applicants with similar circumstances. In the USA, judicial cases set a precedent only when they were
published, and neither Tenorio nor Da Silva's cases were published.[6]

Two precedent cases did affect the gendered and sexualised landscape of queer asylum. The first queer asylum case that was published,
and therefore set a precedent for future LGBT asylum seekers, was Matter of Toboso-Alfonso v. INS.[7] Fidel Armando Toboso-Alfonso was a

Cuban national who gained entry into the USA in June 1980 as part of the Mariel boatlift.[8] During his immigration hearing, Toboso-Alfonso testified that he was part of a registry of known homosexuals maintained by the Cuban authorities and was required to appear before them every few months. During these visits, he was subjected to physical exams and questioned about his sexual activities and was often detained for days for no apparent reason other than to be harassed for being gay. The immigration judge granted Toboso-Alfonso a withholding of deportation based on his membership in the social group of homosexuals, but he was denied asylum because of his criminal record in the USA (he had been convicted of possession of cocaine). Granting a withholding allows an immigrant to remain in the country without being deported. Unlike a grant of asylum, which allows immigrants the opportunity to apply for legal permanent residence one year after their approval and eventually for citizenship, a withholding offers no status advancement. Nor does a withholding allow immigrants the option of petitioning for relatives.

The INS appealed the decision, in part, because of Toboso-Alfonso's criminal record, but also because it did not believe that his experiences amounted to persecution, and they did not accept homosexuals as a social group as defined by the US Refugee Act of 1980. This Act is based on the 1951 United Nations Refugee Convention, which outlines five grounds of persecution: race, religion, nationality, political opinion and membership in a social group. The INS argued that 'socially deviated behaviour' does not constitute a social group.[9] In 1990, the immigration judge's findings were upheld by the Board of Immigration Appeals (BIA), the appellate board for all immigration courts in the USA. In 1994, Attorney General Janet Reno ordered the BIA to publish Matter of Toboso-Alfonso v. INS.

Once the Toboso-Alfonso case was published it set a precedent, paving the way for other immigrants to gain asylum if they too were persecuted for being homosexual. Although Toboso-Alfonso was granted the immigration status of withholding rather than asylum, his case codified homosexuals as a social group for the purposes of immigrants seeking asylum in the USA. This signalled a turn in US immigration history, as it for the first time rejected the exclusion queer migrants and recognised and made possible a way for them to enter and remain lawfully in the USA.

A second significant case for queer migrants is Hernandez-Montiel v. INS. This Ninth Circuit Court of Appeals case was published in 2000.[10] Hernandez-Montiel v. INS paved the way for transgendered women to gain asylum. I refer to Hernandez-Montiel as 'her' and 'she' even though she was born male, but I retain the masculine pronoun 'he' when quoting others. Geovanni Hernandez-Montiel, a Mexican national, was aware of her attraction to boys at an early age and dressed in girls and women's clothing before she reached adolescence. Hernandez-Montiel had a fraught home and school life because of her perceived sexual orientation, and she was threatened by a classmate's father for 'perverting his son'. She was eventually asked to leave home after her expulsion from school due to her sexual orientation. After being raped by police officers and hospitalised for injuries from an attack by a group of men, Hernandez-Montiel's sister arranged for her to enter into a counselling programme to 'cure' her of her sexual orientation by cutting her hair and fingernails and discontinuing her hormone regimen (Cox 2001).

During her immigration hearing, an expert witness testified that in Mexico 'gay men with female sexual identities' are at greater risk of persecution than gay men who are 'male acting homosexuals' (Cox 2001: 191). The judge denied Hernandez-Montiel's claim, arguing that her identity was not 'immutable because he was able to change his appearance from male to female and vice-versa' (ibid.: 191). The Ninth Circuit Court of Appeals overturned the judge's rejection, asserting that gay men with female sexual identities constitute a social group.[11] Soon after, *The New York Times* published a story with a headline that reinforced the idea that Hernandez-Montiel's claim was about behaviour that one could control, rather than identity: 'Court Rules Cross-Dresser Can Stay in the US on Asylum Claim'.[12] While as a precedent case, the ruling would had vast implications for transgendered women fleeing persecution, the gendered language in the case made it particularly relevant for protecting transgendered claimants who were born male and wish to dress and act like women and not those born female who express their gendered identities in masculine ways. Although the term 'transgender' was not used by Hernandez-Montiel, by the immigration judge or by the appellate judges of the Ninth Circuit, immigrant advocates later capitalised on the language of 'gay men with female sexual identities' as a basis for transgendered migrants to make claims.

The significance of these cases is that they recognise both homosexuals and transgendered women (albeit masked in the language of 'gay men with female sexual identities') as a social group. This is one of the five grounds on which immigrants may rely upon as the reason for their persecution or fear of persecution in order to gain asylum. While the USA was obligated to admit asylum seekers who feared persecution because of their membership in a particular social group since the passage of the 1980 Refugee Act, acceptance of homosexuals and transgendered people as a social group for the purpose of asylum was only recognised in 1994 and 2000, respectively, with the publication of Matter of Toboso-Alfonso and Hernandez-Montiel v. INS.

Other nation-states that are signatories to the 1951 United Nations Convention Relating to the Status of Refugees too must admit asylum seekers who have been persecuted or fear persecution based on their membership in a social group. Yet only a handful of countries that are signatories to the Refugee Convention have admitted asylum seekers based on sexual orientation. As of October 2008, only 19 countries had granted asylum to homosexual immigrants (Austria, Australia, Belgium, Canada, Denmark, Finland, France, Germany, Greece, Ireland, Italy, Latvia, the Netherlands, New Zealand, Norway, Sweden, Thailand, the UK and the USA).[13] The fact that so few countries have accepted queer asylum seekers is in part because nation-states that have signed the Refugee Convention decide who may gain asylum and under what circumstances. Moreover, as sexual minorities gain rights in their own countries, seeking asylum may become more difficult.[14]

Together, Matter of Toboso-Alfonso and Hernandez-Montiel v. INS dramatically altered the sexual and gendered terrain of immigration law in the USA. Soon after these cases were published a number of other precedent cases emerged from the US Circuit Court of Appeals that have allowed asylum based on sexual orientation and transgendered identity. Immigration Equality, the largest non-governmental organisation (NGO) working to end discrimination against LGBT and HIV (human immunodeficiency virus) positive immigrants in the USA, maintains a list of current cases on its website.[15] Of the 30 precedent asylum cases that are currently listed, only one involves a lesbian. The remaining 29 were brought forward by gay men, transgendered women or asylum seekers who are HIV positive. The only precedent asylum case involving a lesbian is Pitcherskaia v. INS.[16] No precedent cases to date have been brought forward by transgendered men or bisexual men or women. There is a dearth of information about bisexual asylum claims in general, in part, because there are so few of them (Rehaag 2009).

Because precedent cases stem from asylum claims that were initially denied by immigration judges or asylum officers it is difficult to know whether there are so few precedent cases involving lesbians, bisexuals and transgendered men because their claims are more likely to be granted by immigration officials, if there are fewer lesbians, bisexuals and transgendered men seeking asylum than gay men and transgendered women, or possibly both. Yet this systematic absence of claims by certain gendered asylum seekers may have the unintended effect of exacerbating an androcentric asylum process, albeit in the name of progress for those transcending traditional sexual and gender boundaries.

MARRIAGE AND HIV STATUS:
NEW FORMS OF EXCLUSION FOR QUEER IMMIGRANTS

Although asylum emerged as a means to enter and remain legally in the USA, asylum laws alone hardly abolished discrimination against queer migrants. Marriage and HIV status became two new means of excluding sexual minorities. In 1996, the Defence of Marriage Act defined marriage as a union between a man and a woman. Its application in immigration law is aimed at same-sex partners rather than homosexual individuals by discriminating against bi-national couples. Same-sex couples with mixed citizenship statuses are greatly disadvantaged. Unlike heterosexual partners who have the option of adjusting their spouse's immigration status, same-sex couples cannot petition for their non-citizen partner because the federal government does not recognise same-sex marriages.

While US law was path-breaking for queer immigrants regarding asylum, it has hardly been so regarding other forms of immigration, especially family reunification. According to a report issued by Human Rights Watch and Immigration Equality (2006), 'Family Unvalued: Discrimination, Denial, and the Fate of Binational Same-Sex Couples under U.S. Law', 19 countries allow various forms of queer immigration that include but are not limited to asylum (Australia, Belgium, Brazil, Canada, Denmark, Finland, France, Germany, Iceland, Israel, the Netherlands, New Zealand, Norway, Portugal, South Africa, Spain, Sweden, Switzerland and the UK).[17] Of these countries, Belgium, Canada, the Netherlands, Norway, South Africa, Spain and Sweden, have also legalised same-sex marriage. Conversely, sexual minorities who are in a relationship with a US citizen and seek to immigrate to the USA are disadvantaged because of how US immigration law defines a family. Since 1965, family reunification has been the bedrock of immigration law. Yet family is limited to immediate relatives (spouses, children, parents and siblings) and is defined by heteronormative notions of marriage. This affects same-sex partners, as well as immediate family members, such as children, who otherwise would be allowed to immigrate to the USA. 'Family Unvalued' details how these legal constraints lead to family separation for these couples. One means of rectifying this problem is the Uniting American Families Act, introduced in February 2009. If the US Congress passes this Act, US citizens in same-sex bi-national couples will be eligible to sponsor their partners and children of their partners so that they may immigrate legally to the USA.[18]

Strictures on family unification take many forms across the globe. As Catherine Raissiguier argues in her chapter in this volume, France has implemented physical proof of 'blood' relatives in its immigration policies.

Although the US federal government does not recognise same-sex marriage, five US states had legalised same-sex marriage as of January 2010: Connecticut, Iowa, Massachusetts, New Hampshire and Vermont. Same-sex couples who reside in these states may take advantage of state and local resources that are available to married couples, but they cannot receive federal resources or benefits, even if they live in a state that recognises same-sex marriage.

No data are available on LGBT immigrants in the USA because no immigration office collects it.[19] However, according to the 2000 census, there were 35,820 bi-national couples in the country. Of these, 58% are lesbian couples and 42% are homosexual men. Nearly half (46%) are raising children.[20] These are national data and are not available by state. Therefore, while queer bi-national couples may be more likely to settle in states that recognise same-sex marriage, it is impossible to substantiate this claim with the available data.

In addition to exclusionary practices regarding marriage, queer immigrants have been prohibited from entering and remaining in the USA if they are HIV positive. Beginning in 1987, immigrants testing positive for the HIV virus were excludable on the grounds of contributing to a public health crisis. While this law includes anyone who is HIV positive, regardless of their gender and sexual identity, it particularly affects homosexual men, as they are amongst the populations most affected by the virus. For asylum seekers, the significance of their HIV status is that they must prove that being HIV positive has resulted in persecution. Unfortunately, lack of access to health care is not a basis for an asylum claim.[21] HIV positive immigrants in other nations too have faced discrimination and even deportation, most notably in the UK (Hitchings 2004). Unlike the struggle for equality for same-sex bi-national couples, which continues today, the ban on HIV positive immigrants was effectively overturned on 2 November 2009.[22]

## Queer identity and persecution

This section draws on interviews, asylum applications and asylum preparation manuals to show the ways in which queer asylum is organised in the USA. The focus is on three themes. The first two, homophobia and transphobia in immigrant advocacy networks and queer identity as a social group, scrutinise how being 'out' can impede or facilitate queer migrants' ability to gain asylum. The third theme, queer persecution,

underscores the pervasiveness of sexual and family violence against gay
men and transgendered women.

Although it is certainly arguable that immigrants come to the USA
from all regions of the world, they hardly come in equal numbers by
nationality or region. The USA's proximity to Mexico, Central and
South America and the Caribbean explains, in part, why there may be
higher concentrations of queer asylum seekers from these geographic
areas. For example, 15 of the 30 precedent cases listed on Immigration Equality's website relate to immigrants from Mexico, Costa Rica,
El Salvador, Guatemala, Peru, Cuba and Haiti. The demographics of
immigrant communities also vary by location within a country. In Los
Angeles, California, where much of the research presented here was
done, there is a higher concentration of immigrants from Mexico and
Central America. The examples cited are asylum claims by gay men and
transgendered women from Mexico, Honduras and Guatemala. Since
the Department of Homeland Security does not maintain data on LGBT
asylum claims (neither did its predecessor, the INS), it is impossible to
know exactly how many LGBT immigrants seek asylum or how many
claims were granted or denied.

## MATERIALS AND METHODS

The research presented here is based on interviews with asylum seekers, immigration attorneys and human rights organisation employees,
in addition to asylum applications. The research was done in Los Angeles, San Francisco and New York City in 2001-2003 and 2009. All
interviewee names are pseudonyms.

In Los Angeles from 2001 to 2003, I interviewed immigration attorneys at the Central American Resource Center (CARECEN), an immigrants' rights organisation established in 1983 through grassroots activism by Salvadoran refugees, and the Gay and Lesbian Center, which
since 1996 has offered a range of services to the LGBT community,
including legal assistance and referrals for immigrants. The four asylum
applications discussed in this chapter were procured from CARECEN.

In 2002, I met with a programme director at the International Gay
and Lesbian Human Rights Commission (ICLHRC) in San Francisco.
This human rights organisation was set up in 1990 and was the first to
systematically document human rights violations against sexual minorities and people living with HIV and AIDS worldwide. ICLHRC's asylum
documentation programme issued country reports of violations and
made them available for inclusion in asylum applications from 1993 to
1997. In 2009, I interviewed an attorney at Immigration Equality (for-

merly known as the Lesbian and Gay Immigration Rights Task Force) in New York City. Founded in 1996, this is the largest NGO working to end discrimination against LGBT and HIV positive immigrants in the USA.

### HOMOPHOBIA AND TRANSPHOBIA IN IMMIGRANT ADVOCACY NETWORKS

It is not uncommon for migrants to leave one country for another because they have been persecuted or fear that they will be persecuted, and yet to be unaware that they are eligible for asylum when they arrive in the destination country.[23] Seeking asylum is a daunting task for anyone. For queer migrants, becoming aware that they are eligible for asylum and learning how to apply is particularly difficult because they often face homophobia and transphobia from immigrant advocates. Many immigrants learn about the possibility to apply for asylum in their own national, racial and religious communities. If members of these communities do not circulate stories of queer persecution as reason for asylum, queer migrants might never learn that they are eligible for asylum through traditional support networks. During an interview, Rafael, an employee of ICLHRC, said that 'queer immigrants often have difficulty getting support for being gay in their own immigrant communities.'[24]

Unfortunately, the homophobia and transphobia that is pervasive in some immigrant communities also extends to advocates, such as attorneys and service providers. Immigrant advocates may be sympathetic to stories of persecution based on one's ethnicity or religion, but not be open to hearing about harm based on gender and sexual identity. Attorneys and service providers often approach asylum from a heteronormative position such that they never explore persecution for being queer (or just being queer) as a conduit for gaining asylum. Heteronormative understandings of identity maintain ignorance of LGBT people and their plight by those who are often otherwise proactive in helping immigrants gain asylum. Moreover, some immigrant service providers know that asylum based on sexual orientation or gender identity is available but refuse to work with clients who have these types of claims.

According to Gloria, a paralegal at CARECEN, a psychiatrist who evaluated many of their clients was 'uncomfortable' with transgendered cases, and her calendar was suddenly full when Gloria called seeking help with transgendered clients.[25] Marcos, an attorney who works with CARECEN, revealed during our interview that organisations that provide mental health assistance for sexual minorities are unfamiliar with asylum and cannot complete the assessment required for asylum applications.[26] According to Marcos, organisations that provide mental health services for asylum seekers are often homophobic and nearly always transphobic, making them incapable or unwilling to assess persecution based on sexual orientation or gender identity. Conversely, organisations that offer support services for queer clients are typically unfamiliar with the needs of queer immigrants, including asylum seekers. Establishment of the Immigration Law Project at the Los Angeles Gay and Lesbian Center created networking opportunities for queer asylum seekers.[27] However, many asylum seekers still suffer the repercussions of gaps in the services offered as they are shuffled amongst organisations.[28]

Homophobia spills over into the realm of human rights movements and organisations. Part of the difficulty in situating persecution against queers as a human rights abuse has been the struggle to convince mainstream human rights organisations that queers are a group deserving of protection. According to Rafael, ICLHRC was 'formed in 1990 to prove to Amnesty International that there were human rights violations against sexual minorities'. Many human rights organisations, such as Amnesty International and Human Rights Watch, now routinely issue reports on abuses against LGBT populations, but they have not always done so. ICLHRC's asylum documentation programme marshalled information on human rights abuses against LGBT individuals long before the mainstream human rights organisations did so.[29] According to Rafael, as recently as 2001, NGO networks in the USA tried to prevent ICLHRC from meeting with United Nations officials about HIV because 'we support homosexuals'.

As these examples show, LGBT immigrants face obstacles specific to their status as sexual minorities due to homophobia and transphobia in their own immigrant communities. Consequently, queer immigrants often never learn about asylum. Even if they do discover that they are eligible they may face additional barriers for gaining asylum, as immigrant advocates may be either oblivious to the notion that people are persecuted for being queer or refuse to work with LGBT clients.

## QUEER IDENTITY AS A SOCIAL GROUP

Homophobia and transphobia amongst immigrant advocates can discourage asylum seekers from being open about their sexual or gender identity. Such reluctance can ultimately discourage them from seeking asylum. Conversely, even if migrants are able to locate supportive advocates, being 'out' about one's sexual or gender identity is compulsory in order to gain asylum. Being out is mandatory because queer asylum seekers must convince an immigration official that they were persecuted or fear persecution based on their membership in the category of 'homosexual' or 'gay men with female sexual identities', language codified in the cases of Matter of Toboso-Alfonso and Hernandez-Montiel v. INS.

Applying for asylum entails completing an I-589 asylum application, a declaration that details why one is requesting asylum. Applicants must then marshal evidence, such as letters from doctors and mental health practitioners attesting to physical signs of bodily torture or conditions such as post-traumatic stress disorder (PTSD). Asylum seekers whose application is filed by an immigration attorney and who seek the support of other immigrant advocates must tell their story repeatedly until a legally convincing narrative of persecution is ready for review by an immigration official. In the USA, after one is granted an interview, asylum seekers must tell their story again to either an asylum officer or an immigration judge. A fundamental component of gaining asylum is expressing verbally why one fears returning to her or his country. All asylum seekers are subjected to this process.

For queer migrants, sexuality is at the forefront of their narrative of persecution. Most queer immigrant advocates stress that it is paramount for attorneys, service providers and most importantly immigration officials, to think of homosexuality and transgenderedness as part of one's identity, rather than as behaviour that one can change – as implied in *The New York Times* headline mentioned earlier. This is an important feature of gaining asylum because immigrants must prove that they are part of the homosexual and transgender social group. Yet this strategic move on the part of immigrant advocates may reproduce an essentialised notion of identity in order to prove that it is immutable (Hanna 2005).

For example, the Midwest Human Rights Partnership for Sexual Orientation and the Lesbian and Gay Immigration Rights Task Force issued a handbook for immigrants and their advocates (McClure, Nugent & Soloway 2000). The handbook distinguishes sexual identity based on one's geographic location:

> [W]hile it is not necessary that the applicant was 'out' or experienced persecution in the country of origin, it is essential that the applicant clearly describe his/her homosexual identity, and his/her particular well-founded fear of persecution because of this identity (McClure, Nugent & Soloway 2000: 12).

This statement captures the sentiment of immigrant advocates who recognise that immigrants may have same-sex partners but not necessarily identify as homosexual. According to Elisabeth, an attorney with Immigration Equality in New York City, 'for people in countries where there is not a gay rights movement, their sexuality is defined by who they have sex with; sexual orientation is incomprehensible'.[30] Elisabeth's understanding of sexual behaviour and identity reinforces the advocacy handbook's notion that asylum seekers do not necessarily arrive in the USA with a sense of their own identity. Yet it is precisely the embracing of one's sexual identity that is a necessary component to gain asylum.

One aspect of being out for asylum seekers is offering proof that they are queer. Elisabeth explained how immigrants do this: 'In many of our cases we can prove someone's sexual orientation if someone has a partner or someone is willing to provide an affidavit for them. It is a more difficult issue for people who are not openly gay or have not had a significant relationship.' Therefore, unlike other forms of identity that nearly all asylum seekers must prove, such as their nationality or religion, queer migrants' identity is only made visible when one has entered into a sexual relationship. However, gay men and transgendered women asylum seekers articulate their sexual and gendered identities in ways that underscore gender non-conformity and early childhood persecutory acts as those that formed their sexual identities.

In four of the asylum declarations of gay men and transgendered women discussed here, the claimants' earliest experiences with sexual identity were circumscribed by being 'outed' by relatives and classmates, not for being homosexual per se but instead for being effeminate.[31] The following vignettes are from the written asylum declarations of Carlos, Ernesto, Hector and Marlina (who was born male but was transitioning to female at the time she submitted her asylum application). While their declarations are nearly identical, each is quoted to emphasise the inextricable link between ideals of masculinity and heteronormative expectations for boys and men in Mexico and Central America:[32]

> Since I looked effeminate, many of the kids at school used to tease me and call me names like *hueco* [fag]. Three of my cousins used to harass me constantly about my effeminate mannerisms. My stepfather used to shout and yell crude names at me because I was effeminate. (Carlos, an immigrant from Guatemala)

> When I was about seven years old my brothers and my school companions began to reject me, calling me faggot and telling me that I had

to get into fist fights in order to prove that I was a man. I was thin and small and effeminate and was teased and beaten up by other school children. My brothers told me that I looked like a faggot and that I had to do things like play football and work in the field to act like a man. (Ernesto, a Mexican asylum seeker)

When I was a little boy I always wanted to dress in my mother's clothes and shoes. I always wanted to play with dolls. Even as a little boy, I was perceived as effeminate. I was always much more interested in playing with the other girls than with the boys. My brothers and family members often called me faggot and other derogatory names. (Hector, an asylum seeker from Mexico)

Although I was not attracted to girls, I liked playing and doing girl things. I would rather jump rope with the girls than play soccer with the boys. I would play with dolls and when we played house, I always wanted to be the mother. The boys would harass me and call me names such as *maricon* [sissy] and *culero* [faggot]. (Marlina, a transgendered woman from Honduras)

In these examples, sexual identity followed gender non-conformity. Moreover, sexual identity was created through the means of persecutory acts, such as taunting, beatings and sexual violence. The process of seeking asylum for queer immigrants requires that the applicant be open about her or his sexual and gender identity. When queer migrants do locate sympathetic advocates, they are required to identify as either 'homosexual' or as 'gay men with female identities' in order to qualify for asylum.

The similarity of these narratives may be explained by the fact that they were all represented by the same attorney at CARECEN. As Walaardt points out, in this volume, conformity across asylum seekers' narratives can be traced to specific actors, such as immigrant advocates, who elicit such stories in order to secure a grant of asylum (see also Oxford 2005, 2008).

### QUEER PERSECUTION

In the declarations of Carlos, Ernesto, Felix, and Marlina, sexual violence and family violence emerge as dominant narratives of persecution for gay men and transgendered women.[33] Carlos and Ernesto trace their experiences of persecution to sexual violence by neighbours and family members. Carlos said that at the age of twelve he inquired about how 'homosexuals have sexual relations' to his neighbour, a trusted friend. He described his neighbour's response:

> [He] grabbed a mop I was using to clean the floor and he asked me
> if I would like him to rape me with the wooden part of the mop. He
> threw me on the bed and pulled my pants down. Before he raped me,
> he told me that since I was a fag I deserved what he was going to do to
> me. While he was raping me, I cried and I begged him to stop. He told
> me to stop crying because he knew I was enjoying the rape because I
> was a *maricon*.

Carlos continued his declaration by relating several instances of being raped by his neighbour, as well as by a friend of the neighbour. Ernesto dated his first sexual assault to the age of ten when he was 'sexually abused' by his cousin:

> My cousin told me that we should pretend that we were cows, and
> walk on all fours. He told me I should pull down my pants. He said
> that he was going to play the part of the bull. I didn't think anything
> because I didn't know about sex. The next thing I knew he was pen-
> etrating me. I began to cry. I was bleeding. He threatened me and told
> me that if I told anyone he would tell them that I had asked him to
> do it.

Ernesto also described his being raped by other cousins through-out his childhood. According to their declarations, unlike Carlos and Ernesto, Felix and Marlina were not raped. Instead, they were beaten repeatedly by family members for being perceived as gay. Felix was beaten throughout his childhood by his mother and brothers. After commenting to his male teacher that he 'liked his eyes', at the age of eleven, Felix arrived home to discover that the teacher had told his mother what he had said:

> When I got home, my mother began to hit me with a belt and with a
> spoon. My nose began to bleed. My brother said that he did not want
> to have a homosexual for a brother. He hit me and kicked me. My
> mother watched and she did nothing to stop him.

Felix continued his declaration, describing when he was older a police beating of himself and his boyfriend, who died three days later in the hospital. Marlina first experienced family violence at the age of eleven:

> One day I was outside on the patio when my older brother said that he was tired of people saying that I have a fag for a brother. He punched me in the face and began to beat me. When my mother arrived, my brother told her that I was gay and my mother said that she did not want a queer for a son. She grabbed me by the hair and hit my head against the wall.

Marlina escaped from her family soon after and lived with a neighbour until she left for the USA 12 years later.

These four asylum seekers share a narrative that traces their experiences of persecution to childhood and identifies family members, classmates and neighbours as persecutors.[34] Unlike the claims of most male asylum seekers, gay men and transgendered women divulge being raped or beaten by family members for being perceived as gay or effeminate. As discussed by Boyd and Nowak in this volume, personal violence perpetrated by family members is a hallmark of refugee women's experiences, both creating women's migration flows and accounting for their experiences during flight.

These examples further underline the emphasis in asylum claims on producing a convincing narrative adorned with horrific details rather than the failure of the state to provide protection. The latter, however, according to the Refugee Convention, is the core of an asylum claim. This manoeuvre by immigrant advocates obscures the multiplicity of ways that the state fails in this regard. States may be the agent of persecution (as in the case of Toboso-Alfonso where he was required to register with the government) or states may be unwilling or unable to protect their citizens from the persecution of others, such as the familial violence endured by the asylum seekers discussed in this section.

## Conclusion

The introduction raised the idea that gender and sexuality are constitutive of one another rather than merely additive components of one's identity. Sexual orientation and transgender asylum complicate this notion further in two ways that contribute to migration studies.

First, narratives of persecution by gay men and transgendered women are similar to women's claims in that sexual and family violence is common across their stories of harm. The dominant narrative of queer persecution for gay men and transgendered women is one of sexual and family violence, making the content of these claims similar to those of gender-based asylum claims espoused by women. This is a valuable finding for future research on asylum, as familial and sexual violence is shown not to be relegated solely to women's experiences of persecution.

Second, the findings suggest that persecuted queers follow a similar androcentric path to that forged by heterosexual asylum seekers. This is not because the claims are made by men, but because they are made by those whose experiences of persecution are inextricably linked to gender non-conformity regarding ideals of masculinity. The examples highlighted in this chapter may lead one to think that only those born biologically male (even if some eschew this essentialised gendered identity and consider themselves transgendered women) constitute queer subjects deserving of asylum in the USA.

While lesbians, bisexual women and men, and transgendered men may gain asylum based on their membership in the social group of homosexuals, current precedent cases are dominated by stories of queer immigrants being persecuted vis-à-vis normative ideas of masculinity, simultaneously entailing non-conformist displays of femininity that are both gendered and sexualised. The absence of asylum claims by lesbians and transgendered men may contribute to the invisibility of narratives of persecution based on a lack of conformity to normative ideals of femininity that too would include non-conformist performances of masculinity that are also both gendered and sexualised. In this sense, queer asylum is perhaps following the same trajectory as other forms of migration with a new twist. Similar to 'women' following 'men' in both actual migration movements and studies of migration, in many ways, masculine subjects seem to be at the forefront of queer asylum. Yet they are very different masculine subjects from their heterosexual counterparts because their border crossers lay bare the ways in which masculinity *and* femininity can simultaneously organise migration, revealing how queer asylum is as gendered as it is sexualised.

### Notes

1   While studies of sexuality existed prior to Foucault's work, the 1984 English language publication of *The History of Sexuality* laid the groundwork for a plethora of scholarship on sexuality (Foucault 1984). Butler (1990) and Sedgwick (1990) too have greatly influenced studies of sexuality.

2   See Halberstam (2005) and Currah, Juang & Price (2006) for a discussion of the use of the term queer as it applies to transgendered people.

3   Exclusionary immigration laws were hardly specific to homosexuals during this time. Beginning in the late 19th century and continuing through today, US immigration law has been characterised by restrictive policies (Gerstle 2004).

4   In keeping with Rand's analysis, which denaturalises gender, I too refer to Wood-hull as 'he'.

5   In 1933, the Immigration and Naturalization Service (INS) was created. It was originally located under the Department of Labour, but moved to the Department of Justice in 1940. On 1 March 2003, the INS was divided into three agencies – the US Citizenship and Immigration Services (CIS), the US Immigration and Custom Enforcement (ICE), and the Bureau of Customs and Border Protection (CBP). It then moved from the Department of Justice to the newly created Department of Homeland Security. I refer to the federal office that oversees immigration as the INS until its dissolution in March 2003.

6   This applies to all published cases in the USA and is not specific to immigration law.

7   Matter of Toboso-Alfonso 20 I&N Dec. 819 (BIA 1994).

8   In 1980, approximately 125,000 Cuban nationals left Cuba for the USA via the Mariel boat harbour. This mass immigration is known as the Mariel boatlift.

9   Matter of Toboso-Alfonso.

10   Hernandez-Montiel v. INS, 225 F.3d 1088 (9th Cir. 2000).

11   See O'Dwyer (2008) for a discussion of the variation in US asylum cases by circuit regarding sexual orientation claims. For a more general discussion of asylum claims by all circuits see Ramji-Nogales, Schoenholtz & Schrag (2009).

12   D. Stout, 'Court Rules Cross-Dresser Can Stay in the US on Asylum Claim', *New York Times*, 26 August 2000, p. 14.

13   See Swetha Sridharan, 'The Difficulties of US Asylum Claims Based on Sexual Orientation', MigrationInformationSource www.migrationinformation.org/Feature/display. cfm?id=700 (accessed 31 January 2010). See also Millbank (2008) and Millbank (2009) for an in-depth analysis of how sexual orientation claims are adjudicated in Australia and the UK.

14   Ceci Connolly, 'As Latin Nations Treat Gays Better Asylum is Elusive', *Washington Post*, 12 August 2008 www.washingtonpost.com/wp-dyn/content/article/2008/AR2008081102038.html (accessed on 31 January 2010).

15   www.immigrationequality.org/manual_template.php?id=1066 (accessed on 18 October 2009).

16   A 9th Circuit Court of Appeals case that was published in 1997. Pitcherskaia v. INS, 118 F.3d 641 (9th Cir. 1997).

17   See appendix B of Human Rights Watch and Immigration Equality (2006).

18   See appendix A of Human Rights Watch and Immigration Equality (2006).

19   See appendix C of Human Rights Watch and Immigration Equality (2006).

20   See appendix C of Human Rights Watch and Immigration Equality (2006). These data are based on the 5% Public Use Microdata Sample (PUMS), a random sample of households.

21   See www.immigrationequality.org.

22   J. Preston, 'Obama Lifts a Ban on Entry into US by HIV-Positive People', *New York Times*, 30 October 2009 http://topics.nytimes.com/topics/reference/timestopics/people/p/julia_preston/index.html (accessed 31 October 2009).

23   Since the passage of the Illegal Immigration Reform and Responsibility Act of 1996 asylum seekers must file their applications within one year.

24 Rafael (San Francisco, California, 17 November 2002). Interview conducted by Connie Oxford. Interview tape on file with author.
25 Gloria (Los Angeles, California, 6 August 2002). Interview conducted by Connie Oxford. Interview tape on file with author.
26 Marcos (Los Angeles, California, 9 December 2002). Interview conducted by Connie Oxford. Interview tape on file with author.
27 John (Los Angeles, California, 26 September 2002). Interview conducted by Connie Oxford. Interview tape on file with author.
28 Elizabeth, an attorney with Immigration Equality, articulated that the Lesbian, Gay, Bisexual, and Transgender Community Center in New York City was familiar with the needs of queer migrants and that, although it did not offer immigration services, its staff referred immigrants to Immigration Equality. Elisabeth. (New York City, 9 July 2009). Interview conducted by Connie Oxford. Interview tape on file with author. See Heller (2009) for a discussion of how social workers can help queer asylum seekers.
29 International Gay and Lesbian Human Rights Commission. *Transgender Issues #1, 1989-1995* (San Francisco, 1995). International Gay and Lesbian Human Rights Commission. *Lesbian Packet* (San Francisco, 2001).
30 Elisabeth (New York City, 9 July 2009). Interview conducted by Connie Oxford. Interview tape on file with author.
31 These examples are two gay men from Mexico, one gay man from Guatemala, and one transgendered woman from Honduras.
32 Masculinity is hardly uniform across the globe. See Gutmann (1996) for a discussion of the multiplicity of meanings of masculinity in a culture that is known for hegemonic views of masculinity commonly referred to as *machismo*.
33 I limit my discussion to sexual violence as the basis of an asylum claim. Transgendered migrants face sexual violence in the USA as well. See Solomon (2005) on the case a transgendered woman raped by guards in an INS detention facility.
34 See Ramirez (2003) for further examples of how gay Latino men experience persecution.

## References

Alexander, M.J. (1994), 'Not just (any) body can be a citizen: The politics of law, sexuality, and postcoloniality in Trinidad and Tobago and the Bahamas', *Feminist Review* 48: 5-23.
Butler, J. (1990), *Gender trouble: Feminism and the subversion of identity*. New York and London: Routledge.
Cox, J. (2001), 'Redefining gender: Hernandez-Montiel v. INS', *Houston Journal of International Law* 24 (1): 188-207.
Currah, P., R.M. Juang & S.P. Minter (eds) (2006), *Transgender rights*. Minneapolis: University of Minnesota Press.
Donaldson, M. et al. (eds) (2009), *Migrant men: Critical studies of masculinities and the migration experience*. New York: Routledge.

Espín. O. (1997), *Latina realities: Essays on healing, migration, and sexuality*. Boulder: Westview Press.

Foucault, M. (1984), *The history of sexuality: An introduction*. Volume i. New York: Pantheon.

Gerstle, G. (2004), 'The immigrant as threat to American security: A historical perspective', in J. Tirman (ed.), *The maze of fear: Security and migration after 9/11*, pp. 87-108. New York: The New Press.

Gutmann, M. (1996), *The meanings of macho: Being a man in Mexico City*. Berkeley: University of California Press.

Halberstam, J. (2005), *In a queer time and place: Transgender bodies, subcultural lives*. New York: New York University Press.

Hanna, F. (2005), 'Punishing masculinity in gay asylum claims', *Yale Law Journal*, 114: 913-920.

Heller, P. (2009), 'Challenges facing LBGT asylum-seekers: The role of social work in correcting oppressive immigration processes', *Journal of Gay & Lesbian Social Services* 21: 294-308.

Hitchings, E. (2004), 'Insufficiently inhuman: Removing AIDS patients from the UK', *Journal of Social Welfare and Family Law* 26 (3): 281-288.

Human Rights Watch and Immigration Equality (2006), 'Family unvalued: Discrimination, denial, and the fate of binational same-sex couples under u.s. law'. New York: Human Rights Watch and Immigration Equality.

Luibhéid, E. (2005), *Queer migrations: Sexuality, us citizenship, and border crossings*. Minneapolis and London: University of Minnesota Press.

Luibhéid, E. (2002), *Entry denied: Controlling sexuality at the border*. Minneapolis and London: University of Minnesota Press.

Manalansan iv, M.F. (2006), 'Queer intersections: Sexuality and gender in migration studies', *International Migration Review* 40: 224-249.

McClure, H., C. Nugent & L. Soloway (2000), 'The midwest human rights partnership for sexual orientation and the lesbian and gay immigration rights task force', *Preparing sexual orientation-based asylum claims: A handbook for advocates and asylum seekers* (2nd Edition). Chicago: Heartland Alliance for Human Needs and Human Rights.

Millbank, J. (2009), 'From discretion to disbelief: Recent trends in refugee determinations on the basis of sexual orientation in Australia and the United Kingdom', *International Journal of Human Rights* 13 (2/3): 391-414.

Millbank, J. (2008), 'A preoccupation with perversion: The British response to refugee claims on the basis of sexual orientation, 1989-2003', *Feminist Legal Studies* 16 (2): 141-167.

O'Dwyer, P. (2008), 'A well-founded fear of having my sexual orientation asylum claim heard in the wrong court', *New York Law School Law Review* 52: 185-212.

Oxford, C. (2005), 'Protectors and victims in the gender regime of asylum', *National Women's Studies Association Journal* 17: 18-38.

Ramirez, L.A.P. (2003), 'Immigration and trauma: A study with Latino gay men asylum seekers'. PhD thesis, Wright Institute Graduate School of Psychology.

Ramji-Nogales, J., A.I. Schoenholtz & P.G. Schrag (2009), *Refugee roulette: Disparities in asylum adjudication and proposals for reform*. New York: New York University Press.

Rand, E.R. (2005), *The Ellis Island snow globe*. Durham: Duke University Press.

Randazzo, T.J. (2005), 'Social and legal barriers: Sexual orientation and asylum in the United States', in E. Luibhéid & L. Cantu Jr. (eds), *Queer migrations: Sexuality, US citizenship, and border crossings*, pp. 30-60. Minneapolis and London: University of Minnesota Press.

Rehaag, S. (2009), 'Bisexuals need not apply: A comparative appraisal of refugee law and policy in Canada, the United States, and Australia', *The International Journal of Human Rights* 13 (2-3): 415-436.

Sedgwick, E.F. (1990), *Epistemology of the closet*. Berkeley and Los Angeles: University of California Press.

Somerville, S.B. (2005), 'Sexual aliens and the racialized state: A queer reading of the 1952 US immigration and nationality act', in E. Luibhéid & L. Cantu Jr. (eds), *Queer migrations: Sexuality, US citizenship, and border crossings*, pp. 75-91. Minneapolis and London: University of Minnesota Press.

Solomon, A. (2005), 'Trans/migrant: Christina Madrazo's all-American story', in E. Luibhéid & L. Cantu Jr. (eds), *Queer migrations: Sexuality, US citizenship, and border crossings*, pp. 3-29. Minneapolis and London: University of Minnesota Press.

# 6 Belonging and membership

## Postcolonial legacies of colonial family law in Dutch immigration policies

*Sarah van Walsum, Guno Jones and Susan Legêne*

## Introduction

In recent years, the Netherlands drew international attention by being the first country to require that family unification migrants pass a language and integration test in their countries of origin before being admitted into the Netherlands.[1] Member of Parliament Rita Verdonk (VVD), who in 2006-2007 would become the Dutch Minister for Immigration and Integration Affairs, in 2005 defended these policies in parliament by linking threats to the stability of Dutch society with assumed differences between Dutch norms regarding family relations and sexuality and those of 'non-Western' migrants:

> [F]ailed integration can lead to marginalisation and segregation as a result of which people can turn their back on society and fall back on antiquated norms and values, making them susceptible to the influence of a small group inclined to extremism and terrorism … Ongoing radicalisation implies a real risk that non-integrated migrants will take an anti-Western stance and will assail fundamental values and norms generally accepted in Western society such as equality of men and women, non-discrimination of homosexuals and freedom of expression.[2]

In the context of a debate concerning family migration from 'non-Western' nations, Verdonk's message was clear. Unless family migrants could be screened for 'proper' norms, values and skills before being granted entry, they posed a threat to the Dutch nation. Migrants' norms and values are represented as archaic and backwards, whereas the Netherlands, as a 'Western society', is deemed a place where emancipation is complete. Opponents dubbed this aspect of Dutch family migration policies as racist, because the Dutch language and integration test requirement applied only to people originating from the less industrially developed nations of Africa, Asia and South America. Human Rights Watch, in a 2008 report, qualified the Dutch policies as 'discrimination in the name of integration' (Human Rights Watch 2008; cf. Terlouw 2005; Groenendijk 2011; De Vries 2011, 2012). In more general terms, Dutch family migration policies have been compared to the racist policies that distinguished the rulers from the ruled in the former colony of the Dutch East Indies (De Hart 2003). Other authors have argued that the racial divides of the colonial past are part of the genealogy of current European modes of exclusion (Stoler 1995, 2011; Balibar 2004; Legêne 2011).

This chapter investigates the legacy of colonial discourses and practices in current discussions of belonging and practices of exclusion in the Netherlands, with a special focus on their gendered dimensions. Nonetheless, depicting the present as an automatic sequel to a past racist order in overseas colonial states and society is too simple a rhetoric for two reasons. First, jumping from the colonial era to the present day ignores post-Second World War society in the Netherlands. Yet this was an era of significant developments in which colonialism and racism were contested and sexual morality thoroughly changed. An important achievement of that period is the constitutional principle of equal treatment, which states that everyone in the Netherlands should be free from discrimination, regardless of race, creed or ethnic background. In 1983, this article replaced the original first clause, which since 1815 had served to define the territory of the Netherlands. The new non-discrimination clause thus changed the legal focus from indicating *where* the constitution was effective (it had not been effective for the colonial subjects in the overseas colonies) to *to whom* it applied: to anyone living in the Netherlands. The clause thus reflects changing views in Dutch society and in the international legal order (Legêne 2011: 245-247). We are well aware that formal equality is a necessary, but not a sufficient, condition for equal treatment in a broader sense. For successive post-war Dutch governments, it was not always easy to live up to the enacted ideal of equality regardless of 'race' or 'ethnicity'. This is demonstrated, for instance, by political discourses and restrictive policies concerning the right of free migration of overseas Dutch citizens from the former Dutch East Indies (in the 1950s) and West Indies (from the 1970s onwards) (Schuster 1999; Jones 2007). In that sense, colonialism certainly left its 'postcolonial' marks. However, depicting the present as an automatic sequel to the colonial past risks undermining the attention and activism needed for this constitutional principle of non-discrimination to survive as a vital element of Dutch politics, law and society.[3] It further ignores the impact of the sexual revolution, which ousted marriage as the sole legitimate site of sexuality while rejecting, or at least challenging, the hierarchies between genders and generations that were laid down by *Dutch* family law of the pre-war period. If we wish to gain insight into current Dutch exclusionary immigration discourse and practices by tracing its genealogy back to the colonial past, we have to take these post-Second World War normative shifts into account.

In addition to focusing on recent changes within Dutch politics, law and society, we must more closely analyse the legacies of colonial racism and their gendered dimensions as such. What do we know about 'Dutch' overseas colonial citizenship regimes, both within the Dutch East Indies and in Suriname? How do we assess the plural legal systems in which these were based? And, what legacies can we find in contemporary immigration law? The overall picture seems clear. Stoler has argued that the racist regime of the former Dutch East Indies was grounded in assumptions concerning biologically determined differences deemed relevant to the quality of citizenship (Stoler 1995). Cribb (2010) states that, in a legal sense, this regime 'blurred' colonial pluralism and multiculturalism, ruling its subjects in ways that essentialised cultural differences, respected religious autonomy, recognised plural family law, and patronised specific communities within the archipelago. Establishing and maintaining cultural and racial distinctions within a plural legal order depended on the regulation of biological and cultural reproduction through the control of sexuality. The gendered and racist nature of this regime protected European men's privileges, as men and as Europeans. They were the ones who determined whether the children of their 'native' concubines could acquire the European status and full Dutch citizenship, while a marriage between a 'native' man and a European woman resulted in her losing the privileged status of European – not in his gaining it (De Hart 2003; Stoler 1995). Cribb (2010) concludes that legal pluralism and multiculturalism, at least in their colonial manifestation, amounted to a refusal by the Dutch to share their political morality with their subjects in the Indonesian archipelago. In addition, legal pluralism in a colonial context amounted to a refusal by the ruling colonial class to share its political and socio-economic privileges – such as senior positions in the colonial bureaucracy – with the 'native subjects' (Heijs 1991, 1994; Somers 2005; Jones 2007).[4]

Cribb, Stoler and others have analysed the effects of these Dutch colonial exclusive and gendered notions of citizenship in colonial and postcolonial *Indonesian* society. For our discussion it is relevant to investigate whether these citizenship regimes also influenced citizenship elsewhere: both in the colonies of Suriname and the Netherlands

Antilles, or in the Netherlands, and with respect to citizens who, in the process of decolonisation, were trapped between a former colonial and a new Dutch citizenship. Colonial family law turned out to produce various racial and gendered excluding effects for those who wanted to obtain Dutch citizenship and migrate to the Netherlands, both from Indonesia after 1945 and from Suriname and the Netherlands Antilles after 1954. But we argue here that the postcolonial paradigmatic shift away from the overseas racist mode of exclusion of the colonial period in the 1970s also created new including effects relevant for anyone living in the Netherlands. We discuss how both the decolonisation of Suriname and the sexual revolution in the Netherlands challenged Dutch immigration and family law based on a Western Christian sexual morality and its related institutions, like marriage and heteronormativity. As sexual norms became more contested, it became more difficult for the Dutch state to justify the exclusion of (postcolonial) migrants from its territory on the grounds of their 'non-European' sexual behaviour. At the same time, as the moral dominance of Western Christian norms became less self-evident in the (former) colonial powers, other normative orders acquired more legitimacy and could also serve to inspire those who, in what once had been the superior colonial metropole, were struggling to imagine and establish a new sexual order.

While Verdonk (as quoted in the introduction to this chapter) in 2005 suggested that the liberal, egalitarian and secular morality of current Western European (and specifically Dutch) society is inherent to those societies, our argument is that she ignores how, in the Netherlands, as probably in other Western European countries, the paradigmatic shift towards this new sexual order was also the result of a *two-way* decolonisation process. Decolonisation, and the immigration questions that came with it, helped make Dutch society receptive to normative orders that, only a few decades before, had been labelled within the Dutch overseas racial colonial order as 'non-European', backwards and morally reprehensible.

## Materials and methods

We focus our argument on the dynamic interaction between Suriname's decolonisation, Dutch postcolonial migration and integration policies, and changes in Dutch family law. Our contention is that colonial history is important to understand recent migration policies in the Netherlands, both as a gendered history of segregation, exclusion and heteronormativity and as a history of legal pluralism and inclusion. Family law, used within the colonial setting to regulate 'belonging', has played a key role in this history. It formed a normative system for regulating legitimate family bonds, and hence for establishing a person's legal status. Given that, from 1892 on, Dutch nationality was determined through the *jus sanguinis* principle, family law came to form part of the system for determining formal citizenship. However, grounded in culturally and religiously informed assumptions concerning gender norms and sexuality, family law also could serve to establish substantive cultural norms of citizenship (Stoler 1995; Van Walsum 2008). In the current postcolonial context, family law similarly interacts with migration law, and thus plays a role in both formally and culturally determining who is included and excluded from residence in the Netherlands (Van Walsum 2008).

A telling example of this dynamic interaction between family and migration law was provided in the 1980s by the Berrehab case (ECHR, 21 June 1988, application 10730/84). Abdellah Berrehab, a man of Moroccan nationality, had been admitted to the Netherlands on the grounds of his marriage to a Dutch woman, but had lost his residence permit two years later following a divorce. By then, he and his former wife had had a daughter, Rebecca. Although no longer living with his former wife, Berrehab devoted four days a week to his daughter's care. Nonetheless, the Dutch state refused to extend his residence permit, claiming that he and his daughter did not share family life. The European Court of Human Rights (ECHR) did not agree, and ruled that the Dutch state had violated the right to respect for family life of both father and daughter. Berrehab became a landmark case, not just in migration law, but also – perhaps even more so – in family law. By establishing that co-habitation is not a necessary prerequisite for family life, this case formed an important element in a series of later court judgements, both national and international, developing the concept of the right to respect for family life. This case law ultimately led to legislative reforms introduced in the 1990s that radically changed the nature of Dutch family law (Holtrust 1993; Loenen 2003).

This chapter focuses on the dynamic interaction between family law, immigration law and discourses of national belonging from the colonial past. Its methodology is grounded in the cross-disciplinary collaboration of its three authors, based in family migration law (Van Walsum), historical anthropology (Jones) and political history (Legêne). The overarching research question of this volume concerns implicitly gendered rules, explicit sexual norms, and the changes in migration policy in an era (1917-2010) that saw the heyday of imperialism, decolonisation, massive migration moments, the end of empires and establishment of 'single nations in a single territory', together with the emergence of a global sphere of international justice (Cooper 2005; Stuurman 2010). In addition to this volume's other chapters in which colonialism and decolonisation is not an issue, this chapter widens the scope of gender, sexuality and migration policy, by explicitly suggesting, with the example of the Netherlands, a legal-historical continuity between European colonialism and contemporary European immigration policies. The colonial history is especially instructive for understanding how pluralism in family norms and law and the associated differences in the regulation of gender relations and sexuality have interacted with regimes of inclusion and exclusion in the past. Awareness of these historical dynamics enriches our understanding of both political and legal discourses in the ex-colonial metropolis of today.

An international comparison of colonial legacies in postcolonial citizenship regimes in Europe should emphasise two aspects: colonial cross-overs and legal continuities. Both are vital to understanding recent migration policy issues. By cross-overs we mean, for instance, how the development of legal pluralism in the Dutch East Indies, after the introduction of the 1892 laws that revised Dutch nationality law and established various categories of colonial subjects, was 'applied' in Suriname in the first decades of the 20th century, and how experiences with Dutch citizenship for immigrants from Indonesia between 1950 and 1958 influenced provisions for Surinamese immigrants to the Netherlands after 1975. Such cross-overs and legal continuities must have existed *within* each of the other European empires, as well as *between* these empires in the broader European context, as suggested by Balibar (2004). Our focus is on the Dutch case, by tracing transnational legal continuities in the development of Dutch family law after Surinamese independence. Sources for this approach are, next to secondary literature, primary sources like legislative texts, published court judgements in migration law cases[5] and Dutch parliamentary proceedings.

With respect to the secondary sources, this implies that we also address current debates on Dutch 'depillarisation', or the secularisation process and the loosening of the confessional or ideological bonds that after 1945 were dominant in Dutch civil society (Kennedy 1995; Vuysje 1997; Van Dam 2011).[6] We argue that the impact of decolonisation should be analysed more thoroughly within the fragmentation of this pillarised society. The Treaty of 1975 concerning the admission of Surinamese nationals to the Netherlands, following Suriname's independence, provided for the admission of unmarried partners, both heterosexual and homosexual, at the request of the Surinamese and in recognition of the plurality of conjugal norms prevalent in the former colony

(Van Walsum 2008). Van Walsum has claimed that these treaty provisions – the first statutory regulations to acknowledge the legitimacy of
(homosexual) non-marital relations – helped to pave the way for further reform in Dutch family migration policy, and that these reforms in
turn formed a point of reference in legal debates that preceded reforms
of Dutch family law. In another historical study of Dutch family migration policies in the post-Second World War period, Bonjour (2009)
refutes this claim. In her view the reverse was the case: the Netherlands
had been prepared to admit the unmarried (homosexual) partners of
Surinamese residents thanks to emancipatory processes that had taken
place within the Netherlands. We would like to re-examine this issue
and its relationship to depillarisation, not because we want to prove
Van Walsum right and Bonjour wrong. In the contemporary context of
the Netherlands in which government policy's claim to a higher moral
ground in the realm of sexuality once more serves to justify the exclusion of the putatively morally backward, we believe that it is important
to critically examine the historical validity of that claim. Approaching
decolonisation as a two-way process enriches our analysis of the paradigmatic shift in Dutch family law that has taken place since the 1970s,
a shift that cannot just be explained as a result of the fragmentation of
Dutch pillarised society.

## Colonial cross-overs between East and West:
## The normative Surinamese landscape

In describing the Surinamese normative landscape in terms of family
regulations prior to decolonisation, a periodisation of Surinamese state
formation is needed. Until 25 November 1975, when the country became independent, Suriname was part of the Kingdom of the Netherlands. In the preceding period, political milestones had been the conservative *Staatsregeling* of 1936 that abandoned the word 'colony', but
continued colonial bonds and contained many regulations that were
contradictory to the Dutch Constitution, and the more liberal *Statuut*
of 1954 allowing Suriname an autonomous status within the Kingdom
of the Netherlands (Buiskool 1954: 17-41). After 1901, the Dutch government and colonial legislators, which differed in their degrees of interaction with Dutch legal systems, also worked on family law regulations
that would serve the plural society of Suriname, while also accounting
for the legacies of the past colonial organisation of plantation labour.
The Dutch colonial authorities, via family law and socio-cultural regimes in general, were the dominant 'actors' in creating the Surinamese

plural society and the ethnic divisions therein. Colonial socio-cultural regimes, the subsequent regimes of labour by enslaved and indentured workers on the plantations, the support for small farming in the districts, and finally the emergence of male wage labour for (multinational) companies that exploited natural resources far away from the urban centres of Suriname, all had a deep and lasting influence on the organisation of social and family life in the colony.[7]

In the 19th century the regime of plantation slavery had an impact on the marital status of the enslaved African plantation workers. Despite the critique of Christian missionaries like the Hernhutters, enslaved Africans were not allowed to marry; a child born from an enslaved woman was legally classified as a slave, and the enslaved parents could not recognise the child as theirs. The protection of family life was socially weak and legally non-existent, since the enslaved were legally not 'persons' but 'goods'. In a number of cases, European fathers made possible the manumission of both the enslaved mothers and their children (Van Lier 1977). But enslaved mothers of a child whose biological father was a European, conceived in any form of enforced or voluntary intercourse and relationship, remained highly dependent on paternal decisions concerning the future of the child. The racist colonial regime of African slave labour had accommodated various forms of intimate relationships between people, many of whom had adopted Christianity as (a part of) their beliefs, who were none the less denied access to a decent family life.

Runaway Maroons, who since the 18th century had organised their communities with (almost) no involvement from colonial authorities, as well as Amerindian Surinamese, developed their own norms and customs that the authorities only after the *Staatsregeling* of 1936 tried to integrate into a common legal framework. Chinese, Hindustani and Javanese indentured labourers had since the middle of the 19th century been recruited in order to replace enslaved workers. They became large groups in Suriname. Most of these plantation labour immigrants in the early 20th century had become small farmers or middle-class entrepreneurs. Many were Muslim, Hindu or adherents of Confucianism, and hence initially did not adhere to the dominant Christian family norms. Containing those groups that did not share 'Western' values had been an argument for the conservative character of the 1936 *Staatsregeling* (Buiskool 1954: 27).

Pluralist marital law that would allow for differences with respect to especially Hindu and Muslim beliefs and customs was much-discussed from the beginning of the 20th century. Special provisions concerning marriages of Hindustani and Javanese were drawn up in 1907, but legal unity remained the guiding principle in Suriname (Van Lier 1977: 144). Cultural and legal pluralism that would acknowledge all different population groups, while still favouring (Dutch) Western and Christianity-based family law, turned out to be a very complicated legal issue. Its contested implementation in Suriname was partly based on the example from the Dutch East Indies. Colonial family law in the Dutch East Indies had been an experiment with legal pluralism, which acknowledged *adat* and *sharia* combined with an affirmation of strict citizenship distinctions. The population in the Dutch East Indies was legally classified in three distinct groups: Europeans and those decreed equal to Europeans, foreign Orientals, and indigenous people. Qua nationality status, the population of the Dutch East Indies was classified as Dutch citizens (all of whom were also Europeans) and Dutch subjects (most of whom belonged to the category of indigenous people or foreign Orientals) from 1892 and 1910 onwards. As mentioned before, this legal order implied unequal career patterns for people in different categories.

The legal pluralism of the colonial Dutch East Indies was adapted in Surinamese society from 1937 onwards. However, the context was essentially different. In the Dutch East Indies, 300,000 Europeans ruled over 20 million indigenous persons in 1940. Suriname was a small settlement colony with population groups that, except for the community of Amerindian Surinamese, had been brought from Africa and Asia to Suriname under colonial labour regimes of slavery or indentured labour. The migration histories, the cultural and religious backgrounds of the various population groups, and their history of forced or indentured labour in the colony, made family law a complicated issue. Moreover, against the backdrop of the dominant cultural policies in Suriname at the time, legal pluralism with regard to family law became a contested issue. From 1863 to 1933, the colonial legal regimes and policies with regard to culture, language, education and family had been aimed at assimilation. The *Koloniale Staten*, the colonial representative body consisting of members of the influential local political elite, supported Dutch colonial policies. Assimilation policy, which after emancipation in 1863 was initially targeted at the formerly enslaved, was subsequently also directed at the indentured labourers who came from China, the Dutch East Indies and British India (Van Lier 1977; Ramsoedh 1995; Marshall 2003). The aim of these policies was, as Governor A.A.L. Rutgers stated in 1922, 'to re-melt the entire population, white, brown, black or yellow, regardless if they are Europeans, Americans, Africans or Asians, into one single language and culture community within one legal framework, even in the case of matrimonial law and law of succession'. This policy was very different from that in the Dutch East Indies, which aimed to separate groups rather than to meld them into one. The Dutch colonial authorities were well aware of this difference. The Minister of Colonies J.C. Koningsberger in 1928 stated explicitly that 'preservation of language, morals and customs' was the aim in the Dutch East Indies, whereas 'the fusion of all races, including the Javanese, into one Dutch language and culture community' was the goal of colonial policies in Suriname (Van Lier 1977: 143).

The administration of Governor G.C. Kielstra (1933-1944) signalled a paradigmatic shift away from assimilation policies (Ramsoedh 1995). Before Kielstra became governor in Suriname, he held senior positions in the Dutch East Indies. Around 1914, as the Deputy Advisor for Administrative Affairs of the Outer Provinces (of the Dutch East Indies) he had been involved in the legal description in Christian by-laws for Toba Batak Christians, of customary or *adat* law concerning marriage and family arrangements (Van Bemmelen 2012: ch. 10). His relocation in 1933 from the Dutch East Indies to the West Indies meant a partial transposition of colonial policies from one colony to the other. Inspired by the regime of legal pluralism in the Dutch East Indies, Kielstra wanted to introduce 'Asian marital law', the establishment of separate villages and separate schools for the 'Asian' part of the population, in accordance with the Dutch East Indies model (Van Lier 1977: 143-146, cf. Van Walsum 2000: 29-37). He met fierce opposition from the representative body, which after 1936 was called the *Staten* and by then was dominated by members of the local 'white, Jewish and Creole elite'. These representatives[8] favoured the continuation of equal treatment (*rechtseenheid*) and assimilation, and criticised Kielstra's policies, which they compared with 'apartheid', as an obstruction of national unity. Kielstra, backed by Minister of Colonies Ch.J.I.M. Welter, used the special powers granted to him by the conservative *Staatsregeling* of 1936 to disregard the local representatives and enact his 'Asian marital law' in 1937.

As previously mentioned, legal pluralism in the Dutch East Indies before 1942 did not allow for the development of universal and shared notions of citizenship (Cribb 2010). This had an immediate impact on individual entitlements to, and exclusion from, Dutch citizenship after 1949, when the Dutch East Indies became independent Indonesia. In terms of migration options, the legal pluralism in colonial family law prior to Indonesian independence limited entitlements for migration to the Netherlands, whereas Indonesian society after 1950 established an exclusive Indonesian national citizenship that did not allow for cultural pluralism (Willems 2001: 112). The arrival of postcolonial immigrants from the former Dutch East Indies did not directly impact Dutch family law. On the contrary, meeting the dominant norms of family life formed an important criterion to admitting immigrants from the colonies (Ringeling 1978; Willems 2001: 57-61, 105-111; Bosma 2009). In Suriname, however, legal pluralism with respect to family law between 1936 and 1975, and notably after 1954, when Suriname was an autonomous part of the Kingdom of the Netherlands, developed not only in interaction with Dutch legal reform, but also within an international context of an emerging sphere of global justice based on human rights (Stuurman 2010: 475).

Regardless of existing law, Surinamese society had allowed for cultural and legal pluralism in family regulations, based on the acceptance of Muslim and Hindu private life, as well as the awareness that during the nation's history many had been forced to live in enslavement. Between 1954 and 1975, the social legacies of this past, both for descendants of Afro-Surinamese and for Chinese, Hindustani and Javanese immigrants, were hardly discussed in terms of this history. Dutch perspectives on Surinamese nation-state formation were dominant in schools, in churches and in court. However, in society, cultural pluralism allowed for a family life that was not restricted to Western Christian values. To be sure, during colonial times the model of the 'nuclear' family (husband-wife-children), consisting of spouses married in accordance with civil law (*Burgerlijke Stand*) had been very influential among the Creole and Jewish elite and turned into 'the most frequent model in families, across ethnic groups that have attained or aspire to middle-class status', as observed by Wekker (2001: 187). At the same time, other family systems existed in parallel to the 'Western style nuclear family', such as the marriages according to Hinduism and Islamic faith mentioned above, the 'dual marriage structure' and 'the extended family' (ibid.). In some of these 'alternative' family systems, the husband-wife-children unit is absent. This is the case, for instance, in 'the Creole working-class matrifocal family', in which 'the mother-child and sibling relationships form the durable and dependable network in which an individual is embedded' (ibid.: 188). Matrifocal families can function as the locus for '*matiwerk*' relationships: socio-economic support networks between women, in which 'same-sex' relations can occur. Before Suriname's independence in 1975, a significant number of these 'parallel' family systems had been enacted in law, as in the case of marriage in accordance with Hinduism or Islam, laws recognising the authority of women over their biological children (which is of particular importance for matrifocal families), laws con-

cerning the rights of foster children, and laws concerning concubinage
(Oedayrajsingh & Ahmad Ali 1989).

## Conjugality and family migration policy in the negotiation of Suriname's secession

In the early 1970s, against the backdrop of worldwide decolonisation,
the relationship between the Netherlands and its remaining colonies
(Suriname and the Dutch Antilles) became a topic of parliamentary
debate. This issue was connected to discussions on the regulation of
immigration from Suriname to the Netherlands, which was increasing. The map of the world had changed dramatically. Former colonies,
now a category of independent nations known as developing countries,
played a role in East-West and North-South relationships. The US civil
rights movement and protests against the war in Vietnam added urgency to anti-racism and anti-imperialism movements. In 1971, young
Dutch lawyers and activists supported the American draft resister
Ralph Waver in his claim to political asylum in the Netherlands, marking a renewal of professional support for migrants and refugees seeking
admission to this country (Reurs & Stronks 2011: 15-29; Walaardt 2012;
Walaardt in this volume).

Initial support had been given by NASSI (Nationale Actie Steunt
Spijtoptanten in Indonesië), a volunteer advisory group founded by
Tjalie Robinson and others in 1960, for postcolonial visa applicants who
belonged to the 'last' thousands of people in Indonesia who opted for
Indonesian citizenship and later regretted that choice (Willems 2001:
162; Bibo 2011). Their cases had been closed by the time that Ralph
Waver applied for political asylum, in a context of increasing unem-
ployment following the oil crisis. Following rising immigration from
Suriname, racist violence within the Netherlands became a public issue.
The year 1971 also saw the founding of the extreme right-wing party the
Nederlandse Volks Unie (NVU) (Schuster 1999: 130), the first (and only)
anti-immigrant party in the Netherlands in the post-Second World
War period that anti-racist groups succeeded in having convicted for
promoting racist ideas (Tinnemans 1994: 134-135).

In this polarising context, the debate concerning Suriname's decolonisation not only reflected anti-colonial sentiment, but also concerns
over immigration control. As long as Suriname remained part of the
Kingdom of the Netherlands, the Dutch government could not exclude
Surinamese inhabitants without discriminating between Dutch subjects. Once Suriname was independent, its inhabitants would be for-

eigners, and the Dutch government could legitimately refuse their admission (Jones 2007). Meanwhile, family migration became a political issue connected to labour migrants from the Mediterranean. The centre-left cabinet, elected into power in May 1973 under the leadership of the socialist J. den Uyl appeared to struggle to reconcile both postcolonial and labour migration control with progressive aspirations (Bosma 2009). During a debate with parliament on the issue of labour migration, the cabinet put forward its position as follows:

> Seen from the perspective of the migrant worker himself and from the culture to which he belongs ... it would be unreasonable to refuse entry to family members with whom he feels closely bound and for whom he feels responsible ... The government is of the opinion that – also for moral reasons – it would be unjust to pursue a restrictive policy regarding the admission of family members to stay with foreign workers who, after all, have served the Dutch interest by coming here.[9]

On the other hand, taking the culture of migrant workers into account, raised issues of control:

> Another aspect of family reunification regards applications made, in the case of polygamous marriages, for the admission of more than one wife or of children born out of another marriage than the children who have already been admitted. A similar problem arises when foreign workers request the admission of children born out of wedlock. The list of possible requests that can be made on the basis of family reunification is by no means exhaustive. In practice, we are confronted with even more variations.[10]

It is against this background that the terms concerning family reunification following Suriname's secession would be negotiated. In 1972, a special committee on *Koninkrijkszaken* (the relations within the Kingdom of the Netherlands) was established to address the constitutional relationship between the Netherlands and its former colony Suriname, and to consider alternative regulations in terms of nationality and migration law that could serve to limit the number of persons leaving Suriname for the Netherlands. By then, secession had become an issue of political debate both in Suriname and the Netherlands. Dutch insistence on regulations for migration from Suriname to the Netherlands was to play a major role in the process that would eventually lead to Suriname's independence in 1975 (Jones 2007: 229-234).

Reminiscent of the painful and violent secession of the Dutch East Indies, Den Uyl and his cabinet were determined to have Suriname's independence form a model chapter in the history of decolonisation (Willemsen 1988: 130-131). In determining who was to belong to which nation, the racially neutral criterion of territory was adhered to, rather than the more suspect one of genealogy, which had been the determining factor following Indonesia's secession in 1949 and had turned out to be highly debatable and at times also embarrassing for those who apparently had believed in a strictly segregated colonial society (Ringeling 1978; Van Walsum 2008; Bibo 2010). Anyone who had been born in Suriname and was living there on 25 November 1975, the date of Suriname's independence, acquired Surinamese nationality. Dutch nationals from Suriname, who were resident in the Netherlands on that same date, could keep their Dutch nationality, regardless of parentage or 'cultural orientation' (Heijs 1991: 35-36).

While the ruling left-wing government in the Netherlands saw it as its historical mission to grant Suriname its independence, in Suriname itself secession was contested. To win support, Surinamese politicians had to negotiate guarantees that future Surinamese citizens would continue to have easy access to the Netherlands. During negotiations with the Dutch government, Surinamese representatives strove for a generous regime of admission that would account for family norms that were believed to be characteristic of Surinamese society, including non-marital familial relationships (Jones 2007: 252-254). The final text of the treaty between Suriname and the Netherlands concerning the admission of their respective citizens, which became effective as of 25 November 1975, did in fact include a provision, Article 5, allowing for the admission of the person with whom a citizen of one of the state parties, legally resident on the territory of the other, 'has a long lasting and exclusive personal relationship'. This article also applied to same-sex relationships (Ahmed Ali 1979: 17). This was a significant achievement when we consider that only a decade before, in the wake of Indonesia's secession, Dutch authorities were still being advised by social workers stationed in Indonesia, to refuse 'repatriation' to persons of Indonesian nationality who lived in cohabitation or had illegitimate children. Such practices were considered to be indicative of an 'oriental orientation' that rendered assimilation to Dutch society unlikely (Ringeling 1978: 127). Verton, who worked for the Dutch immigration authorities in the 1960s, reported that if the authorities saw reason to suspect that a foreigner guest worker was engaged in a non-marital sexual relationship with a Dutch woman, this could lead to deportation on the grounds that public order was being threatened (Verton 1971: 45). As late as 1970, the Dutch Council of State ruled that a Turkish worker who had started a relationship with his Dutch landlady, while not having to leave the country, could be required to leave his lover's home.[11]

Swart, in a commentary on the Dutch immigration law of 1965 (published in 1978), remarks that Article 5 of the Dutch-Surinamese treaty concerning the admission of their respective citizens is the first statutory ruling in Dutch law in which persons involved in a non-marital relationship are granted the same rights as married couples. He points out that, by then, Dutch citizens were being enabled by Dutch family migration policies to bring over foreign non-marital partners, but only on the basis of decisions taken by officials with discretionary powers, or following litigation. These were, however, exceptional cases, where marriage was not an option and where the relationship was clearly of a long-lasting nature (Adema & Freezer 1975: 169-170).

In Swart's view, the statutory regulation for Surinamese citizens of a claim to family reunification with a non-marital partner, had to be seen against the background of the specific family norms that prevailed in Suriname at the time (Swart 1978: 411). This view is supported by information provided by Deputy Minister of Justice H.J. Zeevalking to the Dutch parliament in October 1975, one month before the treaty was to become effective (Jones 2007: 254).

Not everyone agrees with that interpretation. Bonjour (2009: 134), for instance, defends the position that the provision in the Dutch-Surinamese treaty allowing for admission of non-marital partners was prompted less by family norms prevalent in Suriname at the time, and more by normative shifts that had, by then, taken place in the Netherlands. These, she claims, had led to changes in Dutch migration policy, and it would have been problematic to impose a more restrictive regime upon former citizens coming from Suriname. It was not Surinamese norms 'imported' via migration law that served as a trigger for normative change in the Netherlands. Rather, normative changes in the Netherlands explain why Surinamese norms could be accommodated in Dutch migration law. Bonjour (ibid.) bases this interpretation on the account of Dutch politician J.F. Glastra van Loon (himself born in the Dutch East Indies) of his experiences as Deputy Minister of Justice in the Den Uyl cabinet between June 1973 and May 1975. He published his account one year after being forced to resign after conflicts with civil servants in his department (Glastra van Loon 1976). In his memoirs he describes how, during his first encounter with the civil servants responsible for immigration, he put forward his position on family migration policies which, among other things, would enable unmarried foreigners, whether heterosexual or homosexual, to stay in the Netherlands as the partner of a Dutch citizen. That statement, he writes, caused a considerable stir in the department, which is understandable given that, until then, non-marital sex had been a grounds for withdrawing residence rights, not granting them.

Glastra van Loon went further than proposing that extra-marital sex (whether heterosexual or homosexual) should no longer lead to loss of residence rights and deportation. His intention was that it should serve as acceptable grounds for admission. Bonjour's (2009: 121) sources indicate that the civil servants of the immigration department accepted this proposal, but with some reservation. Dutch case law indicates that the change in policy was indeed implemented, but in a restrictive fashion. Residence permits were refused to applicants who could not meet income requirements.[12] In effect, this meant that they could only reside with their non-marital partner if they were in possession of a work permit. By then however, given rising unemployment, work permits were generally being refused to foreign workers who had not been officially recruited. As a result, the right to admission on the basis of a non-marital relationship remained illusionary. By contrast, foreign men married to Dutch women were granted work permits so that they could live up to their responsibilities as breadwinners.[13] In a decision of 7 July 1975, the Dutch Council of State advised that since foreigners could be admitted on the grounds of either a marital or a non-marital relationship with a Dutch woman, they should also be equally entitled to a work permit allowing them to fulfil their duties as a breadwinner, regardless of whether they had been officially recruited.[14] The case law referred to above refers only to foreign men living together with Dutch women. The lack of published case law concerning the reverse situation (i.e., a foreign woman living together with a Dutch man), suggests these cases were either less frequent or that foreign women experienced fewer problems in acquiring a residence permit solely on the grounds of their relationship with a Dutch man.

A further indication of the reluctance to implement this new policy, is the fact that an official letter presenting it to the head of the Dutch Immigration Department was only posted on the date of the above quoted decision by the Dutch Council of State, two years after Glastra van Loon had announced it, and after he had already left the Ministry. Furthermore, the letter only refers to the unmarried partners of *Dutch* citizens, not to those of legally resident foreign nationals, while the above quoted case law suggests that the new policy was only being applied to the partners of Dutch *women*. In this light, it is understandable that the Surinamese delegates negotiating the terms of the secession treaties were not convinced that the existing Dutch policies allowing for the admission of foreigners on the grounds of a non-marital relationship would suffice to meet the needs of the future citizens of Suriname, and insisted on the statutory norms which were, in the end, granted (Bonjour 2009: 131).

Following the secession treaties with Suriname, Dutch family migration policies were modified in 1978 to allow for the admission of the non-marital partners of persons with refugee status[15] and in 1980 to allow for the admission of the non-marital partners of migrants with permanent residence status.[16] It is not evident, however, that these reforms were solely prompted by increasingly progressive family norms in the Netherlands, rather than by the relative openness, characteristic of this period, to the normative pluralism that international and post-colonial immigration implied and also needed in order to work out in a proper way. The reverse could equally be argued, namely, that the openness to normative pluralism in the era of decolonisation helped achieve reform in Dutch family law.

## Challenging the institution of marriage in the context of multiculturalism

Thus, in the mid 1970s and nearly ten years before the Netherlands launched its ethnic minorities policy, Dutch politicians and policymakers had accepted the assumption that opening the Netherlands to family migrants from the so-called developing countries, meant opening Dutch society to normative pluralism. As Bonjour (2009) rightly observes, the 1960s and 1970s also marked a period of cultural revolution in the Netherlands. The dominance of religious institutions over family life came to be hotly contested. There was no new normative consensus concerning the merits of the 'permissive society', but Dutch family norms in this period were contested. Once the religious institutions in the Netherlands started to loosen their grip on family norms, a Pandora's Box of conflicting interests and desires opened. After decades of religious tutelage and sectarianism, there was a strong thirst for personal autonomy and normative freedom. Adolescents sought sexual autonomy and release from parental control; women sought freedom from male dominance and a larger say over the upbringing of their children; men sought more sexual freedom and release from the lifelong responsibility of having to provide financial support for dependent family members. Adolescents and women claimed the right to independent shelter and financial security; men insisted on maintaining ties with their children, regardless of the state of their relationship with the mother (Van Walsum 2008: 25-67).

Against this background of contestation, excluding migrants on the grounds that they did not conform to dominant Dutch norms became problematic. Next to an increased openness to normative pluralism outside of the Netherlands, there was therefore also a growing hesitation – embarrassment even – in applying Christian morality as a mechanism of inclusion and exclusion. Ringeling (1978: 127), for example, observes that, shortly before the programme allowing for the repatriation of 'socially Dutch' Indonesians ended in 1963, immigration officials no longer followed social workers' recommendations to exclude candidates on the grounds of co-habitation or promiscuity. And, as mentioned earlier, by the early 1970s legally resident migrants were no longer threatened with loss of status and deportation after having been involved in an extra-marital relationship.

Contrary to Bonjour's (2009) argument, however, non-marital relations were still far from entrenched in Dutch law. Against the background of moral ferment, the major political parties in the Netherlands at the time – the Christian Democrats rooted in the confessional politics of the past, and the Dutch Labour Party under the leadership of Den Uyl – persisted until well into the 1980s in staunchly defending the institution of the family as the keystone of Dutch society. For the Christian Democrats, the family formed the source of altruism that fuelled civil society; for the socialists the family served as a metaphor for national solidarity (Bussemaker 1993: 134). It would take nearly three decades for the dust to settle and a new consensus to be reached on the issue of family norms.

While successive Dutch cabinets continued to promote the institution of marriage, its libertarian opponents rallied forces to claim rights for alternative forms of family life. Interestingly, in pleading their case for regulating co-habitation and other alternatives to marriage, lawyers referred to both the changes taking place in Dutch migration law and the normative pluralism that migration implied. The acceptance, in the 1970s, of the validity of alternative normative systems – however limited and brief it may have been – added new impulses to campaigns for the reform of Dutch family law.

In 1974, the Dutch civil lawyer A.M. van de Wiel compiled an inventory of Dutch laws and policies that took co-habitation into account. These were very few. The still unpublished migration law policy change initiated in 1973 by Glastra van Loon was one of only two policy measures effective on a national level that granted a positive claim on the basis of co-habitation. The few other rules found all related to diminished claims to alimony or welfare benefits, on the grounds of co-habitation (Van de Wiel 1974). In response, J.M. Polak, law professor and later a member of the Dutch Council of State (*Raad van State*), called for more regulation, although he conceded that the Netherlands was a country 'with a rich assortment of lifestyles and convictions', which public authorities would have to take into account (Polak 1974). As demands for change increased, Van de Wiel again provided an overview of the existing regulations, now to inform debate on possible reform. Interestingly, his conclusion – based largely on case law on family migration – was that no regulation of non-marital relations could do justice to the variety of conjugal arrangements that this concept covered. Rather than regulate an alternative to marriage, he recommended a more flexible regulation of marriage itself: 'It will become increasingly clear that the pattern of human relationships is too varied to be caught in a single legal concept' (Van de Wiel 1979: 116).

Five years later, the authoritative Dutch legal journal *Het Nederlands Juristenblad* (NJB), published a manifesto against the legal institution of marriage, written by Professor H. van Maarseveen and two other lawyers: D. Verlegh and S. Korthuis (Verlegh, Van Maarseveen & Korthuis 1984). By then, the Dutch Constitution had been thoroughly revised, including the non-discrimination clause in Article 1. In their manifesto, the three authors expressed their objections to the constrictions imposed by the Dutch state, through the institution of marriage, upon an individual's private affairs. They pointed to the vast variety of conceivable conjugal relations: heterosexual, homosexual, bisexual or non-sexual; monogamous, bigamous, polygamous; temporary or permanent or somewhere in between; living together or living apart. Because a broad array of legal arrangements, from tax benefits to housing permits to social security took marriage as their point of reference, people were more or less forced, in their eyes, to choose this particular form of family life. The authors drew parallels between normative pluralism in the intimate sphere and religious freedom and cultural pluralism in general, pointing out that the Netherlands had become a multicultural society in which a variety of family norms had found a home. By then, Dutch government had launched an ethnic minorities policy indeed, grounded in the principle of cultural diversity (see Schrover in this volume). Verlegh, Van Maarseveen and Korthuis argued that Dutch civil law, in maintaining the institution of heterosexual and monogamous marriage, privileged the normative order of one religion (Christianity) over others, thus violating fundamental principles of freedom of religion, freedom of conscience, privacy and non-discrimination. They warned, 'The government will run into problems since ethnic minorities can now claim acknowledgement of alternative conjugal arrangements on religious grounds' (Verlegh, Van Maarseveen & Korthuis

1984: 859). The authors were apparently unaware of the fact that in another part of the Kingdom of the Netherlands, Suriname, this had already been the case since the 1950s.

## Conclusion: Changing family law and contemporary debates on immigration policies with respect to Muslims

In the fall of 2009, two decades after Abdellah Berrehab contributed to a further reform of Dutch family law by claiming his right to family life with his daughter, even though he did not adhere to the dominant family norms of the time, a Dutch policy document on family migration was published. That document proposed preventing any cross-border form of conjugality that fell short of what was explicitly advanced as the official Dutch norm, based on 'the mutually and equally shared responsibility of partners for each other and for their children':

> The Dutch legal order does not allow for violent forms of parenting, nor for polygamy or marriages contracted under force. All couples are treated equally, regardless of whether or not they are composed of persons of the same or different sexes.[17]

Concerning cross-border unions, this policy document warned that these may be 'concluded under force, and this is unacceptable':

> A forced marriage can indicate honour-related violence; polygamy and marriages between cousins can, in turn, indicate an involuntary union or fraud. Estimates are that roughly 25% of people in the Netherlands of Turkish and Moroccan origin marries within the family. Not only are the children of migrants in the Netherlands being pressured into marrying a cousin from their country of origin so as to help him or her acquire a residence permit; such marriages also result in spouses being forced into providing care to the extended family.

Consequently, any request for family reunification that 'does not concern an already long established relationship, but rather appears to be the result of "matchmaking", with or without the consent of those involved (such as arranged child marriages), should be critically examined by the state. This requires more than controlling for fraudulent marriages.'[18]

The recommended measures not only target the migrating partners or spouses (depicted as 'dependent and uneducated women'), but also the partner or spouse in the Netherlands who, remarkably, is consistently assumed to be heterosexual, male and – generally – of 'non-Western' origin. To the extent that this document acknowledges that men of ethnically Dutch origin also engage in relationships with 'non-Western' women, it assumes they do so because they want a woman who is less emancipated, more compliant, subservient and 'willing to provide sexual services' than a woman raised in the Netherlands. As such, these men are accused of displaying an attitude that 'does not coincide with the Dutch premise of equality within marriage'. Implicitly, like their 'non-Western' countrymen, they are disqualified as proper Dutch citizens.

In the economic and political climate of the first decade of the 21st century, norms concerning family relations and sexuality are again being mobilised to physically exclude specific categories of migrants from legal residence within Dutch territory, while symbolically excluding specific categories among the legally resident population (including Dutch nationals) from substantive citizenship. Ideas about what constitutes family life travel between countries and have travelled between colonies and metropolis. The reforms leading to the current codification of family law in the Netherlands were preceded by an openness to a normative pluralism. This included forms of family life that, at the time, were more common and more widely accepted and legally framed in late colonial societies now referred to as 'non-Western' or developing countries. Immigrants from the Dutch East Indies with its huge Muslim population, and from Suriname, with its complex history of legal pluralism after 1936, rooted in a long history of forced immigration and labour, inspired struggles to legitimate other than dominant forms of (nuclear) family life. Through treaty negotiations or litigation, those with 'non-Western' backgrounds were actively involved in realising these normative changes. Ironically, they (whether as members of other Muslim populations, or of postcolonial immigrant communities), were portrayed in official documents as a threat to the new normative order in the Netherlands, which in different roles they themselves helped to create.

Conservative political and policy rhetoric suggests that emancipation is a one-way street, starting in 'the West' and leading to 'the rest'. Our analysis suggests that the emancipatory changes that occurred in Dutch family law during the second half of the 20th century arose from cross-border and cross-cultural interaction between 'the West' and 'the rest', based on a dynamic colonial relationship that reaches back into the 19th century. Taking 'the West' seriously, implies the need for a European comparative approach to the impact of the various colonial citizenship regimes on postcolonial immigration policies, both national and at a European level. We see more when we approach the road to emancipation, which is implicitly connected to the intention of immigrants to apply for citizenship in Europe, as a two-way street, or, maybe even a roundabout, if we apply this metaphor to the cross-overs between Indonesia, Suriname and the Netherlands in the colonial era and in the aftermath of decolonisation. The Dutch and their immigrants have walked that road before. We propose to explore it again.

## Notes

1 Wet Inburgering Buitenland, *Staatsblad* 2006: 26 & 75. This legislation was made effective as of 15 March 2006.

2 Proceedings Lower House session 2004-2005, 29 700, no. 6: 46-47. These and other quotes from Dutch sources have been translated by the authors of this chapter.

3 There is at present in the Netherlands, no research programme that focuses on legal instruments against racism.

4 Proceedings Lower House, session 1892-1893: 156-158.

5 Unless otherwise indicated, the cases quoted have been published in the annual overview of Dutch migration case law, *Rechtspraak Vreemdelingenrecht* (RV).

6 We thank the organisers of the Amsterdam conference on Dutch 20th century history *Uitsluitend emancipatie* (Excusively emancipation, 14-15 October 2011) for the opportunity to discuss drafts of this chapter in a panel session on decolonisation and migration.

7 Inspired by postcolonial theory, we consciously opt for the term 'enslaved' instead of 'slaves', since the latter term (slaves) naturalises the condition and the identity of the people concerned, whereas the former (enslaved) represents their condition as a result of colonial policy.

8 Christian Hindustani representatives, like Clemens Biswamitre, opposed the policies of Kielstra as well.

9 Proceedings Lower House, session 1973-1974, 10 503, no. 9-10: 16.

10 Proceedings Lower House, session 1973-1974, 10 503, no. 9-10: 16.

11 KB 4 March 1970, no. 99, RV 1970/2.

12 KB 30 August 1974 no. 65, RV 1974/19; KB 29 March 1974 no. 83, RV 1974/7.

13 KB 13 August 1974, RV 1974/18.

14 KB 7 July 1975, no. 45, RV 1975: 18.

15 Comment by Rb Alkmaar 18 July 1978, RV 1978/57.

16 Comment by ABRvS 2 March 1981, RV 1981/11.

17 Proceedings Lower House, session 2009-2010, 32 175, no. 1: 6.

18 Proceedings Lower House, session 2009-2010, 32 175, no. 1: 7-8.

## References

Adema, W.H. & H. Freezer (eds) (1975), *Rechtwijzer voor de vrouw.* Utrecht: A.W. Bruna & Zoon.

Ahmad Ali, H. (1979), *Een handleiding over toelating – verblijf – vestiging van Surinaamse staatsburgers in Nederland: De hoofdregels van de Toescheidingsovereenkomst nationaliteiten; afschaffing visumplicht tussen Suriname en de Benelux.* Utrecht: Stichting Landelijke Federatie van Welzijnsorganisaties voor Surinamers.

Balibar, E. (2004), *We, the people of Europe? Reflections on transnational citizenship.* Princeton: Princeton University Press.

Bibo, A. (2011), 'Een tijd van spijt: Een verkenning van de postkoloniale geschiedenis, intersectionele verhoudingen en categorieën en criteria van het "spijtoptantenbeleid" in Nederland (1957-1965)'. Master's thesis, VU University Amsterdam.

Bonjour, S. (2009), *Grens en gezin: Beleidsvorming inzake gezinsmigratie in Nederland, 1955-2005.* Amsterdam: Aksant.

Bosma, U. (2009), *Terug uit de koloniën: Zestig jaar postkoloniale migranten en hun organisaties.* Amsterdam: Bert Bakker.

Buiskool, J.A.E. (1954), *De staatsinstellingen van Suriname in de hoofdzaken mede vergeleken met die van Nederland en de Nederlandse Antillen.* The Hague: Martinus Nijhoff.

Bussemaker, J. (1993), *Betwiste zelfstandigheid: Individualisering, sekse en verzorgingsstaat.* Amsterdam: Socialistiese Uitgeverij Amsterdam.

Cooper, F. (2005), *Colonialism in question: Theory, knowledge, history.* Berkeley, Los Angeles, London: University of California Press.

Cribb, R. (2010), 'Pluralism and Dutch colonial policy in Indonesia'. Paper prepared for the 21st International Congress of Historical Sciences, Amsterdam, 22-28 August.

De Hart, B. (2003), *Onbezonnen vrouwen: Gemengde relaties in het nationaliteitsrecht en het vreemdelingenrecht.* Amsterdam: Aksant.

De Vries, K.M. (2012), 'The Dutch act on integration abroad: A case of racial or ethnic discrimination?', in S. Morano-Foadi & M. Malena (eds), *Integration for third country nationals in the EU: The challenge of equality,* pp. 324-345. Cheltenham: Edward Elgar.

De Vries, K.M. (2011), *Integration at the border: The Dutch act on integration abroad in relation to international immigration law.* PhD dissertation. VU University Amsterdam.

Glastra van Loon, J.F. (1976), *Kanalen graven.* Baarn: In den Toren.

Groenendijk, K. (2011), 'Pre-departure integration strategies in the European Union: Integration or immigration policy?', *European Journal of Migration and Law* 13 (1): 1-30.

Heijs, E. (1994), 'De Nederlandse nationaliteit van Indische Nederlanders: Een historische terugblik', in W. Willems & L. Lucassen (eds), *Het onbekende vaderland: De repatriëring van Indische Nederlanders,* pp. 58-66. The Hague: SDU.

Heijs, E. (1991), 'Nederlanderschap in de Nederlandse koloniën: Regulering van immigratie vanuit de koloniën door nationaliteitsbeleid in Nederland', *Recht der Werkelijkheid* 12 (2): 21-42.

Holtrust, N. (1993), *Aan moeders knie: De juridische afstammingsrelatie tussen moeder en kind*. Nijmegen: Ars Aequi Libri.

Human Rights Watch (2008), *The Netherlands: Discrimination in the name of Integration*. New York: Human Rights Watch.

Jones, G. (2007), *Tussen onderdanen, rijksgenoten en Nederlanders: Nederlandse politici over burgers uit Oost & West en Nederland 1945-2005*. Amsterdam: Rozenberg Publishers.

Kennedy, J.C. (1995), *Nieuw Babylon in aanbouw: Nederland in de jaren zestig*. Amsterdam & Meppel: Boom.

Legêne, S. (2011), 'Waar blijft de kritiek? Canon tussen politiek, wetenschap en cultuur', in M. Grever, I. de Haan, D. Hondius & S. Legêne (eds), *Grenzeloze gelijkheid: Historische vertogen over cultuurverschil*, pp. 238-254. Amsterdam: Bert Bakker.

Loenen, T. (2003), 'Zorg(e)loze toekomst voor de vrouw in het familierecht', *Nemesis* 5/6: 115-122.

Marshall, E. (2003), *Ontstaan en ontwikkeling van het Surinaams nationalisme: Natievorming als opgave*. Delft: Eburon.

Oedayrajsingh Varma, E.G. & H.A. Ahmad Ali (1989), *Surinaams familierecht*. Utrecht: Nederlands Centrum Buitenlanders.

Polak, J.M. (1974), 'Een administratiefrechtelijke benadering van het huwelijk en andere twee-relaties', in M. Beuckens-Vries et al. (eds), *Twee mensen en het recht*, pp. 79-85. Zwolle: Tjeenk Willink.

Ramsoedh, H. (1995), 'De Nederlandse assimilatiepolitiek in Suriname tussen 1863 en 1945', in L. Gobardhan, M. Hassankhan & J. Egger (eds), *De erfenis van de slavernij*, pp. 114-133. Paramaribo: Anton de Kom Universiteit.

Reurs, M. & M. Stronks (2011), *Pioniers in het vreemdelingenrecht*. The Hague/Utrecht: SDU/FORUM.

Ringeling, A.B. (1978), *Beleidsvrijheid van ambtenaren: Het spijtoptantenprobleem als illustratie van de activiteiten van ambtenaren bij de uitvoering van beleid*. Alphen aan de Rijn: Samson.

Schuster, J. (1999), *Poortwachters over immigranten: Het debat over immigratie in het naoorlogse Groot-Brittannië en Nederland*. Amsterdam: Het Spinhuis.

Somers, J.A. (2005), *Nederlands-Indië: Staatkundige ontwikkelingen binnen een koloniale relatie*. Zutphen: Walburg Pers.

Stoler, A.L. (2011), 'Colonial aphasia: Race and disabled histories in France', *Public Culture* 23 (1): 121-157.

Stoler, A.L. (1995), *Race and the education of desire: Foucault's history of sexuality and the colonial order of things*. Durham: Duke University Press.

Stuurman, S. (2010), *De uitvinding van de mensheid: Korte wereldgeschiedenis van het denken over gelijkheid en cultuurverschil*. Amsterdam: Bert Bakker.

Swart, A.H.J. (1978), *De toelating en uitzetting van vreemdelingen*. Deventer: Kluwer.

Terlouw, A. (2005), 'Discriminatie op grond van nationaliteit: Algemene aanbeveling 30 van het Committee on the Elimination of Racial Discrimination en haar betekenis voor Nederland', *NJCM Bulletin* 30 (1): 119-127.

Tinnemans, W. (1994), *Een gouden armband: Een geschiedenis van Mediterrane immigranten in Nederland (1945-1994)*. Utrecht: Nederlands Centrum Buitenlanders.

Van Bemmelen, S.T. (2012), *Good customs, bad customs in North Sumatra: Toba Batak, missionaries and colonial officials negotiate the patrilineal order (1861-1942)*. PhD dissertation, VU University Amsterdam.

Van Dam, P. (2011), *Staat van verzuiling: Over een Nederlandse mythe*. Amsterdam: Wereldbibliotheek.

Van Lier, R. (1977), *Samenleving in een grensgebied: Een sociaal-historische studie van Suriname*. Amsterdam: S. Emmering.

Van de Wiel, A.M. (1974), *Samenleven buiten huwelijk: Over het juridisch lot van concubine en concubijn in binnen- en buitenland*. Deventer: Kluwer.

Van de Wiel, A.M. (1979), 'De relatie in het recht – enkele actualia', *NJB* 54 (6): 109-116.

Van Walsum, S.K. (2008), *The family and the nation: Dutch family migration policies in the context of changing family norms*. Newcastle upon Tyne: Cambridge Scholars Publishing.

Van Walsum, S.K. (2000), *De schaduw van de grens: Het Nederlandse vreemdelingenrecht en de sociale zekerheid van Javaanse Surinamers*. Gouda: Gouda Quint.

Verlegh, D., H. van Maarseveen & S. Korthuis (1984), 'Het huwelijk de rechtsorde uit', *NJB* 59 (28): 857-861.

Verton, P.C. (1971), 'Vreemdelingenbeleid op de weegschaal: deel 2'. *Intermediair* 45.

Vuysje, H. (1997), *Correct: Weldenkend Nederland in de jaren zestig*. Amsterdam: Contact.

Walaardt, T. (2012), *Geruisloos inwilligen: Argumentatie en speelruimte in de Nederlandse asielprocedure, 1945-1994*. Hilversum: Verloren.

Wekker, G. (2001), 'Of mimic men and unruly women: Family, sexuality and gender', in R. Hoefte & P. Meel (eds), *Twentieth century Suriname: Continuities and discontinuities in a new world society*, pp. 174-197. Leiden: KITLV Press.

Willems, W. (2001), *De uittocht uit Indië 1945-1995*. Amsterdam: Bert Bakker.

Willemsen, G. (1988), 'Sociaal-democratie, kolonialisme en dekolonisatie: Suriname 1900-1975', in M. Hisschemöller (ed.), *Een bleek bolwerk: Racisme en politieke strategie*, pp. 119-136. Amsterdam: Pegasus.

# 7 Blood matters

Sarkozy's immigration policies and their gendered impact

*Catherine Raissiguier*

In some countries, like Senegal, Ivory Coast, the two Congos, Togo, Madagascar and the Comoro Islands, 30% to 80% of family documents are fraudulent.
*Dans certains pays, comme le Sénégal, la Côte d'Ivoire, les deux Congo, le Togo, Madagascar ou les Comores, de 30 % à 80% des actes d'états civils sont frauduleux.*[1]
– Adrien Gouteyron

## Introduction

The quote that opens this chapter is from a Senate report published in June 2007. Part of a larger study on the administration of visa applications in French consulates, the report urges consulate agents to focus on the review of visa applications, outsourcing non-essential tasks to the private sector (*en externalisant au secteur privé les tâches annexes*). It also recommends that a common work culture be promoted across the various agencies in charge of controlling immigration in France. The average processing cost for a visa application is €35, concludes Gouteyron, while the average cost for the deportation of an illegal immigrant can reach €1,800. By suggesting that a streamlined and more efficient processing of visa applications would result in a higher rejection rate and savings in the long term, the report clearly places the management of visa applications within the broad politics of immigration control urged by the Sarkozy administration. Nicolas Sarkozy campaigned on a political platform that called for the tightening of immigration policies and promotion of 'chosen' migration (*immigration choisie*), which favours economic migration over family reunification. The 2007 immigration law made good on both promises.

The passage above was drawn from a section of the report titled 'Document Fraud: An Endemic Problem' (*La fraude documentaire, un phénomène endémique*) and has been widely quoted to justify and legitimise the use of genetic testing in the context of immigration. By documenting that some countries are prone to produce fraudulent and unreliable civil documents – in this case, African countries that were part of France's former colonial empire – Gouteyron provided the argument that would enable French legislators to target certain immigrants and 'offer' them differential treatment in the visa application process.

This chapter analyses the 2007 immigration law and its introduction of DNA testing as a move toward the re-inscription of 'blood' and 'bloodlines' into discussions of national belonging in France. This move is neither new nor exceptional within the French republican tradition. However, it is troubling at a time of intensified anti-immigrant sentiment and the normalisation of radical right nationalist agendas throughout Europe. For this reason, it is worthy of closer scrutiny. This chapter's analysis of the 2007 law brings to light striking features of French politics of immigration since the mid-1970s. These features include the contestation of *jus soli* as a determinant of national belonging and inclusion and the particular importance given to families and familial linkages in accessing rights of entry and sojourn in France. Both should not simply be seen as new developments threatening a generous and inclusive French republican tradition in matters of immigrants' rights. Instead, they should be understood as a re-articulation of existing exclusionary threads within that tradition. Rather than viewing these features as aberrations within the French Republic, this chapter presents them as troubling elements that have, in fact, existed within that tradition since its inception (Raissiguier 2010).

The goal of this chapter is threefold. First, it places the 2007 law within the context of a growing contestation, since the mid-1980s, of the principle of *jus soli* (citizenship determined by place of birth). It then looks at the law's DNA provision in relation to the tightening of family reunification procedures during the same period. Finally, by looking at some of the narratives (both textual and visual) that emerged around the law, a brief discussion is provided of changing meanings, in France, of the notions of family and familial linkages.

## Materials and methods

The investigation presented here is based on close readings of legal, political and cultural discourses that preceded and accompanied the introduction of DNA testing for immigration vetting purposes in France. More specifically, narratives are analysed for their gendered meanings and for the ways in which they intersect with discursive processes of racialisation and othering. The argument put forward is that the gradual tightening of immigration policies not only adds to the vulnerability of immigrant women and the children who depend on them, but it also advances deployment of racialised thinking in France. In the process, the radical potential of French republican ideals may become compromised through the discursive and material construction and treatment of subjects who only have access to sub-standard rights and who experience various forms of discrimination on a daily basis.

## *Jus soli*, DNA and the question of origins

This chapter takes issue with political (and scholarly) narratives that expound and promote the idea of a French (republican) exception, in which France – for reasons of history, ideology, demography and military ambition – developed a generous and egalitarian tradition of immigrants' rights and national membership. Such narratives point out that the French nation has constructed itself around a foundational ideal that privileges political will, cultural unity and universalism. 'One becomes French through the learning of a language, through the learning of a culture, through the will to participate in the economic and political life' (Schnapper 1991: 63). Equipped with a rather liberal national legislation, a tight linkage between nationality and citizenship, and a strongly assimilationist culture, France managed to successfully take foreigners and their children into the fold. Analysts emphasising the unique power of inclusion of 'the French model' argue that secular institutions such as schools, the military, employment and workers' unions have functioned (at least until recently) as the socialising and assimilating tools for former groups of foreigners and their children (Schnapper 1989: 99-109). Periodic outbursts of violence and the erosion of regional and ethnic traditions are necessary evils, which must be accepted to reap the benefits of integration, particularly social mobility and meritocracy. The automatic link between nationality and citizenship (much touted as the hallmark of the French republican tradition), however, was not present for French women until 1944 and never in place for France's colonial subjects.[2] Both groups, in fact, were nationals without citizenship.

Other narratives tell a slightly more nuanced story in which French nationality has been established since the 17th century around a complex set of criteria: place of birth (*jus soli*), bloodline (*jus sanguinis*), marital status and duration of residence within the national boundaries (Weil 1996). Prior to the French Revolution, *jus soli* was the dominant criterion for acquisition of French nationality, and it has remained so for most of France's modern history (Brubaker 1993; Weil 1996).

Nationality laws were reformed in 1851, 1889 and 1927 to automatically incorporate 'third generation' and then 'second generation' immigrants into the nation and to ease processes of naturalisation. These measures were implemented to make long-term foreign residents accountable to the French state and to deter the emergence of national separatist activities among immigrant communities (Brubaker 1993; Weil 1996). They were also intended to augment the numbers of French workers and nationals and to increase the pool of army recruits (Brubaker 1993). Inclusion of foreign populations, via 'generous' nationality and natu-ralisation laws, was not accomplished, however, without resistance, and political resentment was often expressed through xenophobic and anti-immigration rhetoric. The law of 1889, for instance, was supported by representatives of French industry, with a vital need for workers, by elected officials from industrial areas seeking to stop foreign competi-tion, and by those in the military who wanted to rebuild a powerful army. Those opposing the change were the defenders of the French race and identity, who were heavily recruited from the French aristocracy.

Xenophobic and anti-immigrant feelings also emerged at the turn of the century, in the inter-war period, and in the more recent con-text of the rise of the National Front Party.[3] Each time, ideologues and politicians questioned the ability of some foreigners and their children to assimilate into French culture. Each time they challenged processes that would turn them into French citizens (Schor 1985; Krulic 1988). These sentiments affected Jews at the end of the 19th century, when immigration from Eastern Europe nearly doubled their numbers in France. They targeted Belgians, Italians and Poles in the 1880s and in the 1930s, when these immigrant groups were perceived as a threat to the full employment of French nationals. More recently they have focused on North and sub-Saharan Africans in the context of postco-lonial immigration, global restructuring and the formation of Europe.

Weil (1996) traces the development of French immigration politics to the 1930s, arguing that, with the exception of the Vichy government and the National Front Party today, the French have always refused to accept the logic of a hierarchy of ethnicities. Weil also suggests, how-ever, that there have been great discrepancies between *l'état de droit* (the laws of the state) and *l'état acteur* (the practices of the state). Even though Weil sees basic egalitarian (republican) principles underlying the French politics of immigration, he cannot but note that the actual means of implementing these principles are often lacking. As a result, in highly charged political contexts, the effects of French immigration laws rarely meet their stated objectives. Instead, they often produce exclusionary practices and differential treatments.

Based on a comparative analysis of France and Germany, Brubaker (1992, 1993) stresses the historico-political character of the French notion of citizenship and nationality. Brubaker does acknowledge, however, the existence of a vital counter-hegemonic ethno-cultural discourse at the turn of the century, in the inter-war period, and since the mid-1980s. He argues that this ethno-cultural understanding of the nation has never, with the exception of the Vichy regime, determined the French politics of citizenship (Brubaker 1993: 23).

Thus, the French Republic has had elements of exclusion based on ethnicity within its relatively generous and liberal understanding of nation and nationality. These exclusionary elements, according to the French historian Noiriel, tend to be de-emphasised because 'the French model' is traditionally contrast to the German one and found 'generous' in comparison. Noiriel (1991) argues that, since the first major law on nationality in 1889, there has always been, in France, a political current willing to deny certain actors the right to acquire French citizenship: 'Since Michelet, in the face of what has often been said, the republican reflection on nationality has therefore been haunted by the question of origins.'[4] The 1993 reform of the nationality code with the Méhaignerie Act, inscribes itself and can only be understood in relation to that current. The Méhaignerie Act, among other things, stipulated that children born in France of foreign parents had to request French nationality instead of accessing it automatically through *jus soli*.[5] The Méhaignerie Act must be seen as the result of a decade-long political campaign launched by the extreme right (but from early on embraced by the republican right). It challenged, starting in the mid-1980s, the ease with which one could become French and contested the precedence of *jus soli* in nationality law (Brubaker 1997; Feldblum 1999; Groupe d'Information 2000; Weil 2002).

The contention here is that the immigration law of 2007, like the Méhaignerie Act of 1993, must be placed in relation to an ethno-cultural current within the French republican tradition. Indeed, with its vote on 23 October 2007, the French Parliament codified genetic testing for immigration vetting purposes into law. The law, promulgated on 20 November 2007, is often referred to as the Hortefeux law. Brice Hortefeux was the Minister of Immigration in the Sarkozy government. The Senate vote was 185 yes, and 136 no, and in the National Assembly 282 yes and 235 no. Socialists voted unanimously against the bill. Under the Hortefeux law, DNA tests may be used by immigration candidates to prove a blood relation with a French person or a legal resident when applying for a long-term visa (over three months) under the legal provision of family reunification. Immigration visas for family reunifications involving children are rather few: 23,000 visas per year are granted for family reunification (9,000 of those go to children). Popular opinion was divided on the issue. A poll published in October in *Le Parisien* indicated that 49% of those surveyed supported the DNA measure compared to 43% who considered it to be 'contrary to the values of the Republic'.[6] Opposition to the law, especially its DNA testing amendment, has been strong among scientists, scholars and civil society. More than 300,000 persons, of all political sensibilities, signed the petition 'Hands off my DNA' (*Touche pas à mon ADN*).[7] (The slogan paraphrases that of the 1984 French anti-racism NGO called 'SOS Racism', *Touche pas à mon pote* or 'Hands off my pal'.) Thousands of others expressed their outrage and opposition to the bill in large demonstrations on 20 October 2007. Even members of the Sarkozy government, former French ministers from across the French political spectrum, and African leaders voiced their concern about the Hortefeux immigration law. Fadela Amara, who became Secretary of State in the Ministry of Urban Affairs in 2007, called the DNA amendment 'disgusting' and threatened to resign over it. Bernard Kouchner, foreign minister under Sarkozy, also expressed concerns. Edouard Balladur, Jean-Pierre Raffarin and Dominique de Villepin – former prime ministers on the right – as well as Lionel Jospin, Pierre Mauroy, Michel Rocard and Laurent Fabius – former prime ministers on the left – came out publicly against the amendment. Aimé Césaire, the poet, Alpha Oumar Konare, the president of the African Union, and Senegalese President Abdoulaye Wade also spoke against the DNA provision.

The National Assembly nonetheless adopted the law on 19 September 2007. It was then sent to be examined by the Senate. In response to mounting criticism against the bill, a bicameral commission – made up of seven representatives from the Senate and the Assembly (*commission mixte paritaire*) – met and introduced modifications to the DNA testing provision. The commission mandated that the DNA tests should be voluntary and paid for by the French government (the original amendment demanded that applicants pay for the tests); the blood relation should be checked only against the mother's DNA (this modification was introduced to avoid unexpected revelations about the actual biological composition of the family); the need for the test should be authorised by a civil court; and informed consent should be mandatory from all concerned persons. Finally, the genetic testing provision in the new immigration law was to be implemented as a pilot to be revisited after 2009.

Following those modifications, the bill was voted into law in October 2007. The French Constitutional Council ruled that the Hortefeux law was in conformance with the French constitution. Several observers noted that the modifications diluted the major substantive provisions of the bill. Despite the changes and the softening of its most radical elements, the Hortefeux law challenged both the equality and the human dignity principles that France claims to expound. Because DNA testing was to be proposed only when documents were believed to have been forged and when consular agents doubted the validity of the documents produced, applicants from certain countries would be especially affected by the measure. As pointed out at the beginning of the chapter, Adrien Gouteryon's report provided the rationalisation for this differential treatment of visa applicants. By maintaining the possibility of genetic testing for one specific group of individuals (Africans), the Hortefeux law established a symbolic demarcation between French nationals and foreigners and between different immigrant groups. In October 2007, the National Consultative Ethics Committee declared that an 'inscription in the law of a biological identification reserved only for foreigners' stands 'in contradiction to the spirit of French law'. In a context of increased anti-immigrant sentiment and heightened securitisation, such a symbolic ranking was feared to fuel existing racialised thinking and practices in France. Selective genetic testing wrote racialised discriminatory practices into French law in order to control immigration.[8]

La haute autorité de lutte contre les discriminations et pour l'égalité (HALDE) – an independent administrative unit created by law in December 2004 to fight against discriminatory practices and promote equality in France – did find the Hortefeux law discriminatory. In addition, HALDE noted that several of its provisions violated international agreements signed by France. In particular, it declared the Hortefeux law in violation of the UN Convention on the Rights of the Child.[9] It also found that the law infringed on an individual's right to privacy and was, therefore, a violation of the European Convention on Human Rights.

In September 2009, the Minister of Immigration, Eric Besson, declared that he would not sign the application decree for the Hortefeux law. Besson argued that the law could not be implemented by the French state for a variety of material and ethical reasons: 'Our consulates are not equipped to run these tests, therefore the procedure would have to take place outside', he explained, underscoring the potential threats to the privacy of the individuals tested.[10] For now, DNA testing for the purpose of family reunification is no longer on the French horizon. However, as indicated by recent debates about a French national identity and the place of Islamic scarves and burqas in France, the issues raised by the near adoption of the provision are still very much present.

## DNA testing, family reunification and gendered precarisation

The DNA testing amendment was initially introduced by the Union for a Popular Movement (UMP) deputy Thierry Mariani. 'When serious doubt on the authenticity of the family relation' has been raised, diplomatic and consular agents can offer the 'opportunity' to the visa applicant to request the comparison at their own expense of 'their genetic prints in order to verify the declared biological parentage'.[11] Critics of the bill, and of the Mariani amendment in particular, argued that genetic testing should not be used to verify family links. Parentage, they remind us, cannot be reduced to blood relations. Socialist opponents, in particular, argued that the bill sets a dangerous political precedent. By using genetics rather than human rights principles, the Hortefeux law, they argued, contradicts the very foundations of the French Republic by using blood as the determining factor of who gets to belong in France. 'This law violates the fundamental principles of the Republic which do not define family and affiliation by biology', said Socialist deputy Arnaud Montebourg. Montebourg also warned that the bill would 'create very serious grounds for discrimination' and bring France into a system of 'biocontrol of individuals' where 'genetics will be used as a tool of the administrative police'.[12]

Opponents of the Hortefeux bill also pointed out that, in France, juridical parentage is not the same as biological relations. A heterosexual married woman, for instance, may be inseminated with the sperm of an unrelated male donor, and that child will be considered her and her husband's legal child. A child adopted by a heterosexual family is legally affiliated with the adoptive parents. Finally, the man who 'recognises' a child within a heterosexual family is not always the child's biological father. Indeed, genetic research today clearly documents that declared (and hence juridical) parentage does not always coincide with biological lineage.[13] As reported in the daily *Le Monde* newspaper:

> In the past 20 years, advances in genetic research have allowed demonstration that illegitimate children are far more numerous that once imagined. According to the scientific journal *The Lancet*, at least 2.7% of birth certificates are 'false', in that they do not match the child's biological parents. Researchers who study genetic disease transmission across generations say they have to exclude 5% to 10% of their samples precisely because of such lineage disparities.[14]

France has forbidden open DNA testing in part because of the porous quality of family borders and 'lineage'. The proposed amendment, hence, violates the French civil code, which forbids the use of genetic prints in establishing parentage unless requested by a magistrate. It also violates the provisions of a recent law on bioethics adopted in August 2004, which stipulates that identification by DNA testing can be conducted only in the context of medical or scientific research. As originally proposed by Mariani, genetic testing for family reunification would have to be conducted under an exception (*dérogation*) to Article 16 of the French Civil Code.[15] It is interesting to note here that such legal restrictions in French law have generated a clandestine European market for DNA tests, with French residents using the internet to access DNA tests in less restrictive countries (e.g., Switzerland, Belgium, Spain).

Brice Hortefeux and other supporters of the bill argue for the value and validity of genetic testing for family reunification vetting purposes, pointing out that France is hardly an innovator.[16] Indeed, 12 European countries, including the UK, use it already. Detractors of the bill counter that these countries have not passed the rigorous legislation on biogenetics that France has, and that in many of them the practice is exceptional.[17] The introduction of genetic testing for family reunification then needs to be placed against the backdrop of tighter border controls within the construction of a 'fortress Europe'.

The increasingly restrictive immigration measures that have marked the last four decades in France (and in the rest of Europe) have been accompanied by a general understanding that immigrants are here to stay. As a result, along with tighter immigration laws, policies that facilitate and help processes of integration of already existing immigrant communities have been put in place. Indeed, all countries in Europe guarantee the long-term settlement and integration of legal immigrants and deny entry to new immigrant workers with low-level qualifications from third-world countries, but they authorise the legal entry of family members (Weil 1995).

In the specific context of France, the Hortefeux law illustrates a steady movement, since the mid-1970s, toward stricter regulations on family reunification. Here, it must be noted that France's politics of immigration have been shaped – at least partially – by the recurring issue of its uniquely slow demographic growth (Spengler 1979; Ronsin 1980). It is against this historical background that questions of matrimony, reproduction and descent (and women's role within them) become central to national debates on immigration, nationality and citizenship.

After the Second World War, during three decades of unprecedented economic growth, French governments facilitated the entry and settlement of European immigrants (first from Germany and Italy and later from Spain and Portugal) and their families. During the first few years after the war, European immigrants were entitled to financial help when they settled with their families. Despite the National Office of Immigration's efforts, family settlement was hampered by post-war housing shortages and marked discrepancies between official immigration policies and on-the-ground recruitment practices.

The number of entries through formal family reunification procedures remained low until 1957. Following implementation of *régularisation sur place* in 1960, which allowed family members to change their status after they had settled in France even if they had entered the country illegally, family reunification numbers began to increase. Family reunification policies were designed with the idea that men (as wage earners) migrate first and women (as housewives) follow. In turn, they have affected women and children in specific and unique ways.

In July 1974, France closed its borders to labour immigration. Since then, the vast majority of legal entries have occurred through family reunification. Because most immigrant women entered the French territory through family reunification, their immigration, citizenship, income-generating power and social benefits are connected to the status of a male family member. In other words, it is the legal status of a husband or father that determines a woman's legal status. The severing of familial and marital relationships can put immigrant women and their daughters in a legal bind vis-à-vis the French state and relegate them to illegality. Legal scholars, grassroots immigrant women's organisations and international agencies have underscored and deplored this constructed legal dependence and vulnerability of immigrant women (Rahal-Sidhoum 1987; Rude-Antoine 1996; Scales-Trent 1999; on the perverse effects of feminist campaigns against the dependent status of marriage migrants, see Schrover in this volume).

In the mid-1970s, against the backdrop of an international economic crisis and alarming rates of unemployment, family immigration in France was suspended, re-authorised, recognised as a basic human right, curtailed and allowed again under certain conditions (Raissiguier 2007). Short-term measures restricting the employment of foreign workers' wives and children had emerged in the mid-1970s and continued until the election of François Mitterrand in 1981. Therefore, policies that let women in but denied them the right to be gainfully employed reinforced immigrant women's dependence on men. Historically, then, legal texts on family reunification, and the ways in which they were applied, created a framework in which immigrant women have lacked legal and economic autonomy. This problem lingers today in spite of fundamental changes introduced by the immigration law of 17 July 1984.

Before 1984, spouses and children entering the country through family reunification were granted a residency permit that mentioned their status as 'family members' and did not include the right to seek employment. Residency and work permits were separate documents. Family members who wished to work for a wage needed to request a work permit once they could document that they had secured a job. The law of 1984 established two types of sojourn or work permits: a temporary sojourn permit (for varied lengths of time that cannot exceed one year) and a residency permit valid for ten years. Both permits entitle the recipient to work legally. Since 1984, family members entering the country through the family reunification procedures obtain the same permit as the resident member; renewal is automatic for those who obtain a ten-year residency permit. For those who receive a temporary permit, renewal is tied to their ability to provide for themselves should the familial link be severed.

The immigration law of 24 August 1993 restricted the conditions of entry and sojourn for immigrants and tightened the conditions for family reunification. Immigrants filing a family reunification request on behalf of family members now had to document at least two years (instead of one) of legal sojourn in France, and their ability to meet appropriate housing and resources requirements. The 1993 law furthermore demanded that family reunification occur in one step. Immigrants were prohibited from bringing family members incrementally over time, as their social standing improves and they become better able to meet the necessary housing and income requirements. The Pasqua laws of 1993 prohibited the entry of polygamous families into France through family reunification (only one wife and her children can be brought into the country through the procedure). It also prohibited the renewal of residency permits of foreigners in polygamous situations.

The 1993 law increased the legal vulnerability of immigrant women. It made legal family reunification harder to achieve and stipulated that, in the case of divorce or estrangement within a year of the issuance of residency papers, the papers could be withdrawn for the foreign spouse. If women are determined to be in violation of immigration law, they can be deported to their country of origin. Mothers of French children are protected from such deportations under French law, but as undocumented migrants, they are unable to work legally or to claim and receive certain social and health benefits. Since the passage of the 1993 law, accessing the right to family reunification has become complicated, expensive and time-consuming. As a result, for many, this form of legal immigration is no longer within reach. In this context, many have become undocumented, swelling the numbers of the French *sans-papiers. Sans-papiers*, which literally means 'without papers', have organised since the mid-1990s against this constructed illegality (clandestinisation) and for their collective regularisation (Raissiguier 2010).

In spite of improvements, the 1998 Chevènement law did little to diminish the dependence of women on their spouse's legal status. The law introduced the notion of 'familial and private life' as one of the criteria that would be taken into account for legalising undocumented immigrants. Theoretically, the law opened up the notion of 'family' to include bonds outside those of matrimony, such as common law marriage (*concubinage*) and civil unions of straight and gay couples. Polygamous family members who entered the country prior to 1993 can have their residency papers renewed, as long as they document that they are no longer bound by a polygamous union and are no longer cohabitating. This specific measure has put some women in extremely vulnerable positions, especially given the limited availability of affordable housing.

This brief analysis of family reunification in France since the mid-1970s documents a steady trend towards the tightening of these provisions, despite France's recognition that the right to live with one's family is indeed a basic human right. It also illustrates the ways in which immigration laws often put women and the children who depend on them in vulnerable and precarious situation.

### Reconfiguring French families and France as family through 'blood' metaphors

While the human rights weaknesses and the racist effects of the new law have been discussed at great length in France, little attention has been directed towards the gender and sexual implications of a law that, after all, focuses on blood, bloodlines and descent. It is also important to note the rise of a dominant discourse in France that systematically links certain immigrant youths to violence and insecurity.[18] French sociologist Muchielli traces the emergence of the insecurity thread in French media to the early 1990s. Needless to say, the mantra that links insecurity and immigration has paved the way for the rise of the political right in France and, within it, the successful rise to power of Sarkozy (Muchielli 2001). This discourse was spread by a handful of 'experts' and media pundits and has now become common sense across the political spectrum. Indeed, according to Muchielli, by the mid-1990s both the political right and the left 'appeared to have accepted that many of the problems [of insecurity and allegedly increasing violence] were due to unresolved issues of cultural difference and social alienation.'[19]

In particular, Xavier Raufer and Alain Bauer were regularly featured in various media outlets (especially the right-leaning newspaper *Le Figaro*). They emerged as key architects of a discourse of fear and hatred that has great currency in France today.[20]

This last section of this chapter looks at the often-overlooked subtext of the immigration and insecurity discourse that underwrites the DNA provision of the Hortefeux law. Directly following the social unrest and violent outbursts in the fall of 2005, Sarkozy (then Minister of the Interior) and other right-wing voices blamed polygamous families for the violent behaviour of African male youths from the *banlieues*. Sarkozy himself declared to the French weekly *L'Express* that the youths responsible for the urban violence were 'French by law' but that 'polygamy and the [lack of] acculturation of a certain number of families [made] it more difficult to integrate a French youth of African descent than a French youth of another descent'. Bernard Accoyer (who is also known for his homophobic comments during the *pacte civil de solidarité* debates), then the president of the UMP group in the National Assembly, declared on the French radio station RTL that polygamy 'was certainly one of the causes' of the social trouble. Polygamy, he added, 'is the incapacity to provide the education necessary to an organised society; a society with norms'. Finally, linking the 2005 urban riots with family reunification gone wild, he stated, 'For us to be able to integrate them [the male youths], we need to keep their numbers below our integration threshold'[21] (compare this with the term 'absorption capacity' used by Dutch politicians, see Walaardt in this volume).

Here the spectre of polygamy and of different family structures is conjured up to racialise a particular group of immigrants and to demonise a group of French youths. African mothers (and fathers) are set apart in their incapacity to acculturate and, as a result, to reign in their violent sons. The particular and dangerous violence of these young men is also constructed through the discourse of the abused woman and the over-controlled sister within Muslim and North African immigrant communities. Fadela Amara and her organisation *Ni Putes Ni Soumises* have unfortunately greatly contributed to this very problematic construction.[22]

The discourse of blood is a discourse about kinship and family, but it is also about sexuality and gender. The impulse to exclude certain families from the French nation can also be traced in the debates surrounding French civil unions and more specifically what the French call *homoparentalité* (the capacity for queers to become parents, in particular through artificial insemination and adoption). The parliamentary debates that preceded the passage of the *pacte civil de solidarité*

or French civil union clearly demonstrate strong attachment to heteronormative family structures within republican France. For this chapter's purpose, I simply briefly engage an interesting visual narrative that
connects DNA testing, the Hortefeux law and queer politics in France.
As noted in Michael Petrelis' blog, in September 2007, both the liberal
*San Francisco Chronicle* and the conservative *Washington Times* ran
similar stories about the Hortefeux bill and the opposition it encountered in France.[23] Both newspapers used images of an ACT UP Paris protest against the Hortefeux bill without covering either the demonstration or the specific demands made by the French queer organisation.
On his blog, Petrelis commends the ACT UP Paris activists, but does not
provide any analysis of this peculiar visual illustration of French anti-
DNA law demonstrations by US media. The ACT UP protest focused on
the plight of immigrants suffering from HIV/AIDS, although this was
not addressed in either of the newspaper articles. ACT UP Paris activists were agitating to render visible the plight of queer immigrants, who
will have to live alone if family reunification policy continues to be
tightened and who face deportation under the politics of deportation
quotas deployed under the Sarkozy regime.

Queers in France, like certain immigrants, are often imagined outside of national boundaries. This is particularly true when it comes to
discussions of marriage, family and parenthood. Writing about an earlier immigration law, Eric Fassin, commented in *Le Monde*:

> Indeed, to limit family reunification while casting systematic doubt
> on mixed marriages, as the law of 2006 does on the control of the
> validity of marriages, is to define the immigrant without family, but
> also the family without the immigrant. In other words, when the right
> of blood takes over, it is not only that the Other is being racialised:
> the law slowly reinvents France as a national family; it tends to invent
> French nationals by descent (*Français de souche*).[24]

Building on Fassin's analysis, I would add that when the right of
blood takes over, the law defines the immigrant and the queer without
family, but also the family (and the nation) without the immigrant and
the queer.

Current discussions of immigration in France are replete with sen-
sational narratives about gender and sexuality. The wearing of Islamic
scarves, polygamy, forced marriages, female genital cutting and the
sexual victimisation of young Muslim women, for instance, receive
intense and recurring attention in the French media (compare Cederberg, Andreassen and Schrover in this volume). The impact of these

narratives within French culture, however, has elicited little scholarly attention. Yet sex and gender constitute important threads within anti-immigrant discourses that present Africans and Muslims as undesirable immigrants in France. Nor is the deployment of sex and gender new within discussions of national identity, immigration and racial or ethnic communities. The fact that victimised women and girls and violent men are conjured up to capture the cultural distance between the French and their postcolonial others must, therefore, be read as a redeployment of distant and yet singularly familiar discourses about the fatherland (*la patrie*), the nation and the Republic.

## Conclusion

Because of the polemics generated by the DNA testing provision of the Hortefeux law, other problematic aspects of the law came under scrutiny. Particularly concerning was that the law called for an evaluation of the French language skills of visa applicants. It also asked host immigrant families to sign a contract stipulating specific conditions of hosting and integration (*contrat d'accueil et intégration*). Furthermore, it required sponsoring families to demonstrate that they earned at least the minimum wage (133% of the minimum wage for families of six or more). On the positive side, the new law instituted unlimited sojourn and residency permits for legal immigrants renewing their ten-year permit.

In addition to DNA testing, the law introduced the use of biometrics for would-be immigrants. Article 62 of the law required that foreigners voluntarily returning home (with financial support of the French state), have their photograph and digital fingerprints taken and stored. This provision was introduced with the aim to fight fraud and make it more difficult for these individuals to make their way back into France. Both the increased use of biometrics and the introduction of DNA testing in the Hortefeux law make sense within the broad immigration control logic and generalised suspicion toward certain foreigners promulgated by Senator Gouteyron, whose report opened this essay.

The Hortefeux law is not unique. It is simply the French flavour of a broader European trend in immigration policy (compare Van Walsum, Jones & Legêne in this volume). An EU administrative memorandum requesting the tightening of family reunification policies, for instance, was issued in 2003. The memorandum stipulates that it is appropriate to demand that immigrants joining family members respect national 'norms' and demonstrate a working knowledge of the language of the host country. There has also been a levelling of asylum policies across Europe. The introduction of DNA testing (even if voluntary) in France is simply another piece of the larger European politics of dissuasion of family (and humanitarian) immigration in favour of economic immigration. Sarkozy implemented those policies first during his tenure as Minister of the Interior and later as president of the French Republic.

This chapter discussed the Hortefeux immigration law in relation to the growing contestation of the principle of *jus soli* and the tightening of family reunification procedures in France. The gradual tightening of immigration policies since the mid-1970s has had specific gendered effects on immigrant women and the children who depend on them. It has added to the precarisation and the clandestinisation of many of them. By introducing the tracing of affiliation through 'blood' for some immigrants, the 2007 immigration law inscribed differential treatment of people into French immigration policy. It also anchored a movement toward the racialisation of certain immigrant communities through the discursive construction of some immigrants as unable to assimilate into the French cauldron. Finally, it built on and deepened racist and heteronormative understandings of the 'family' in France.

## Notes

1   All translations from French to English are mine unless indicated otherwise. Adrien Gouteyron is a senator and a member of the *Union pour un Mouvement Populaire* (UMP). A. Gouteyron, *Trouver une issue au casse-tête des visas, Rapport d'information No 353 de M. Adrien Gouteyron, fait au nom de la commission des finances, du contrôle budgétaire et des comptes économiques de la Nation* (27 June 2007). www.senat.fr/notice-rapport/2006/r06-353-notice.html (accessed on 22 March 2010).
2   For a detailed discussion of citizenship and nationality in the context of 'French Algeria' see Stora (1992); Wihtol de Wenden (1994: 41-59).
3   An extreme-right nationalist political party founded by Jean-Marie Le Pen in 1972. Once in the margins of the French political spectrum, it is now a force to be reckoned with, as demonstrated by Le Pen's strong showing in the 2002 presidential election. The National Front's continued success can be seen in the 2010 regional election results.
4   Germany has granted nationality (until 2000) on the basis of *jus sanguini*.
5   The requirement that these youths request the French nationality was abrogated by the Guigou law of 1998.
6   Cited in Agence Presse, 'French Parliament Approves DNA Immigration Bill,' *France24*, 24 October 2007, www.france24.com (accessed 15 October 2009).
7   For the petition and the list of those who signed it, see www.touchepasamonadn.com (accessed 23 March 2010).

8 For an interesting NGO intervention on this topic, see Médecins du Monde, 'Pauvreté-immigration' *Le Monde* (25 October 2007).

9 Article 2 provides for the obligation of states to respect and ensure the rights set forth in the Convention to each child within their jurisdiction without discrimination of any kind.

10 Damien Bouhours, *Le Petit Journal*, 16 September 2009.

11 Anne Chemin and Laetita Van Eeckhout, 'Tests ADN pour certains candidats à l'immigration: Des tests génétiques pour le regroupement familial, *Le Monde*, 14 September 2007.

12 Agence Presse, 'French Parliament Approves DNA Immigration Bill'.

13 Axel Kahn and Didier Sicard, 'Filiation et regroupement familial,' *Le Monde*, 17 September 2007.

14 Chemin and Van Eeckhout, 'Tests ADN.'

15 Chemin and Van Eeckhout, 'Tests ADN.'

16 See Brice Hortefeux 'Nous avons apporté six garanties supplémentaires aux tests ADN', *Le Monde*, 10 October 2007.

17 See Digital Civil Rights in Europe, 'Update on DNA and biometrics in French immigration law', *Digi-Gram*, 5.20 (24 October 2007). It is important to note here that immigration DNA test results are required for most visa applications involving family who immigrate to the USA.

18 See Pam Moore, 'Media demonization, "la fabrique de la haine" and *Le Figaro*'. http://wjfms.ncl.ac.uk/MooresWJ.htm (Accessed 25 March 2010).

19 Moores, 'Media demonization'.

20 Muchielli has challenged the claims, the methodology and even the academic credentials of these so-called experts who published the best-seller *Violences et insécurités urbaines* (Paris 1998).

21 Bernard Accoyer, 'Le Sénat a adopté le projet de loi sur la `maîtrise de l'immigration" *Le Monde*, 5 October 2008.

22 See Catherine Raissiguier, 'Muslim women in France: Impossible subjects?' Darkmatter (2008) www.darkmatter101.org/site/2008/05/02/muslim-women-in-france-impossible-subjects.

23 The *San Francisco Chronicle*'s story ('France seeks to enforce deportation quotas for illegal aliens') appeared on Saturday 22 September 2007. *The Washington Times* ran its story ('Anti-illegals bills sparks uproar in France') on Thursday, 20 September 2007. Both articles and the images that accompany them can be accessed online through links on Petrelis' blog: http://mpetrelis.blogspot.com/search?q=act+up+paris.

24 Eric Fassin, 'Statistiques de la discorde,' *Le Monde*, 6 October 2007.

## References

Brubaker, R. (1997), *Citoyenneté et nationalité en France et en Allemagne*. Paris: Belin.

Brubaker, R. (1993), 'De l'immigré au citoyen: Comment le *jus soli* s'est imposé en France, à la fin du xixe siècle', *Actes de la recherche en Sciences Sociales* 99 (Septembre): 3-26.

Brubaker, R. (1992), *Citizenship and nationhood in France and Germany.* Cambridge: Harvard University Press.

Feldblum, M. (1999), *Reconstructing citizenship: The politics of nationality reform and immigration in contemporary France.* Albany: SUNY Press.

Groupe d'information et de soutien des immigrés (2000), *Guide de la nationalité française.* Paris: Syros.

Krulic, J. (1988), 'L'immigration et l'identité de la France, mythes et réalités', *Pouvoirs* 47: 31-43.

Noiriel, G. (1991), *La tyrannie du national: Le droit d'asile en Europe, 1793-1993.* Paris: Calmann-Levy (Collection Les temps qui courent).

Rahal-Sidhoum, S. (1987), *Eléments d'analyse de statut socio-juridique des femmes immigrées en vue d'un statut pour l'autonomie des femmes immigrées en France.* Paris: Convention CFI/FNDVA.

Raissiguier, C. (2010), *Reinventing the Republic: Gender, immigration and citizenship in France.* Stanford: Stanford University Press.

Raissiguier, C. (2007), 'French immigration laws: The sans-papières' perspectives', in T. Spijkerboer & S. van Walsum (eds), *Women and immigration law in Europe: New variations of feminist themes,* pp. 204-222. Abington and New York: Glass House Publishers.

Ronsin, F. (1980), *La Grève des ventres: Propagande néo-malthusienne et baisse de la natalité française (xixe-xxe siècles).* Paris: Aubier Montaigne.

Rude-Antoine, E. (1996), 'Des épouses soumises à des régimes particuliers', *Migrants-Formation* 105: 45-61.

Scales-Trent, J. (1999), 'African women in France: Citizenship, family, and work', *Brooklyn Journal of International Law* xxiv (3): 705-737.

Schnapper, D. (1991), *La France de l'intégration: Sociologie en 1990.* Paris: Gallimard.

Schnapper, D. (1989), '*La France de l'intégration* and "Un pays d'immigration qui s'ignore"', *Le Genre Humain* (February): 99-109.

Schor, R. (1985), *L'opinion française et les* étrangers. *1919-1939.* Paris: Publications de la Sorbonne.

Spengler, J. (1979), *France faces depopulation.* Durham: Duke University Press.

Stora, B. (1992), *Aide-Mémoire de l'immigration Algérienne: Chronologie, bibliography.* Paris: L'Hartmattan.

Weil, P. (2002), *Qu'est-ce qu'un Français? Histoire de la nationalité française depuis la révolution.* Paris: Gallimard.

Weil, P. (1996), 'Nationalities and citizenships: The lessons of the French experience for Germany and Europe', in D. Cesarani & M. Fulbrook (eds), *Citizenship, Nationality & Migration in Europe,* pp. 74-87. London: Routledge.

Weil, P. (1995), 'L'Europe a-t-elle une politique de l'immigration?', *Working Paper 105.* Barcelona: Institut d'Études Politiques.

Wihtol de Wenden, C. (1994), 'Le cas français', in B. Faiga, C. Wihtol de Wenden & K. Leggewie (eds), *De l'immigration à l'intégration en Allemagne,* pp. 41-59. Paris: Cerf.

# 8 Gender, inequality and integration

## Swedish policies on migrant incorporation and the position of migrant women

*Maja Cederberg*

## Introduction: Gender, migration and policy effects

As feminist migration scholars have highlighted, in contrast to gender-blind conceptions of migration, women have formed, and continue to form, a significant part of migratory flows. Furthermore, the conditions that structure migrants' options, positions and experiences in both sending and receiving countries are gendered (see, e.g., Phizacklea 1983; Morokvasic 1984; Kofman 1999; Kofman et al. 2000). Cultural constraints, in particular, related to dominant ideas about male and female roles in the private and public spheres are underpinned by, and help to reproduce, gendered power relations and inequalities. These affect the nature and extent of men's and women's economic, social and political participation in sending countries and imply differences in their experiences and resources held, in turn impacting upon the migration and settlement process. Furthermore, while there are tendencies to emphasise the (gendered) cultural baggage that migrants bring with them to Western 'host' societies, gender inequalities in the West also continue to shape the position and experience of both migrant and non-migrant women.

Lack of attention to gender differences has meant that migration and migrant incorporation policies in receiving countries have often not considered their potentially gendered effects, particularly ways in which policies may disadvantage women. Migration research has shown that policies regarding asylum, labour migration and family migration have set different conditions for the migration and settlement of men and women (see, e.g., Boyd 1999; Kofman 1999, 2004, 2005, 2007; Kontos 2009; Piper 2006). The pitfalls of a universal, 'gender-neutral', conception of rights have also been underscored in feminist literature on citizenship. This literature has illustrated, amongst other things, that gendered (and racialised) individuals have different levels of access to rights and privileges, and they are differently able to enjoy, in practice, the rights they are granted on paper (see, e.g., Pateman 1988; Boris 1995; Siim 2000; Lister 2003; Yuval-Davis 1997).

This chapter considers the effects of Swedish policies regarding migrant incorporation on the position of migrant women. The term 'incorporation' is used to refer to the range of policies that are designed to facilitate migrants' settlement in the host society. Although the term 'integration' is often generically used to refer to such policies, in this chapter that term is used only in reference to policies that themselves use the term, in order to emphasise the particular values and assumptions involved. The chapter starts with a historical overview of Swedish policy on migrant incorporation. It then discusses the gendered effects of different policy approaches in two key dimensions: the cultural and the socio-economic.

In regard to the cultural dimension, the chapter examines the shift we have seen from a focus on cultural group rights towards a more individual approach emphasising the need for 'integration' and social cohesion. The gendered aspects and potential effects of different policy approaches are considered, as well as the debates that have surrounded them. Insofar as 'other' gender roles and relations are used to represent cultural difference and 'authenticity', this has had particular implications for migrant women, whose imagined difference has been used to both defend and question policies promoting cultural diversity. When it comes to the second dimension, the socio-economic one, the focus is on rights and opportunities related to employment and social welfare. While some policies target newcomers, most affect the broader labour market and welfare policy areas. Here, the shift has entailed greater labour market deregulation and an increasingly restricted welfare regime. Because such policies have been introduced in the context of a labour market and society that is divided along lines of both gender and ethnicity (as well as class), their impacts have been felt, in particular, by groups that were already in a disadvantaged position, including certain groups of migrant women.

## Materials and methods

The chapter draws on two main sources: an analysis of Swedish policies on migrant incorporation undertaken as part of a research project on racism and ethnic discrimination in Sweden (Cederberg 2006), and the Swedish component of the EU-funded project FeMiPol, on the integration process of female migrants in selected European countries (Kontos 2009). Aside from an analysis of policy changes since the mid-

1970s, both research projects included expert interviews (e.g., with policymakers, civil servants, and NGO and trade union representatives),
and biographical narrative interviews with refugees from Somalia and
Bosnia (Cederberg 2006) and with migrant women from a range of
countries outside of Europe (Kontos 2009). Also used were policy documents and official reports, as well as secondary sources (including empirical research) in which different policies and policy approaches are
evaluated or assessed.

## From group rights to individual responsibility:
## A brief history of Swedish policy on migrant incorporation

In 1975, Sweden adopted its first policy concerned particularly with
migrant incorporation. It was based on the three principles of equality, freedom of choice and partnership.[1] The goal of equality had been
established earlier by the 1968 immigration policy, which emphasised
the importance of equal rights and opportunities for migrants and non-
migrants in the labour market and in wider society. The 1975 policy
asserted the possibility of retaining one's cultural heritage as a precondition for such equality (as proposed in the literature on cultural recognition and cultural citizenship rights, see, e.g., Taylor 1994; Kymlicka
1995). In turn, freedom of choice was said to refer precisely to the individual's right to choose whether 'to retain and develop their original
cultural and linguistic identity'.[2] Finally, partnership implied cooperation and mutual solidarity between the majority Swedish population
and different migrant groups. In short, the initial policy emphasised the
equal rights of migrants and non-migrants, including cultural rights.
It developed in a context in which the majority of migrants were labour migrants, and it was strongly related to social democratic ideology, together with the corporatist structure and, particularly, the strong
position of the trade unions (Ålund & Schierup 1991; Soininen 1999;
Schierup, Hansen & Castles 2006).
    Although the three principles of the 1975 policy were retained for
some time, and while policy documents continue to emphasise equality and diversity as the basis for migrant incorporation, a number of
changes were made over time. These relate to both migrant-specific
policies and to other policies that impact on migrants. By the mid-
1980s, some limits were introduced to the freedom to choose one's cultural identity, which at this point, it was emphasised, had to be contained within the limits of the core laws, norms and values of Sweden[3]
(Borevi 2002, 2004). The context is significant, and in policy docu-

ments from the 1980s and early 1990s the changing nature of immigration is emphasised in arguments for revising the initial policy.[4] In the 1970s, migrants came primarily from other Nordic countries, Eastern and Southern Europe and Turkey, while more recent migrants arrived from South America, Asia, the Middle East and Africa. Furthermore, there was a shift from labour migrants to refugees and family migrants. Against this backdrop, both greater cultural differences and the majority population's fear of difference were put forward in support of a more limited 'freedom of choice'.[5] However, the policy documents present this less as a change and more as a clarification, due to the fact that the 1975 policy had failed to specify the types of claims that could be made under the 'freedom of choice' banner, and more problematic claims had been made to cultural rights (that were less amenable to Swedish norms and values) than had been envisaged by the policy.

Although policy was gradually transformed in the 1980s, an explicit shift took place in the 1990s, when the government stated that it had made a mistake in emphasising difference and opting for migrant-specific policies. It proposed instead that the future would be one of *integration*. A 1997/1998 policy document, 'Sweden, the Future and Diversity: From Immigrant Policy to Integration Policy',[6] signalled a change from a targeted to a general approach to migrant incorporation, and also from an emphasis on groups to individual rights and responsibilities (Geddes 2003: 118-122). This was the point at which the immigration and integration policy areas were separated. The shift was meant to imply that aside from some specific measures to support newcomers after their arrival, integration policy would be aimed at society as a whole. Hence, the term integration here is conceived as different from assimilation (denounced since the 1975 policy). The idea was not that 'they' should integrate into 'our' society, but that society should be reshaped to suit the needs of all of its members: in other words, in a process of mutual accommodation.[7]

Despite taking a step back from the previous, more wholehearted, endorsement of cultural diversity, the 1997/1998 document, nonetheless, underlines the value of such diversity. Another core feature was its emphasis on ethnic equality, particularly in the labour market. Although the principle of equality had long been central in Swedish policy, concerns had arisen about increasingly high levels of unemployment amongst migrants. Discrimination was also attracting further attention. Key measures proposed to solve these problems were improvement of the system for validating foreign qualifications, upgrading the complementary education system for cases where training was needed to acquire a license to practice in Sweden, and expanded protection against discrimination. Finally, emphasis was placed on what had in fact already been an important feature of Swedish policy in this area, namely, the idea that the general employment and social welfare policy framework should provide a broad basis for equality and integration.[8] As such, in order to assess different approaches to migrant incorporation, we need to go beyond migrant-specific policy, and take into account broader developments, in particular, regarding the labour market, employment and social welfare.

During the 1980s, the renowned Swedish social model, characterised by a universal welfare policy, corporatism and centralised wage bargaining, as well as the political and ideological dominance of social democracy, started to be revised. The Swedish government sought to give the market more rein while to some extent cutting back on welfare provisions. These changes were part of a shifting political-economic scenario in Sweden, in step with wider global trends and, particularly, their expression in the European context. The economic crisis of the early 1990s hastened these trends, including labour market deregulation and moves towards a less comprehensive welfare regime (Soininen 1999; Schierup, Hansen & Castles 2006).

It is important to note here that during the same period, a number of structural changes took place in the Swedish labour market, as part of the transformation from an industrial to a 'post-industrial' economy. This implied a need for different (and, to some extent, higher-level) skills, which significantly impacted migrants who had come to work in the industrial sector when it was in need of labour. It also affected more recently arrived migrants, as the changing nature of the labour market meant that it was much more difficult for them to get 'a foot in' (the changing nature of immigration flows also played a role here, which will be discussed later in this chapter). The increased importance of 'Sweden-specific' skills were amongst the factors affecting migrants' labour market entry, as well as the rise of informal recruitment practices, in which a greater role was played by social contacts and networks (Bevelander & Lundh 2007; Behtoui 2008; Behtoui & Neergard 2010; Cederberg 2012). Aside from the industrial sector, jobs had been lost in the public sector too, which impacted women in particular (Bevelander 1999, 2005; De los Reyes 2000; Integrationsverket 2006; Schierup, Hansen & Castles 2006).

This broader social and political-economic context accounted for much of the focus of the 1997/1998 integration policy. Exclusion and segregation along ethnic lines was seen as a growing problem, but the government was anxious to counteract simplistic solutions to complex problems, especially in the form of the far-right, anti-immigrant sentiment that had flourished in the early 1990s (Borevi 1998). However, notwithstanding its strong emphasis on mutual accommodation and combating discrimination, the 1997/1998 policy was criticised ten years later by an enquiry into the position of migrants and ethnic minority groups in various societal areas. That enquiry found that despite the strong focus on equality and anti-discrimination, too little had been done to tackle structural forms of discrimination and inequality (SOU 2006: 79).

If 1997/1998 was an important moment in Swedish policy on migrant incorporation, the next took place ten years later, after the social democrats lost power to a centre-right coalition in 2006. The new coalition parties had been critical of the social democrats' integration policy in the opposition,[9] and they introduced what was presented as a major policy shift. This was signalled not least by closing down the Swedish Integration Board, which had been established by the previous government in 2000. A central feature of the centre-right government's approach to migrant incorporation has been a strong focus on employment as the key to wider social integration. Emphasis is on increasing migrants' ability to utilise their existing skills and qualifications in the labour market and on speeding up newcomers' entrance in paid employment. Another central feature concerns language and culture, particularly migrants learning the Swedish language, combined with the promotion of social cohesion through a shared set of norms and values.[10]

In fact, employment has been seen as a fundamental basis for migrant incorporation since the emergence of such policies in Sweden. This is underscored not least by the emphasis long placed on ethnic equality in the labour market. But if the idea that employment is central is not in itself new, the particular approach taken by the current government is distinct, along with the political-economic context in which the idea is now being implemented. Concerning the language and culture component, neither the expectation that migrants learn the language nor the argument for shared norms and values is particularly new. However, the broader discourse within which the current policy is situated is to some extent distinct in that there is greater focus on demands and (individual) responsibilities. In short, the transformation of both the socio-economic and cultural aspects of migrant incorporation and related policies must be understood in relation to the wider shift towards a neo-liberal approach and discourse (Schierup & Ålund 2011).

## From multiculturalism to social cohesion and the (persistent) gendered production of cultural difference

As noted, the 1975 policy was based on principles of equality and co-operation, along with granting newcomers the right to retain their cultural distinctiveness. Moreover, the corporatist tradition in Sweden influenced the shape of early migrant incorporation policies, and social identities were initially conceived largely in terms of collective experiences (Ålund & Schierup 1991, 1993). This corresponded well to the multiculturalist principle of giving rights and voices to different national and ethnic groups, enabling those to reproduce and represent themselves. One particular expression of this concerns the importance granted to migrant associations. These were seen as playing a key role in relation to the 'freedom of choice' principle, but also as channels through which particular interests could be expressed and represented (Borevi 2004). Multiculturalism in the Swedish case thus implied collective and representative rights for migrants, to be exercised through their national and ethnic groups (Schierup, Hansen & Castles 2006). It is, however, worth noting that a simultaneous 'Swedishisation' process took place through the conditions set for associations applying for state funding (Ålund & Schierup 1991).

The policy of leaving minority groups alone to arrange their own, 'traditional' intra-familial and community relations with limited interference from the majority society was the target of much critique. The underlying conception of 'cultures' as bounded and fixed entities, which Schrover (2010) refers to as 'cultural freezing', was challenged, and potentially damaging effects on less powerful members of ethnic minority groups were highlighted. The gendered implications, in particular, have been emphasised, in relation also to the fact that what was often regarded as 'authentic' about cultures were gender roles and family relations. Furthermore, the idea of representing migrants' interests through ethnic associations was problematised, by asking who speaks for whom and whose voice is silenced in the process, with again, the gendered effects emphasised (Anthias & Yuval-Davis 1992; Yuval-Davis 1997). In the Swedish debate on multiculturalism, some have argued that the principle of cultural group rights has implied the exclusion of migrant women from the wider policy of gender equality on which Sweden prides itself (Daragahi 2002; see also De los Reyes et al. 2003).

While the gendered implications are significant, they do not affect migrant or ethnic minority women uniformly. Individuals are differently positioned within migrant and ethnic communities, depending not only on gender but also on their social class and other factors that play a part in shaping intra-group relations and hierarchies. Furthermore, there are differences between (and within) ethnic minority groups both in regard to their cultural traditions and practices, and in terms of how they are positioned within wider society. That latter, in turn, sets the conditions for the 'integration' prospects of individual migrants, but it also impacts upon intra-group relations and dynamics. De los Reyes (2003) relates an account of young immigrant girls in Sweden who are at risk of being exposed to what is commonly referred to as 'honour culture'. Gendered violence and other oppressive cultural practices within minority groups must be considered in the context of a segregated and discriminatory society, where intercultural exchanges are limited and where the powerlessness of individuals in the majority society may result in particular expressions of power within minority communities. Such an approach helps to counterbalance arguments that tend to culturalise such social problems (as discussed by Ålund 1999; Ålund & Schierup 1991). In this chapter, by contrast, they are regarded as complex outcomes of ethnic discrimination, inequality and segregation, in combination with particular intra-group relations and practices.

Gender oppression within minority communities and the tendency to accept or to turn a blind eye to it forms one important line of criticism of multiculturalism. Another has to do with the further obstacles to gender and ethnic equality posed by particular representations that have accompanied accounts of cultural pluralism. Representations of 'other' women and gender relations are especially noteworthy in the case of Sweden, where the discourse on gender equality forms an important part of a Swedish 'imagined community', and as such provides 'a basis for drawing and marking borders not only towards other countries, but also towards the immigrant population in Sweden' (Molina & De los Reyes 2003: 306, my translation). The production of a dichotomy between a (gender-equal) Swedish 'self' and a (gender-oppressed) minority 'other' is facilitated by the tendency to homogenise and generalise about 'others'. This is part of the bounded conception of 'cultures' noted earlier, in relation to which elements of difference and resistance are marginalised (Ålund 1991, 1999). Regarding representations of migrant women, in particular, the popular image portrays them as isolated, passive and as victims of 'patriarchal cultures' (Brune 1998, 2003).

This arguably has impacted the incorporation of migrant women into the Swedish labour market. The policy of equality from 1968 to 1975 did not prohibit development of an ethnically (and gender) segmented labour market (Schierup & Paulsson 1994). Migrant women have, in fact, been disproportionately represented in jobs associated with lower skill levels, poorer pay and less social status (Knocke 1986, 1994, 1999, 2001). Research points towards a range of factors under-lying their position, including differences in human capital, structural features of the Swedish labour market, and ethnic and gender discrimi-nation (Bevelander 1999, 2005; De los Reyes 2000, 2007; SCB 2009; Schierup, Hansen & Castles 2006; SOU 2006: 59, 2006: 60). With regard to that last, Knocke (1994, 1999) argues that the popular image of 'the immigrant woman' as passive, oppressed and uneducated has played a significant role in shaping migrant women's labour market incorpora-tion.

Thus far, this chapter has argued that there are two key gendered effects of multicultural policies. First, the 'leave them alone' policy implied by multiculturalism may have contributed to the reproduction of unequal gender relations. Second, a gendered conception of 'other-ness' that has accompanied multiculturalism, in particular, gendered imagery that forms part of stereotyped representations of 'other' cul-tures, may have impacted on the lives and opportunities of migrant women. Importantly, these effects may not automatically disappear with a shift away from multiculturalism as a policy approach. In regard to the first, I have emphasised the importance of not reducing all gen-dered effects of ethnic boundary-making to multicultural policies per se, but to also consider factors such as ethnic discrimination and segre-gation. As to the latter, the gendered production of difference appears fairly consistent over time: whether it is used to promote ethnic diver-sity or to warn against the oppressive and divisive effects of too much diversity, representations of 'other' women continue to play a central role in Swedish 'integration' policy, as we shall see.

With regard to the gradual transformation of the cultural dimension of migrant incorporation policies, representations of gender roles and family relations in 'other' cultures have been important. In the mid-1980s, when a need was proposed to specify the boundaries of the 'free-dom of choice' principle, cultural differences in approaches to the rights of women and children were highlighted.[11] As part of the move from a promotion of minority ethnic groups and practices to individuals' inte-gration into the majority society (in 1997/1998), examples underscored as potentially damaging to individuals were similarly gendered: tradi-tional roles prohibiting women from accessing paid work, along with gendered violence and oppression.

In recent years, much of the debate about gender and 'integration' has centred on particular cultural practices often associated with Islam and Muslim communities, including female genital mutilation, forced marriages and 'honour culture'. That last became an important political

issue in the early 2000s, following two 'honour murders' that received
abundant mass media coverage. Among the policy proposals made at
that time was a citizenship test, though this faced much criticism from
the government at the time and was not introduced. However, much
of the surrounding discourse continued to influence the debates, as
well as the policy approach adopted by the Liberal Party, which led the
early 2000s debate from the opposition and since 2006 has played a key
role in forming policies in government. Indeed, gender has become an
important feature of integration policy, through the emphasis is on the
risks posed to women by insufficient cultural integration of (certain)
migrant and minority ethnic groups. As such, the discourse has arguably developed in a manner that not only regards migrant women as
'other' to Swedish (and more broadly to Western) culture and society,
but also increasingly as women in need of protection, similar to the
victimhood discourse on migrant women in the Netherlands discussed
by Schrover (2009).[12]

In turn, the debate about gender-oppressive practices in 'other'
cultures forms an important backdrop to the current focus on social
cohesion. A notable initiative is the 'Basic Value Dialogue' which was
introduced in 2008 with the aim of overcoming some supposedly fundamental differences in values and practices existing within Swedish
society. Respect for democratic values, human rights and gender equality, on one hand, and work against discrimination and intolerance,
on the other, form the core of the initiative. The 'dialogue' aspect is
emphasised, meaning that it is intended as a conversation rather than
the imposition of one set of values over another.[13] The Swedish version
of 'social cohesion' policy thus differs from those in countries that have
adopted a more direct assimilatory approach, making it clear whose
values should dominate a cohesive society (the civic integration tests
introduced in countries like the Netherlands, Germany and the UK
are good examples of this). However, the change in policy direction
is nonetheless significant. Although the policy documents themselves
tend to avoid too many direct examples of the kinds of values and practices that might be regarded as less acceptable in the future cohesive
society, these are rather clear in the surrounding political debate. For
instance, the Swedish Minister for Integration and Equality made headlines by taking a hard line on young women wearing a veil, which she
proposed to ban, and on female genital mutilation, for which she suggested compulsory testing. In relation to the debate on honour-related
oppression and violence, a key measure proposed was the 'Basic Value
Dialogue' itself.

As the discourse and policy have moved towards less difference and more cohesion, they have also increased emphasis on demands on and responsibilities of individuals. We see this not least in the transformation of the policy regarding language acquisition – the so-called 'Swedish for Immigrants' course – in relation to which stricter rules have been introduced. Having found that migrants often take years to complete the course (and fearing a potential abuse of the compensatory system attached to it), the government has introduced a time limit, along with a national test. Furthermore, a bonus has been introduced as an incentive for swiftly and successfully completing the course.[14] While regarded as key to the process of cultural integration, language skills have also been increasingly emphasised in relation to migrants' labour market integration, as discussed in the following section.

## From equality to flexibility:
## The centrality of employment in a changing context

Equality in employment and in the wider society was a core principle of the 1968 and 1975 policies. Hence, emphasis was put on adapting general frameworks by considering specific conditions facing different social groups, and especially, dealing with any factors limiting newcomers' access to rights and benefits.[15] Measures included improved access to translation services and a restructuring of the public pension system to ensure some degree of access for newcomers. Social democratic ideology and corporatist structures have long underlied the strong equality focus. More broadly, the aim of full employment was a cornerstone of social democratic policy and regarded as a precondition for an integrated society with a strong welfare state (Schierup, Hansen & Castles 2006).

Though employment equality was a key focus of early migrant incorporation policy, the issue of unemployed migrants did not feature significantly, as the majority of migrants at the time had come to fill gaps in the workforce. However, this was soon to change, due to shifts in the labour market as well as the changing nature of immigration flows. Following those changes, migrants began to experience exclusion from the labour market. Some lost their jobs due to structural transformations, and newer arrivals found it difficult to get a foot in. This then became a significant issue on the policy agenda. Although the central role played by the general policy framework in resolving the problem of unemployed migrants was emphasised in both the mid-1980s and the mid-1990s, it was also suggested that targeted measures were needed to compensate for the additional disadvantage experienced by migrants compared to non-migrants in accessing employment.[16]

Aside from the increased cultural and ethnic diversity discussed previously, another effect of the change in immigration flows was a much greater variety in educational and skill levels amongst immigrants in Sweden. The migrant population became increasingly polarised in this regard, including people with limited education and work experience, as well as those with very high levels of qualifications (Nelander, Acchiardo & Goding 2004; Cederberg & Anthias 2006). The arrival of people with high educational levels led to an emphasis on proper validation of foreign qualifications, combined with the provision of complementary education. This policy was strengthened as frequent mismatches were identified between migrants' skills and the jobs they did (along with unemployment amongst highly-educated migrants). This was presented as a waste of valuable resources.[17] The government also emphasised the importance of helping migrants with lower levels of skills to enter the Swedish labour market. One general measure put in place to raise educational levels amongst less-educated groups, including newcomers, was 'The Knowledge Lift', which involved basic and further education. Migrant-specific measures included intensified activities in immigrant-dense neighbourhoods, as well as a range of work experience programmes designed to introduce newcomers to Swedish workplaces.[18]

Despite the explicit aim of the 1997/1998 'integration' policy to target society as a whole and not just migrants, the enquiry mentioned earlier (SOU 2006: 79) suggested that rather than contributing to an equal and integrated society, the policies had contributed to an 'us' versus 'them' mindset, while insufficiently dealing with structural inequalities and discrimination. Discrepancies between the policies themselves and their implementation was one issue raised by the integration board (Integrationsverket 2004, 2005). Another problem concerned uneven implementation across different groups, and especially, gender inequalities found when examining how policies had been implemented in practice. For example, women were found to have had less access to work experience programmes than men. This was particularly the case for women with lower levels of education. In the expert interviews for the FeMiPol project, one person suggested that this might have been the result of certain (gendered) assumptions operating within the institutions that were there to help facilitate migrants' 'integration' (Cederberg & Anthias 2006).[19]

To understand the impact of policy on the socio-economic dimension of migrant incorporation, we need to look beyond migrant-specific policy and consider the general policy framework surrounding the labour market and welfare state. Earlier, this chapter described some of the main changes that took place over time in regard to the labour market, employment and social welfare. Although the move towards a more flexible labour market and a more restricted welfare regime had a longer history than the current government, the speed of this transition increased after the new government came into power in 2006. The Conservative Moderate Party, the largest party in the coalition, presented itself as the 'new labour party', suggesting that the welfare systems in place under social democratic governments had gone too far in supporting people outside of work and they had done too little to provide incentives for labour market integration and reintegration.

Measures introduced to achieve the goal of full employment included tax cuts for wage earners and a tightening of the social insurance system with regard to both unemployment and illness. Stricter conditions were introduced, with more limited compensation provided and increased cost of participating in the unemployment insurance scheme. The general idea was to increase incentives for people to work. In terms of labour demand, measures included reducing worker costs for employers and expanding options for employing people on fixed-term contracts. Both of these measures are regarded as advantageous for people currently outside of the labour market, as it enables them to more easily get a 'foot in'.[20] The active labour market measures that had played an important role in the social democratic policy vision, such as providing training opportunities for people out of employment, do not feature as much in the current approach. Since 2006, Sweden has seen a decline in such measures, with the focus instead primarily on matching people's skills and qualifications with existing job opportunities, coaching and increasing demands on job-seeking activities – all centred on the aim of swiftly getting unemployed people (back) into work[21] (for a critical discussion see Syrén 2010).

In regard to migrant-specific policies in this area, the current government has retained the view of the previous government, that despite the commitment to general rather than targeted policies, additional measures are needed to support newcomers in the initial period after their arrival in Sweden. It has therefore introduced some labour market measures aimed at newcomers in particular. One of these is called 'step-in jobs'. These jobs are subsidised by the government and tied to participation in the 'Swedish for Immigrants' language course. They are intended to stimulate employers to hire more people and to get newcomers into the Swedish labour market as soon as possible.[22] In line with the general policy emphasis on coaching and job-seeking activities, another measure introduced is the 'development plan' designed for each newcomer. Aside from language training and further educational activities, these plans include a survey of the individual's previous qualifications and employment experience, and various forms of support designed to facilitate employment entry provided by private actors to which the public labour agency has subcontracted the work.[23]

While some of these policies target migrants specifically, as we have seen, most are general policies aimed at the population as a whole. As such, their impact is felt across the board. Though policies do not affect everyone uniformly, they do have differential impacts on different groups, given that they are introduced in the context of a society and labour market that is divided along lines of gender, ethnicity and class and where (gendered, racialised and classed) individuals have different access to rights and opportunities. For example, increased flexibilisation of the labour market and the work force has different impacts on the different groups (Cook 1998). Those who are in a weaker position in the labour market and socio-economically tend to be more strongly affected by, for example, employment instability and the economic insecurity that follows from it. In turn, those effects are exacerbated by a less generous welfare regime, as the protection available for those outside of employment for the short or longer term is less accessible to certain groups. The changes to the social insurance system discussed earlier are a case in point. They imply reduced access for some groups (those who do not fulfil certain criteria, such as employment continuity, and those who have opted out of the unemployment insurance scheme due to its increased cost). For those who are eligible, more limited compensation is available. In short, groups that display a more marginal position in the Swedish labour market are more likely to experience the negative effects of the changes. Amongst those groups are young people, women and non-European migrants (Jonsson & Wallette 2001; Cederberg & Anthias 2006; Mulinari 2006; Nelander, Acchiardo & Goding 2004; Schierup, Hansen & Castles 2006; Larsson 2009; Schierup & Ålund 2011).

In the case of migrant women, and especially women from non-European countries, statistics show that over time, they have become particularly prone to exclusion from the labour market. As already noted, this is the result of a variety of factors, including their qualifications and structural changes in the Swedish labour market that have made it more difficult for migrants to find a place therein, but also ethnic and gender discrimination. Aside from being severely affected by unemployment, migrant women from outside of Europe exhibit disproportionately high levels of temporary employment (Jonsson & Wallette 2001; Nelander, Acchiardo & Goding 2004; De los Reyes 2007; SCB 2009).[24]

The government asserts that it is precisely the groups that hold a weaker position in the labour market that will benefit from the measures introduced, in the sense that they will be more easily incorporated. However, we must ask what this might mean in the longer term. Research evaluating the government's labour market policy since 2006 already suggests that the situation of vulnerable individuals and groups, including migrants, has not improved, and that gender inequalities persist both within the migrant population and within society more widely (Syrén 2010). It is too early to know the long-term consequences of all these policy changes, but it seems important to consider some potential implications.

In times when the ability to be flexible is a great asset to employers, who need to respond to changing demands and economic fluctuations, could the increased leeway given to employers to dictate the terms and conditions of employment function to exacerbate rather than to solve the problem of exclusion? After all, a growing segment of the population may come to experience a *permanent* instability and insecurity as a result of their *temporary* employment position. Furthermore, in such a scenario, increased restrictions on welfare and greater demands put on job seekers to enter *any* employment are likely to further limit employees' bargaining power in relation to employers. In a discussion about migrant incorporation, what needs to be considered is the influence of labour market and socio-economic insecurities on migrants' lives and integration prospects. These policies and structures have implications not only in terms of limited employment opportunities and vulnerability to unemployment (as well as the reproduction of structural inequalities in the labour market), but also in terms of people's ability to plan for the future and develop a sense of stability and security (Nelander, Acchiardo & Goding 2004; Integrationsverket 2006; Mulinari 2006; Anthias et al. 2009).

## Conclusion

This chapter considered the gendered effects of Swedish policies on migrant incorporation, focusing on two dimensions: the cultural and the socio-economic. In regard to the cultural dimension, it traced the policy shift from cultural group rights to an emphasis on the individual and the promotion of social cohesion. Despite some important changes, the gendered dimensions of the policies and the surrounding debates have remained significant over time. The multicultural approach was found to be problematic from a gendered perspective for two reasons. First it provides for insufficient consideration of internal differences and power relations within migrant and ethnic minority groups. Second, it may contribute to 'other' gender roles and relations – represented through images of migrant women – being regarded as the 'authentic core' which should be protected and reproduced. Furthermore, despite official commitment to cultural pluralism and ethnic diversity, policies have in reality been closely bound up with social hierarchies, processes of inclusion and exclusion, and a general tendency to regard migrant or minority groups as 'other' to the majority Swedish society. While this has implications for all members of minority groups, the gendered effects have been emphasised precisely because of the centrality of women to the representation of ethnic groups and boundaries.

Regarding the shift away from the multicultural approach, the fact that 'other' women are used as markers of cultural difference continues to have negative implications for migrant women, whose lives and opportunities remain constrained by stereotypes – despite concerns about the welfare of migrant women being prominent in the discourse. Furthermore, despite the common tendency to culturalise gendered violence and oppression within minority groups, this chapter emphasised the importance of considering the structural context of such practices, and thus not to 'blame' multicultural policies for their existence, nor to assume that abolishment of multiculturalism will automatically cause such practices to disappear. In other words, the issue is not merely one of allowing more or less cultural difference. It also involves improving the structural conditions under which migrants are supposed to 'integrate', and in particular, building a more inclusive, equal and less discriminatory labour market and society.

In regard to the socio-economic dimension of migrant incorporation policies, this chapter focused in particular on rights and opportunities in the areas of employment and social welfare. It underscored that although employment has been regarded as central to migrant incorporation throughout the history of Swedish policy in this area, the wider context in which this idea has been introduced has changed over time, as have the details of how it has been implemented. Although previous policies centred on workers' rights and equality did not prohibit the development of gender and ethnic divisions in the Swedish labour market (in part due to the 'othering' practices just discussed), accelerating deregulation and a more restricted welfare regime impacts particularly negatively groups that already occupy the margins of the labour market. Migrants – especially those from non-European countries and women – are disproportionately located in those margins.

It therefore seems important to go beyond the anti-exclusion rhetoric of the current government and consider the actual effects, or potential effects, of policies that set out to 'include'. As those policies are in part designed to provide less security and protection for workers in order to 'encourage' entry into employment, they do not appear to improve the structural conditions referred to above. Furthermore, to the extent that women migrants are particularly exposed to such lack of security and protection, the policies risk reproducing or even reinforcing the disadvantage that they experience. As such, the current approach appears problematic when considered from the perspective of the long-term 'integration' of migrant women, not only in the labour market, but also in society more widely, where economic stability and security play an important role.

## Notes

1 Proposition 1975:26 Regeringens proposition om riktlinjer för invandrings – och minoritetspolitiken m.m.
2 Proposition 1975:26 Regeringens proposition om riktlinjer för invandrings – och minoritetspolitiken m.m., 15, my translation.
3 Proposition 1985/86:98 Om invandrarpolitiken.
4 Proposition 1985/86:98 Om invandrarpolitiken; Proposition 1990/91:195 Om aktiv flyktings- och immigrationspolitik m.m; SOU 1984:58. Invandrar – och minoritetspolitiken. Stockholm: Allmänna förlaget.
5 Proposition 1985/86:98 Om invandrarpolitiken; Proposition 1990/91:195 Om aktiv flyktings- och immigrationspolitik m.m.
6 Proposition 1997/98:16 Sverige, framtiden och mångfalden – från invandrarpolitik till integrationspolitik.
7 Proposition 1997/98:16 Sverige, framtiden och mångfalden – från invandrarpolitik till integrationspolitik.
8 Proposition 1997/98:16 Sverige, framtiden och mångfalden – från invandrarpolitik till integrationspolitik.
9 In particular, see the 'Exclusion Maps' produced by the Liberal Party to emphasise the growing problem of social and labour market exclusion and the alleged failure of the Social Democrats' integration policy, e.g., Folkpartiet (2004).
10 Skrivelse 2008/09:24 Egenmakt mot utanförskap – regeringens strategi för integration; Proposition 2008/09:1:13 Förslag till statsbudget för 2010. Integration och jämställdhet. Utgiftsområde; Proposition 2009/10:60 Nyanlända invandrares arbetsmarknadsetablering – egenansvar med professionellt stöd.
11 Proposition 1985/86:98 Om invandrarpolitiken.

12  See also Spivak (1993) and Mohanty (1988) on the gendered production of difference in colonial discourse.
13  Skrivelse 2009/10:106 Dialog om samhällets värdegrund.
14  Proposition 2009/10:188 Nationell sfi-bonus.
15  Proposition 1975:26 Regeringens proposition om riktlinjer för invandrings- och minoritetspolitiken m.m.
16  Proposition 1985/86:98 Om invandrarpolitiken; Proposition 1997/98:16 Sverige, framtiden och mångfalden – från invandrarpolitik till integrationspolitik.
17  Proposition 1997/98:16 Sverige, framtiden och mångfalden – från invandrarpolitik till integrationspolitik; Integrationsverket (2006).
18  Proposition 1997/98:16 Sverige, framtiden och mångfalden – från invandrarpolitik till integrationspolitik.
19  See Schierenbeck (2004) for an interesting discussion of the role of 'front-line bureaucrats' in meetings between migrants and Swedish public institutions.
20  Proposition 2006/07:89 Ytterligare reformer inom arbetsmarknadspolitiken, m.m; Swedish Government Offices (2008) The Swedish Reform Programme for Growth and Employment 2008-2010; Skrivelse 2008/09:24 Egenmakt mot utanförskap – regeringens strategi för integration.
21  Proposition 2009/10:60 Nyanlända invandrares arbetsmarknadsetablering – egenansvar med professionellt stöd.
22  Proposition 2008/09:1:13 Förslag till statsbudget för 2010. Integration och jämställdhet. Utgiftsområde 13.
23  SOU 2008:58 Egenansvar – med professionellt stöd. Stockholm: Fritzes.
24  Skrivelse 2008/09:24 Egenmakt mot utanförskap – regeringens strategi för integration.

## References

Ålund, A. (1999), 'Feminism, multiculturalism, essentialism', in N. Yuval-Davis & P. Werbner (eds), *Women, citizenship and difference*, pp. 147-162. London & New York: Zed Books.
Ålund, A. (1991), *Lilla Juga*. Helsingborg: Carlsson.
Ålund, A. & C.U. Schierup (1993), 'The thorny road to Europe: Swedish immigrant policy in transition', in J. Wrench & J. Solomos (eds), *Racism and migration in Western Europe*, pp. 99-115. Oxford: Berg Publishers.
Ålund, A. & C.U. Schierup (1991), *Paradoxes of multiculturalism*. Aldershot: Avesbury.
Anthias, F., M. Cederberg, T. Barber & R. Ayres (2009), 'Welfare regimes, labour market policies, and the experiences of female migrants', in M. Kontos (ed.), *Integration of female immigrants in labour market and society: A comparative analysis*, pp. 15-21. Frankfurt Am Main: Institute of Social Research at the Goethe Institute.
Anthias, F. & N. Yuval-Davis (1992), *Racialised boundaries: Race, nation, gender, colour and class and the anti-racist struggle*. London: Routledge.

Behtoui, A. (2008), 'Informal recruitment methods and disadvantages of immigrants in the Swedish labour market', *Journal of Ethnic and Migration Studies* 34 (3): 411-430.

Behtoui, A. & A. Neergaard (2010), 'Social capital and wage disadvantages among immigrant workers', *Work, Employment and Society* 24 (4): 761-779.

Bevelander, P. (2005), 'The employment status of immigrant women: The case of Sweden', *International Migration Review* 39 (1): 173-202.

Bevelander, P. (1999), 'The employment integration of immigrants in Sweden', *Journal of Ethnic and Migration Studies* 25 (3): 445-469.

Bevelander, P. & C. Lundh (2007), 'Employment integration of refugees: The influence of local factors on refugee job opportunities in Sweden', IZA Discussion Paper 2551. Bonn: Institute for the Study of Labor.

Borevi, K. (2004), 'Den svenska diskursen om staten, integrationen och föreningslivet', in *Föreningsliv, makt och integration*, pp. 31-65. Governmental Report DS 49.

Borevi, K. (2002), *Välfärdsstaten i det mångkulturella samhället*. PhD dissertation, Uppsala University.

Borevi, K. (1998), 'Svensk invandrarpolitik under (om)formulering', *Politica* 30 (2): 168-182.

Boris, E. (1995), 'The racialized gendered state: Constructions of citizenship in the United States', *Social Politics* 2 (2): 160-181.

Boyd, M. (1999), 'Gender, refugee status and permanent settlement', *Gender Issues* 17 (1): 5-25.

Brune, Y. (2003), '"Invandrare" i mediearkivets typgalleri', in P. de los Reyes, I. Molina & D. Mulinari (eds), *Maktens (o)lika förklädnader: kön, klass och etnicitet i det postkoloniala Sverige*, pp. 150-181. Stockholm: Atlas.

Brune, Y. (1998), *Mörk magi i vita medier*. Stockholm: Carlssons.

Cederberg, M. (2012), 'Migrant networks and beyond: Exploring the value of the notion of social capital for making sense of ethnic inequalities', *Acta Sociologica* 55 (1): 59-72.

Cederberg, M. (2006), *Everyday racism in Malmö, Sweden: The experiences of Bosnians and Somalis*, PhD thesis, Nottingham Trent University.

Cederberg, M. & F. Anthias (2006), 'National report: Key informants' interviews – the Swedish case', *Report WP 2, FeMiPol Project*. www.femipol.uni-frankfurt.de/docs/working_papers/wp2/Sweden.pdf.

Cook, J. (1998), 'Flexible employment: Implications for gender and citizenship in the European Union', *New Political Economy* 3 (2): 261-277.

Daragahi, H. (2002), '"Hedersmodets" anatomi. Om integrationspolitik, kultur och kvinnors rättigheter', in *Törnrosalandet. Om tillhörighet och utanförskap*. Norrköping: Integrationsverket.

De los Reyes, P. (2007), *Etnisk diskriminering i Arbetslivet: Kunskapsläge och kunskapsbehov*. Stockholm: Swedish Trade Union Confederation.

De los Reyes, P. (2003), *Patriarkala enklaver eller ingenmansland? Våld, hot och kontroll mot unga kvinnor i Sverige*. Norrköping: Integrationsverket.

De los Reyes, P. (2000), 'Folkhemmets paradoxer: Genus och etnicitet i den svenska modellen', *Kvinnovetenskaplig tidskrift* 2: 27-47.

De los Reyes, P., I. Molina & D. Mulinari (2003), *Maktens (o)lika förklädnader: Kön, klass och etnicitet i det postkoloniala Sverige.* Stockholm: ATLAS Förlag.

Folkpartiet (2004), *Utanförskapets karta: En kartläggning över utanförskapet i Sverige.* Stockholm: Folkpartiet.

Geddes, A. (2003), *The politics of migration and immigration in Europe.* London: Sage.

Integrationsverket (2006), *Rapport Integration 2005.*Norrköping: Integrationsverket.

Integrationsverket (2005), *Introduktion för nyanlända invandrare – enkätundersökning 2004,* Integrationsverkets rapportserie 2005: 01.

Integrationsverket (2004), *Integration var god dröj,* Integrationsverkets rapportserie 2004: 01.

Jonsson, A. & M. Wallette (2001), 'Är utländska medborgare segmenterade mot atypiska arbeten?', *Arbetsmarknad & Arbetsliv* 7 (3): 153-168.

Knocke, W. (2001), 'Att vara kvinna och invandrare i det svenska arbetslivet' in L. Gonäs, G. Lindgren & C. Bildt (eds), *Könssegregering i Arbetslivet,* pp. 25-36. Stockholm: Arbetslivsinstitutet.

Knocke, W. (1999), 'The labour market for immigrant women in Sweden: Marginalised women in low-valued jobs', in J. Wrench, A. Rea & N. Ouali (eds), *Migrants, ethnic minorities and the labour market: Integration and exclusion in Europe,* pp. 108-131. London: Macmillan.

Knocke, W. (1994), 'Kön, etnicitet och teknisk utveckling', in C.U. Schierup & S. Paulson (eds), *Arbetets etniska delning: Studier från en svensk bilindustri.* Stockholm: Carlsson.

Knocke, W. (1986), *Invandrade kvinnor i lönearbete och fack.* Forskningsrapport nr 53. Stockholm: Arbetslivscentrum.

Kofman, E. (2007), 'The knowledge economy, gender and stratified migrations', *Studies in Social Justice* 1 (2): 122-135.

Kofman, E. (2005), 'Gendered migrations, livelihoods and entitlements in European welfare regimes', UNRISD Working Paper. Geneva: United Nations Research Institute for Social Development

Kofman, E. (2004), 'Gendered global migrations: Diversity and stratification', *International Feminist Journal of Politics* 6 (4): 642-664.

Kofman, E. (1999), 'Female "birds of passage" a decade later: Gender and immigration in the European Union', *International Migration Review* 33 (2) (Summer): 269-299.

Kofman, E., A. Phizacklea, P. Raghuram & R. Sales (2000), *Gender and international migration in Europe: Employment, welfare and politics.* London: Routledge.

Kontos, M. (ed.) (2009), *Integration of female immigrants in labour market and society: A comparative analysis.* Frankfurt Am Main: Institute of Social Research at the Goethe Institute.

Kymlicka, W. (1995), *Multicultural citizenship.* Oxford: Oxford University Press.

Larsson, M. (2009), *Anställningsformer år 2009: Fast och tidsbegränsat anställda efter klass och kön år 1990-2009.* Stockholm: Landsorganisationen.

Lister, R. (2003), *Citizenship: Feminist perspectives.* New York: New York University Press.

Mohanty, C. (1988), 'Under Western eyes: Feminist scholarship and colonial discourses', *Feminist Review* 30 (August): 61-88.

Molina, I. & P. de los Reyes (2002), 'Kalla mörkret natt! Kön, klass och ras/etnicitet i det postkoloniala Sverige', in P. De los Reyes, I. Molina & D. Mulinari (eds), *Maktens (o)lika förklädnader. Kön, klass & etnicitet i det postkoloniala Sverige*, pp. 295-317. Stockholm: Atlas

Morokvasic, M. (1984), 'Birds of passage are also women', *International Labour Review* 18 (4): 886-907.

Mulinari, P. (2006), 'Den andra arbetskraften: Exotisering och rasism på arbetsplatsen', in SOU 2006:59 *Arbetslivets (o)synliga murar*. Stockholm: Fritzes.

Nelander, S., M. Acchiardo & I. Goding (2004), *Integration 2004: Fakta och kunskap*, Stockholm: Swedish Trade Union Confederation.

Pateman, C. (1988), *The sexual contract*. Palo Alto: Stanford University Press.

Phizacklea, A. (ed.) (1983), *One way ticket*. Routledge: London.

Piper, N. (2006), 'Gendering the politics of migration', *International Migration Review* 40 (1): 133-164.

SCB (2009), *Integration: Utrikes födda på arbetsmarknaden*. Stockholm: Statistics Sweden.

Schierenbeck, I. (2004), 'En Välfärdsstat för alla? Frontlinjebyråkrater och invandrarklienter' in SOU 2004:49 *Engagemang, mångfald och integration*. Stockholm: Fritzes.

Schierup, C.U. & A. Ålund (2011), 'The end of Swedish exceptionalism? Citizenship, neoliberalism and the politics of exclusion', *Race & Class* 53: 45-64.

Schierup, C.U., P. Hansen & S. Castles (2006), *Migration, citizenship, and the European welfare state: A European dilemma*. Oxford: Oxford University Press.

Schierup, C.U. & S. Paulsson (1994), *Arbetets etniska delning. Studier från en svensk bilindustri*. Stockholm: Carlssons Bokförlag.

Schrover, M. (2010), 'Pillarization, multiculturalism and cultural freezing', *BMGN/ LCHR* 125 (2-3): 329-354.

Schrover, M. (2009), 'Family in Dutch migration policy 1945-2005', *The History of the Family* 14: 191-202.

Siim, B. (2000), *Gender and citizenship: Politics and agency in France, Britain and Denmark*. Cambridge: Cambridge University Press.

Soininen, M. (1999), 'The "Swedish model" as an institutional framework for immigrant membership rights', *Journal of Ethnic and Migration Studies* 25 (4): 685-702.

SOU (2008: 58), *Egenansvar: Med professionellt stöd*. Stockholm: Fritzes.

SOU (2006: 79), *Integrationens svarta bok: Agenda för jämlikhet och social sammanhållning*. Slutbetänkande av Utredningen om makt, integration och strukturell diskriminering. Stockholm: Fritzes.

SOU (2006: 60), *På tröskeln till lönearbete: Diskriminering, exkludering och underordning av personer med utländsk bakgrund*. Rapport av Utredningen om makt, integration och strukturell diskriminering. Stockholm: Fritzes.

SOU (2006: 59), *Arbetslivets (o)synliga murar*. Rapport av Utredningen om makt, integration och strukturell diskriminering. Stockholm: Fritzes.

SOU (1984: 58), *Invandrar- och minoritetspolitiken*. Stockholm: Allmänna förlaget.

Spivak, G. (1993), 'Can the subaltern speak?', in P. Williams (ed.), *Colonial discourse and post-colonial theory*, pp. 66-111. Hemel Hempstead: Harvester Wheatsheaf.

Syrén, M. (2010), *Vad har hänt med den aktiva arbetsmarknadspolitiken?* Stockholm: Swedish Trade Union Confederation.

Taylor, C. (1994), *Multiculturalism and the politics of recognition.* Princeton: Princeton University Press.

Yuval-Davis, N. (1997), *Gender and nation.* London: Sage.

## 9  Take off that veil and give me access to your body

### An analysis of Danish debates about Muslim women's head and body covering

*Rikke Andreassen*

## Introduction

This chapter analyses two Danish debates about Muslim women's head and body covering. One of these debates focuses on a 2007 prohibition of fully-veiled women from working in the Danish public sector; the other involves a 2009 proposal to outlaw full veiling (burqas and niqabs) in Denmark. These debates function as a window to a broader understanding of how categories of race and ethnicity, gender, sexuality, religion and nationality are constructed. The chapter shows that these debates have played important roles in excluding Muslims from the Danish community, and that within them, gender, gender equality and sexual liberty became hostages in nationalist constructs of the Danish nation as white.

## Materials and methods

Over the past decade, Muslim women's head and body covering has been an integral part of Danish debates about migrants and integration. Most debates have been about the 'hijab', the headscarf that covers the hair and shoulders and represents the most prevalent type of headwear among Danish Muslims. Recently the debate has changed from a focus on hijabs to an emphasis on niqabs and burqas, which are the veils that fully cover a woman's face and body (Siim & Andreassen 2010). Most Nordic research on veiling has concentrated on the hijab.

This chapter expands on previous research and sheds light on recent debates about full facial veiling. The sources for the analyses are mainly media representations of debates (on television, in newspapers and on websites), especially politicians' utterances in these debates. Based on the theoretical foundation of social constructivism (Foucault 1990: 93 ff; Butler 1999: 43 f.) and intersectionality (Crenshaw 1991), the meth-

odological approach is a combination of discourse analysis (Laclau &
Mouffe 1985) and frame analysis (Verloo & Lombardo 2007). Media
reports on these debates function as a window to a broader understanding of how categories of race and ethnicity, gender, sexuality and
nationality are constructed and contested. The study analyses how
these constructions play into minorities' inclusions or exclusions in the
national community. As the chapter will demonstrate, the two cases
studied imply a demand that women be physically accessible in order
to receive citizenship rights and to be included in the national community. It argues that debates about veiling are not simply about 'white
men wanting to save brown women from brown men', as Spivak (1993)
put it, even though that is at play. Debates about and representations of
veiled Muslim women also contribute to the construction of the Danish
nation as racially and ethnically white.


## The stereotype of the 'oppressed migrant woman'

To fully understand the significance of debates about veiling, it is ben-
eficial to examine how Muslim women have been represented during previous decades in Denmark. For the majority of Danes, the
media constitute the main source of information about racial and
ethnic minorities (Andreassen 2005: 5). The term 'racial and ethnic
minorities' refers to migrants and their descendants of colour or of
a non-Danish ethnicity. This chapter underscores the racial aspect of
migration and integration by explicitly referring to the raciality of migrants and their descendants instead of simply referring to migrants
and their descendants as 'ethnic', as most researchers do. Analyses of
the Danish news media have shown that communications about racial and ethnic minorities have been replete with negative stereotypes
(Andreassen 2007). Since the 1970s, one dominant stereotype has
been the 'oppressed migrant woman'. This stereotype is constructed
via stories about female racial and ethnic minorities as victims of domestic violence, arranged and forced marriages, and honour killings.
The news media often explain these oppressions with reference to migrants' culture or to Islam. In other words, women are being oppressed
because of their culture or religion, and the men who oppress them
are characterised as typical representatives of their culture or religion.
This differs from the news reports of domestic violence and murders
committed by Christian, ethnically Danish men. Here, the men are
not described as representatives of Danish culture or of Christianity;
rather they are presented as individuals for whom something has gone

wrong. In the 1990s, stereotypes about the oppressed migrant woman gained a new feature; namely, her portrayal as veiled. Numerous news reports, especially during the 2000s, focused on female Muslim migrants' and their descendants' headscarves and veils. Many of these stories involved veiled women and employment. The news media have primarily presented headscarves and veils as oppressive to women. An integrated part of the news media's construction of female racial and ethnic minorities as oppressed is a parallel construction of ethnically Danish women as liberated. Most news stories compare these minority women directly or indirectly to ethnically Danish women. Since racial and ethnic minority women are presented as oppressed and as victims of a patriarchal culture, the ethnically Danish women, who are presented in binary opposition to the minority women, appear as liberated and as living in a female emancipated culture (Andreassen 2005: 124 ff., 2007: 28 ff.).

These news stories leave television viewers and newspaper readers with the impression that the racial and ethnic minority population and the ethnically Danish majority population are each others' opposites and live very different lives. In other words, the news is reported in an 'us' versus 'them' way. In the news stories, racial and ethnic minorities, as well as ethnic Danes, are presented as a homogenous group, and the news seldom differentiates between the minorities' different national, racial, ethnic and religious affiliations or their citizenship status.

## Veiling and employment

During the spring of 2007, the debate about veiled women and employment took a new turn. The debate began when the alderperson from Odense, the third largest city in Denmark, Jane Jegind, of the right-wing Liberal Party (*Venstre*), and the vice major, Alex Ahrendsen, of the right-wing, populist Danish People's Party (*Dansk folkeparti*), announced that the municipality would not give financial support to fully veiled day-care providers. In Denmark, municipalities cover 75% of private day-care expenses. The introduction to a prime-time news clip aired by the Danish public service station DR described the situation:

> Can one be covered like this, in a burqa, when one is working as a day-care provider? That question has cause a stir among the municipality politicians in Odense. The City Counsel's Children and Youth Alderperson will prevent a burqa-covered Muslim woman from being a day care provider. The then Minister of Family Affairs, Carina

Christensen, supports her [the alderperson] and is working towards a
ban [of burqa-dressed day care providers].[1]

The leader of the Office for Space and Capacity Management of the
Centre for Children and Youth in Copenhagen, Jan Dehn, also spoke
in the news clip. He explained why he believes that day-care providers
should not be veiled:

> Pedagogically, one needs to relate to children. And the child needs to
> be able to mimic happiness, sadness, worry, fear, pleasure. That can,
> among others, be read in the face, and that is why we [the Copenha-
> gen municipality] have chosen to say that it is not compatible with the
> work of a day care provider to wear a burqa.[2]

The Odense day-care controversy quickly spread to other municipalities and cities. A few days later, the municipalities of Copenhagen,
Frederiksberg (part of greater Copenhagen), Aarhus (the second largest city in Denmark) and Odense proclaimed that they did not want
veiled women as employees in the public sector. They would therefore revoke social welfare benefits (*bistandshjælp*) of women in burqas, because the women's way of dressing was interpreted as preventing
their availability to enter the workforce. According to news reports, 'If
she is unemployed because she insists on her burqa, then she has in
reality resigned from the labour market. And then she and her sisters
can lose social welfare benefits.'[3] Interviews were broadcast of municipal politicians representing the right-wing liberal party and the social
democrats, who stated that veiled women did not want to be active participants on the labour market. Gert Bjerregaard, alderperson for Social
Affairs in Aarhus municipality, representing the liberals, argued, 'If one
is at the labour market's disposal, then one needs to send a signal that
one wishes to enter the labour market, and one does not do that if one
is covered and wearing a burqa.'[4]
    A majority of journalists and politicians refer to full facial cover-
ing as a 'burqa'. Burqa is, however, the term for a traditional Afghani
piece of clothing that covers the face and body. In Denmark, very few
women wear burqas, although some wear niqabs (the piece of clothing
that covers the face except for a narrow opening in front of the eyes).
Journalists and politicians are likely actually referring to niqabs when
they speak about 'burqas', as it makes little sense to legislate the wearing
of burqas when there are virtually no burqas in the Danish cityscape.
This confusion of terms illustrates politicians' and journalists' lack of
knowledge about veiling.

In the media, no journalists questioned the politicians' claim that it is the individual woman's responsibility whether she is employed or not. Neither did any journalist suggest that one reason for veiled women's unemployment could be that some employers may discriminate against veiled women. Instead journalists, like the politicians, blamed the women for their lack of employment. This is an illustration of the so-called 'blame the victim' rhetoric.

Similar to the municipalities' demand that their employees should not be covered, the then Minister of Employment, Claus Hjort Frederiksen, representing the liberals, argued that all women working in state or municipal jobs must show their faces and shake hands with men. A news clip about the handshake requirement opened with footage of Claus Hjort Frederiksen happily shaking hands with a woman news reporter.[5] After this he said, 'Public employees are not allowed to discriminate between men and women. Therefore all employees need to greet men and women similarly, and in this country we greet by shaking hands with one another ... We are demanding just three things: that we can see who you are; that one does not discriminate between men and women; and then of course we can make demands for social security reasons.'[6] The social democrats' spokesperson on integration issues, Henrik Sass Larsen, argued that there can be variation in the demand for handshakes: 'In situations where we as citizens meet the service in the public sector, it is fair to demand that we can see who we are talking to. And I also think it is very fair that people shake hands. But in all other job situations, it must be the individual workplace that decides the rules.'[7]

It is interesting that it is the liberal party that wants to dictate national rules for clothing and behaviour, and the social democrats, who would leave clothing and behaviour regulations to the individual workplace. This illustrates that in debates where race and ethnicity, religion, gender and nationality intersect, traditional political viewpoints and divisions seem to disappear. Traditionally, the liberals have argued that employers and employees should decide working rules and regulations among themselves, whereas the social democrats have argued that rules and regulations ought to be centralised. The traditional division between right-wing (the liberals) and left-wing (the social democrats) in relation to the labour market is subverted in discussions about Muslim women's veils.

Interestingly no complaints have emerged about publicly employed women wearing burqas or niqabs. And no problems have been documented with publicly employed women refusing to shake hands. Therefore, the Danish public witnessed a series of debates and discussions about Muslim women's wearing of veils and refusal to shake hands, even though it was never an actual problem. Similarly, in December 2007, intense debate and discussions followed a decision by the high school *Egaa Gymnasium* in Aarhus to ban students from dressing in burqas, despite the fact no student had actually worn a burqa or niqab at the school.

## Women must be physically available in order to gain citizenship rights

Applying feminist analysis, one can interpret the demand for women to remove full body covering and be willing to shake hands as a demand for accessibility. Women have to be physically accessible in order to be full members of Danish society and to be included in the Danish welfare system. The municipal politician as responsible for taking social benefits away from fully veiled women, the liberal Gert Bjerregaard, argued, 'We do not think it promotes integration to wear a burqa in situations where one is about to enter the labour market. To me it is about being open and accessible, and one does not signal that [openness and accessibility] with a burqa.'[8] Apparently, it is not possible for a woman to be part of Danish society if she cannot be seen or touched. This means that a woman can only be a fully included member of Danish society and the welfare system if she is bodily available for the male gaze and the male touch.

Quite literally the politician Søren Espersen, representing the Danish People's Party, argued against veiling because he wants to gaze at women. He said, 'I want to be allowed to see Muslim women's nice breasts.'[9] This comment was uttered in a debate about multiculturalism, which Espersen, along with his party, argues against. Apparently, one of the benefits of the monocultural ethnically Danish society is, according to Espersen, the free access to (viewing) women's bodies (see also Thuesen 2009).

## No burqas allowed

The prohibition of full facial coverage among public employees was followed by a suggestion of a complete burqa ban in 2009. The ban was a vital aspect of the Conservative Party's integration initiative 'Democratic Integration.'[10] The then conservative spokesperson on integration issues, Naser Khader, launched the initiative with the comment, 'We do not want to see burqas in Denmark. We simply cannot accept that some of our citizens are covering their face.'[11] This prohibition was not targeted at a specific group of veiled women, (e.g., women in public employment), but at all covered women. Fully veiled women were not to be allowed anywhere in Denmark. The 'Democratic Integration' initiative states, 'We do not like clothing that signals oppression, as the burqa does. We will work towards a prohibition against burqas.'[12] Originally, Khader argued that burqas should be prohibited even in people's private homes: 'If we were to allow people to wear burqas in their own backyard then we would have to allow many exceptions [from the prohibition]. Therefore we need to be consistent and argue that the burqa does not belong in Denmark.' However, it was never the party's official policy to prohibit burqas in all private spheres; officially the proposed prohibition aimed at prohibiting burqas in all Danish public spaces.[13] As with the previous prohibition of 'burqas' in the public sector, this prohibition was mainly targeted against niqabs, which mistakenly were named burqas. The Danish People's Party and the social democrats supported the prohibition, whereas the other governing party, the liberals, opposed it. As a compromise, the government (made up of both liberals and conservatives) decided to appoint a 'burqa committee', to map the burqa situation in Denmark. The committee delivered its report in 2009, concluding that just 100 to 200 women were fully covered (wearing niqabs or burqas) in Denmark (Thuesen 2009).

The proposed prohibition of burqas is a serious encroachment on people's privacy, as well as on the right to freedom of religion. A general prohibition of burqas and niqabs would likely violate the Danish Constitution, which guarantees freedom of religion (paragraph 67) and prohibits religious discrimination (paragraph 70). It would also violate the Universal Declaration of Human Rights, as this similarly guarantees freedom of religion (article 18) and prohibits discrimination (article 7). In the end, the conservatives never proposed their burqa ban in parliament, both because liberals were against it and because legal advisors told them that such ban would violate constitutional rights. Traditionally, a political party checks with its legal advisors to determine if a proposal is legal before proposing it. Therefore, one can question why this procedure was not followed in the burqa case; one reason could be that members of the Conservative Party knew that the proposal could not pass but wanted the publicity gained from suggesting it. The Danish People's Party, which initially supported the ban, and whose members are known as the most Islam-critical in the Danish Parliament, will now propose the burqa ban in parliament. The social democrats, who similarly supported the ban initially, ended up arguing in favour of a general ban, while arguing against voting for such a ban: 'We still find that burqas are a violation of women and we initially found that a ban was a good idea. But all experts that we have spoken to, tell us that such ban most likely would violate the Constitution. And we have to accept that.' Henrik Sass Larsen, who was the social democrats' political spokesperson at the time, adds, 'I understand the Danish People's Party's intention [of proposing the ban in parliament], which I sympathise with.'[14] In order words, the social democrats would ban full veiling if it was legally possible to do so.

## Gender equality as a hostage in a nationalist struggle

All parties in favour of a burqa ban argue against veiling because they consider it oppressive to women. At the same time they hold veiled women themselves responsible for their supposed oppression. In these debates, Muslim women and their clothing or veils become not only the symbol of the oppression but also its essence. The solution to end the oppression is the removal of their clothing and a forced bodily integration onto the unveiled Danish society. The debates are illustrative of a 'blame the victim' rhetoric; the women are blamed for their own oppression. Veiled women are held responsible for their religious community's supposed female oppression. This implies a perception of women as the bodily reproducers of the community (Lutz, Phoenix & Yuval-Davis 1995: 9). Veiled women mark with their bodies the imagined separation between an imagined Danish (liberated female) community and an imagined Muslim (oppressed female) community.

During the previous decade's debates about headscarves, one of the dominant arguments against hijabs was the perception that headscarves are oppressive to women. A remark by Peter Skaarup, the vice-president of Danish People's Party, is illustrative of politicians' arguments against veiling:

> In Denmark, we have experienced a change in our society during the previous 20, 30, 40 years, where women and men have become equal, and according to Danish norms it is discriminatory to wear a veil. The fact that women must hide their sexuality, cover their hair, that is, in a Danish context, an expression of a devaluation of the woman ... and that is what we have fought against with our struggle for gender equality, and therefore the veil is a problem for our society ... We have been fighting for this women's emancipation and gender equality ...

Ill. 9.1 *Danish Muslim women demonstrate for the right to veil. The sign says, 'The headscarf is my choice, my right, my freedom'. The man in the picture is the liberal Bertel Haarder, who was Minister of Integration at the time.* Photo: Freddy Hagen

The right thing is therefore to ban the veil and live accordingly to our customs here in Denmark.[15]

Skaarup represents a growing number of white, Christian male politicians who recently became very engaged in debates about Muslim women's rights and Islam as a religion that oppresses women. These politicians did not previously participate in feminist struggles, nor did they express feminist views. But when arguing against veiling, they inscribe themselves into the historical women's struggle. Skaarup argues, '[W]e have fought against [discrimination] with our struggle for gender equality … We have been fighting for this women's emancipation and gender equality.' In so doing, he presents himself and his party as active participants in women's emancipation over the previous decades. This is not historically accurate. The Danish People's Party has not voted in favour of laws or proposals aimed at limiting the oppression of women or at increasing gender equality in Denmark. Neither has the Danish People's Party's predecessor, the Progressive Party. Generally these politicians were not involved in women's rights before they became engaged in debates about veiling. Therefore they seem to speak in favour of women's rights and feminism when feminism can be used as an anti-Muslim tool. For these politicians, arguments about gender and gender equality seem to be used to support their anti-Muslim and anti-immigrant agendas. Such politicians, and the initiatives they represent (e.g., a burqa ban), commonly presume that gender equality already exists in Denmark. They present Danes as living in a society with gender equality, ignoring the numerous remaining gender inequalities, such as lack of equal pay, lack of women in leadership positions, lack of women in politics and domestic violence.

These politicians' rhetoric and claims about Islam as a religion that is oppressive to women and about Danish Muslim women as living gender-oppressed lives illustrate what Spivak (1993) has called 'white men wanting to save brown women from brown men'. But in the Danish situation, it is not only white men who want to save brown women, but also brown men, including conservative spokesperson Khader, who is of Syrian origin. I have argued elsewhere that Khader's attack on veiled women is a way for him to demonstrate whiteness and Danishness; hence, his exclusion of veiled women from the Danish community becomes his own way into the Danish community (Andreassen 2010a). Common among these Danish men (white and brown) is their wish to save brown women (i.e., veiled women), without including their voices in their politics and without listening to their reasons for veiling.

Frantz Fanon (1965: 63) has described the Algerian war of independence (1954-1962) as a French struggle aimed at 'unveiling Algeria'. Fanon (ibid.: 46 f) argued that 'it was the colonist's frenzy to unveil the Algerian woman, it was his gamble on winning the battle of the veil', because unveiling would imply 'bring[ing] this [Algerian] woman within his reach, to make her a possible object of possession' (ibid.: 44). This seems to parallel Danish politicians' attempts to unveil Danish Muslim women in order to liberate them from supposed oppression and in order for the women to be fully – bodily accessible – subjects in the Danish nation. Indeed, to be a fully integrated subject in the Danish nation and to receive full citizenship rights, one must unveil and become an object of possession for these men's gaze and touch.

The Danish political battle against veiling is about gender, but in the battle gender and gender equality became hostages in a nationalist struggle. This struggle is not as much about gender equality as it is about excluding certain people, Muslim migrants and their descendants, from the Danish community. Among the ways that the struggle is being played out is by presenting ethnically Danish, white, Christian culture as positive and liberated through a negative stereotypical presentation of the 'other', the Muslim, coloured culture as oppressive to women. It is interesting to note how gendered crimes like domestic violence, honour killings and forced marriages are vocalised in debates about racial and ethnic minorities while the same gendered crimes are made invisible in relation to migration policies, as documented by Boyd & Nowak in this volume. Both situations (visibility in debates about multiculturalism and invisibility in migration policies) result in minority women's exclusion.

## White sexual liberation and the colour of homophobia

This national struggle is not only taking place in the arena of gender and minority women but also in debates about sexual minorities. Since 2001, when the Copenhagen Gay (LGTB) Pride Parade was attacked by a small group of men of Middle Eastern origin, Danish media and politicians have tended to associate discrimination of sexual minorities with racial minorities, and especially with Muslim racial minorities. The attack took place in Noerrebro, where there is a high concentration of racial and ethnic minorities among its residents. The leader of the Danish People's Party, Pia Kjærsgaard, wrote the following about the Noerrebro attack:

> Today Noerrebro has changed ... The tolerance is gone. And one of the main reasons is because Noerrebro has become a Muslim enclave. And where Islam goes in, tolerance goes out ... Last summer, a procession called Gay Pride was harmed. It is gays and lesbians in a festive manifestation. It is a little wild but rather harmless. But the Muslim brotherhood out there did not think so – and the homosexuals had to run the gauntlet ... We [the Danish People's Party] will work towards getting Noerrebro back. So the tolerance and broad-mindedness again can exist [there].[16]

According to Kjærsgaard, homophobia in Denmark is a result of recent (Muslim) immigration.

For the first time in Danish history, a young Muslim woman with a hijab, Asmaa Abdol-Hamid, ran for a seat in parliament in 2007. During the election, Abdol-Hamid was repeatedly asked by Danish journalists about her attitudes towards gender equality and homosexuality. She answered repeatedly that she is a feminist and in favour of gender equality and sexual minorities' rights. Despite this, the news media continuously treated Abdol-Hamid as if she was against gender equality and as if she disliked homosexuals and opposed giving them equal rights.[17]

Homosexuality and sexual minorities' rights have never been domi-
nating issues in Danish elections. But they apparently became a hot
topic with a hijab-wearing Muslim candidate running for office. The
hijab seems to convey notions of homophobia and gender oppression;
notions that stick so strongly that they seem impossible to get rid of
verbally (Ahmed 2004: 44 f.). None of the ethnically Danish candidates
were questioned about their support – or lack of support – for gender
equality or sexual minorities' rights during the 2007 election campaign.
No candidates with headscarves or veils ran for office during the 2011
election.

Similar to the debates about veiling, where gender equality becomes
constructed as a national Danish value, sexual liberty and tolerance
towards sexual minorities are framed as integrated features of Danish society, and ethnic Danes are presented as tolerant towards sexual minorities. Hence, homophobia and discrimination against sexual
minorities become features of the racially and religiously diverse society.

In Kjærsgaard's representation, (white) homosexuals come to represent Denmark, and an attack on them is therefore an attack on the
nation. In this racialised narrative, harming the white gay or lesbian
body equates with harming the whole nation. Often homosexuals have
been excluded from the national community and have had limited citizenship rights and welfare state rights (Richardson 1998). Historically,
homosexuals have been framed as 'the other', against which mainstream heterosexual society has constructed itself. In recent Danish
narratives, the homosexuals' race appears to dominate at the expense
of their sexuality. The whiteness of the homosexual body compensates
for the alienation of the minority sexuality. In these debates, Danish
nationality is constructed around an inclusion of the white homosexual against the exclusion of the potential homophobic person of colour.
Raissiguier's chapter in this volume, as well as that of Oxford, correctly
indicate that nations tolerant of homosexuality and homosexual family
formations might be more inclusive in their family migration politics.
However, as these Danish narratives show, inclusion of national sexual minorities does not necessarily lead to inclusive attitudes towards
migrants and their descendants, as tolerance towards sexual minorities
might mirror an exclusion of migrants and their descendants, since
inclusion is accompanied by the national, white understanding of sexual freedom.

When arguments of gender and sexual equality are used to present
Islam and Muslim migrants and their descendants as homophobic and
oppressive to women (i.e., less democratic and civilised than ethnic

Danes), they do more than influence the construction of a prejudiced and racist political climate. They also contribute to a racialised understanding of gender, sexuality and gender equality. In the debates, gender equality and sexual tolerance are constructed as white, Christian and ethnically Danish values. In Denmark, there is a linguistic difference between 'being Danish' and 'holding Danish citizenship'. Consequently, migrants and their descendants do not become Danish by obtaining citizenship. In these debates, 'being Danish' is synonymous with practicing gender equality and being liberal towards sexual minorities – despite the fact that there is gender discrimination and homophobia in Danish society. The argument that others are not practicing equality, for instance due to the wearing of a Muslim veil, becomes a tool for excluding veiled women, and Muslims in general, from participating in the national Danish community. In the political rhetoric, the discourse of gender and sexual equality becomes a mechanism of in- and exclusion.

## Conclusion: Maintaining power structures

Scott (1999: 42) has argued that gender is a relation of power, defining it as 'a constitutive element of social relationship based on perceived differences between the sexes, and ... [as] a primary way of signifying power'. I would like to expand her argument by suggesting that in the political debates about veiling gender plays a part in constructions of power, not only between men and women, but also between the white majority population and the minority population of colour. Scott (1999: 45) has argued that 'gender is a primary field within which or by means of which power is articulated'. This is particularly true if we expand the argument to gender's intersections with race and ethnicity and with religion, as a primary field in which power is articulated. In the debates about veiling, gender intersects with race and ethnicity and with religion, in particular, through the constructed binary oppositions between the veiled, oppressed minority women and the non-veiled, liberated, white, majority ethnic Danish women. Power is articulated and constituted at different levels within the fields of gender, race and ethnicity, and religion. It is ascribed and constituted via the utterances that privilege 'Danish culture' over 'migrant minorities' and 'Islamic culture'. But power is also inscribed more ingeniously, by maintaining the hegemonic discourse that there is gender equality among the ethnically Danish population and that this gender equality involves free accessibility to the female body.

Ill. 9.2 *Europeans demonstrate against the European Union at the 2001* EU *Summit in Gothenburg. In front of the demonstration is a woman of colour with her own demonstration against the exclusion of minorities in Europe.* Photo: Spacecampaign

## Notes

1  DR1 prime-time news programme TV-*Avisen* 2 May 2007.
2  DR1 prime-time news programme TV-*Avisen* 2 May 2007.
3  DR1 prime-time news programme TV-*Avisen* 5 May 2007.
4  DR1 prime-time news programme TV-*Avisen* 5 May 2007.
5  DR1 prime-time news programme TV-*Avisen* 4 May 2007.
6  DR1 prime-time news programme TV-*Avisen* 4 May 2007.
7  DR1 prime-time news programme TV-*Avisen* 4 May 2007.
8  Søren Nielsen, 'Kontanthjælp taget fra to kvinder', *Politiken*, 9 May 2007, see http://politiken.dk/indland/article301320.ece.
9  Søren Espersen, DR2 *Deadline*, 28 September 2008.
10 'Demokratisk integration', Konservativt folkeparti, 18 August 2009, www.konservative.dk/nytogdebat/nyheder/august/sider/integrationsudspil.aspx.
11 'K kræver forbud mod burka', *Politiken*, 17 August 2009.
12 'Demokratisk integration', Konservativt folkeparti, 18 August 2009, www.konservative.dk/nytogdebat/nyheder/august/sider/integrationsudspil.aspx.
13 Troels Evold Widding & Signe Højgaard Nielsen, 'JP hjalp Naser Khader i burka-sag', *Journalisten*, 15 September 2009, www.journalisten.dk/jp-hjalp-naser-khader-i-burka-sag.
14 Christian Lehmann, 'Socialdemokraterne skifter mening om burkaforbud', *Information*, 6 September 2009.

15  Peter Skaarup, DR *P1 Morgen*, 23 May 2006.

16  Pia Kjærsgaard, 'Giv os Nørrebro tilbage', *Pias ugebrev*, 23 November 2003.

17  For a longer analysis of the media's treatment of Abdol-Hamid, see Andreassen (2007: 146 ff.) and Andreassen (2010).

## References

Ahmed, S. (2004), *The cultural politics of emotion*. Edinburgh: Edinburgh University Press.

Andreassen, R. (2010a), 'Burka og bryster: Debatter om tørklæder, tilgængelighed, ligestilling og nationaliteti', in I. Degn & K.M. Soeholm (eds), *Tilsløring og demokrati i en globaliseret verden*, pp. 80-95. Aarhus: Aarhus Universitetsforlag.

Andreassen, R. (2010b), 'Sing a song but stay out of politics: Two cases of representations of racial/ethnic minorities in the Danish media', in K. Nikunen & E. Eide (eds), *Media in motion: Cultural complexity and migration in the Nordic region*, pp. 163-181. Aldershot: Ashgate.

Andreassen, R. (2007), *Der er et yndigt land: Medier, minoriteter og danskhed*. Copenhagen: Tiderne Skifter.

Andreassen, R. (2005), *The mass media's construction of gender, race, sexuality and nationality: An analysis of the Danish news media's communication about visible minorities from 1971 to 2004*. PhD dissertation, University of Toronto, Canada.

Butler, J. (1999), *Gender trouble: Feminism and the subversion of identity*. New York: Routledge.

Crenshaw, K. (1991), 'Mapping the margins: Intersectionality, identity politics and violence against women of color', *Kvinder, køn og forskning* 2-3 (2): 7-20.

Fanon, F. (1965), *A dying colonialism*. New York: Grove Press.

Foucault, M. (1990), *The history of sexuality: An introduction*. Vol. 1. New York: Vintage Books.

Laclau, E. & C. Mouffe (1985), *Hegemony and socialist strategy: Towards a radical democratic practice*. London: Verso.

Lutz, H., A. Phoenix & N. Yuval-Davis (eds) (1995), *Crossfires: Nationalism, racism and gender in Europe*. London: Pluto Press.

Richardson, R. (1998), 'Sexuality and citizenship', *Sociology* 32: 83-100.

Scott, J.W. (1999), *Gender and the politics of history*. New York: Columbia University Press.

Siim, B. & R. Andreassen (2010), 'Debatter og reguleringer af muslimske tørklæder: Populisme og symboler', *Politik* 13 (4): 15-24.

Spivak, G. (1993), 'Can the subaltern speak?', in P. Williams & L. Chrisman (eds), *Colonial discourse and post-colonial theory*, pp. 66-111. Hemel Hempstead: Harvester Wheatsheaf.

Thuesen, I. (2009), *Rapport om brugen af niqab og burqa*. Copenhagen: University of Copenhagen.

Verloo, M. & E. Lombardo (2007), 'Contested gender equality and policy variety in Europe: Introducing a critical frame analysis approach', in M. Verloo (ed.), *Multiple meanings of gender equality: A critical frame analysis of gender politics in Europe*. New York: CPS Books, Central European University Press.

# 10 Multiculturalism, dependent residence status and honour killings

## Explaining current Dutch intolerance towards ethnic minorities from a gender perspective (1960-2000)

*Marlou Schrover*

## Introduction

This chapter analyses how issues pertaining to the Turkish minority in the Netherlands have been framed in parliamentary discussions and in newspapers (see also Schrover 2011).[1] It focuses, in particular, on three issues that dominated debates between the 1960s and the 2000s. The issues are described here separately, but they are very much related. They occurred more or less in parallel and influenced one another. The first was the multicultural policy in the Netherlands, which included provisions for granting subsidies to Turkish organisations. Dutch multicultural policy thus stimulated and subsidised differences. In the 1980s, ideas about multiculturalism changed, and organisations lost most of their subsidies. One exception was a Turkish women's organisation. However, that organisation's exceptional position led to a coup which heralded its end. Second was the large-scale publicity campaigns conducted to prevent the deportation of Turkish women with a dependent residence status after they had been left or divorced by their husbands. There was a strong emphasis in the campaigns on the risks these women faced, within the Netherlands and after their return to Turkey. Third was the so-called 'honour killings'. Before the 1970s, Turkish men and women, like Dutch men and women and others, were occasionally involved in crimes of passion and related violence. Until the 1970s, however, these were never framed as honour killings. In the 1970s, newspapers systematically specified whether a perpetrator or a victim was Turkish and ran headlines like, 'Turk kills man', 'Turk shoots man', or 'Jealous Turk kills girlfriend'. In the mid-1970s, the term 'honour killing' entered debates after experts had used this notion to explain and predict violence among Turks in the Netherlands. The leading question of this chapter is how and why the problematisation of these three issues occurred.

## Materials and methods

Problematisation is the process in which actors (academics, politicians and journalists) analyse a situation, define it as a problem, expand it by attaching issues to it, finally suggesting a solution (Foucault 1984: 388-389). Problematisation always serves a purpose. In earlier research I showed how problematisation, via an emphasis on the vulnerability of migrant women, enabled rules to be bent without changing them (Schrover 2009a, 2010a, 2011).

This chapter uses records of parliamentary debates and newspaper articles to analyse the discourse on the issues mentioned above and, more specifically, nodal points within it. In general, nodal points appear in the process of articulation and give a discourse stability and coherence (Laclau & Mouffe 1985: 105; Hoving, Dibbits & Schrover 2005). A nodal point is a point in a discourse at which another meaning is defined (De Cillia, Reisigl & Wodak 1999: 157). In this chapter, the three focal issues are regarded as nodal points. Apart from the nodal points, there are routine combinations, for instance, of fairness on the one hand and firmness on the other (Van Dijk 1988, 1989, 1992: 92; Prins 2002). Nodal points and routine combinations form the intersection between discourse analysis and frame analysis. Within text, packets of organised knowledge, called 'frames', 'scripts' or 'topoi', are commonly used. These packets, referred to here as 'frames' for the sake of brevity, are determinants of the inferences necessary to understand sentence connections (Van Dijk 1983: 30; Entman 1996: 77-78). Frames support an argument without constituting it. They make text 'recognisable' and make it possible to omit information, because it is an inherent part of a packet of knowledge (Scheufele 1999; Van Gorp 2005; Matthes & Kohring 2008). Frames play a role in the process of problematisation via what is called the 'tactical linkage' of issue areas (such as, e.g., trade, climate, safety or migration), which are clustered in negotiations as 'areas of joint gain' (Rhodes 1997; Betts 2006).

The sections below analyse how in political debates and newspaper articles issues were linked and groups of arguments were clustered. The materials drawn on in this chapter come from three main sources: parliamentary debates, newspaper articles and archives of immigrant organisations. Newspaper articles were collected from all major national newspapers and a large number of regional newspapers in the Netherlands.[2] The main immigrant organisation archive used was that of the Turkish women's organisation Hollanda Türkiyeli Kadinlar Birligi (HTKB).[3]

## Multiculturalism and a Turkish women's organisation

Multicultural policy, as it was introduced in a number of Western countries in the 1960s, stimulated individuals to organise into groups on the basis of perceived cultural similarity. The struggle for recognition by organisations within this policy spurred ethnic group formation, organisation and mobilisation. Ethnic brokers worked to obtain recognition by making cultures or cultural difference visible. Since recognition claims were based on the supposed uniqueness of a group's culture, institutionalisation of multiculturalism led to an overemphasis on differences between groups, underplaying diversity within groups. Because of assumptions about group homogeneity, Dutch authorities encouraged the formation of representative bodies for migrants per country of origin. This not only denied differences within groups, but it also increased competition between groups, which tried to legitimise the claim that they spoke on behalf of the 'community' and thus qualified for funding. In the long run, these policies led to 'cultural freezing' – that is, static ideas about the identity of minority groups and about the Dutch majority society. This denied the fluidity of ethnicity, and the fact that ethnicity can be differently experienced within communities along lines of age, gender and class; while it also ignored the influence of state policies, geopolitical constellations and economic change (Volpp 1996: 1588-1589, 1592; Schrover 2010a).

Okin (1999) has shown that multiculturalism can have negative consequences for immigrant or minority women, since an emphasis on authentic identity and traditional values often implies restricted rights for women. Bhadha (2009: 57) demonstrates that a paradox of multicultural vulnerability may be created when the result of what is meant to be the empowering of groups through multiculturalism policies leads to entrenchment of oppressive elements of cultural traditions, placing women in a worse position than they would be without group recognition within multiculturalism. Okin's point of view has been criticised because it promotes stereotypical views of non-Western women. Gender subordination is constructed as integral only to non-Western cultures (Lutz 1997; McKerl 2007: 198). Non-Western cultures are presented as sexist, frozen and static (Volpp 2001: 1185; McKerl 2007: 204-205). Western representations of the East serve not only to define those who are the objects of the Orientalising gaze, but also the West, which is defined through its opposition to the Rest. The West is defined as modern, democratic and progressive; the Rest are seen as primitive, barbaric and despotic. This representation always serves a purpose. Around 1900, for instance, British suffragettes used the image of the 'victimised sisters' in India to bolster their own claims. The victimised sisters symbolised what the suffragettes did not wish to be: immobile, secluded in the home and without rights (Volpp 2001: 1195). In the 1970s, white middle-class Western women justified their claims to equality by constructing non-Western women as helpless subjects of barbaric traditionalism. The 'other' was seen as equal only in Christian rhetoric, but never in reality (Doezema 2001: 30).

In the Netherlands, multicultural policy underwent major shifts over time.[4] Three sets of ideas lay at the basis of the policy. In the first place, a model for living apart together had been developed in a 19th century Dutch colonial context: no conversions, no assimilation, but a pacified segregated coexistence (Snouck Hurgronje 1916; see also the chapter by Van Walsum, Jones & Legêne in this volume). Secondly, there was the consociational model of conflict regulation, known as pillarisation, which characterised Dutch society from the end of the 19th century onwards. Pillarisation linked political parties, civic associations and a wide range of organisations, and immerged individuals in their own (religious) group from the cradle to the grave. A number of groups within Dutch society – most importantly the Catholics, which in the 19th century constituted about half of the population, but encountered obstacles in the political and social domains – achieved emancipation via this form of segregation. The model of 'living apart together' of (denominational) groups dominated Dutch society well into the 1960s. Within it, group rights were granted, for instance, to Orthodox Protestants who were exempted from obligatory inoculations, taxes, insurance and conscription. In the 1960s, the idea of pillarisation gradually lost ground, but its institutional infrastructure survived. It went on to structure the organisation of the new migrants, who came from the 1960s, by ethnicity and religion rather than by class. Provisions dating from the time of pillarisation made it possible, for instance, for migrants to set up their own schools, subsidised by the Dutch government (Schrover 2010b).

Ideas derived from pillarisation made multicultural policies acceptable to the Dutch public, but the initial idea behind multiculturalism was not emancipation via segregation, but to facilitate an easy return of guest workers to their countries of origin (Rijkschroeff, Duyvendak & Pels 2003: 27). A multicultural policy was pursued because it enforced the idea of guest-worker migration as temporary migration. It allowed migrants to function in the Netherlands, while making a return easy. To facilitate a return, it was believed essential that migrants preserved their language, cultural identities and internal group structures (Scholten 2007: 78; Obdeijn & Schrover 2008). Authorities felt that there was no need to encourage or facilitate integration (Rijkschroeff, Duyvendak & Pels 2003: 22).[5] The government maintained this idea long after it had become clear that not all guest workers would return, because this made it possible to legitimise continuation of guest-worker recruitment (Bonjour 2008: 11).

Within the multicultural policy, integration was seen as a group process. This led to subsidies for immigrant organisations.[6] Dutch government policy strongly influenced the number of organisations that were established, their nature, goals and continuity (Penninx & Schrover 2001). Most of the immigrant organisations that were formed were men's organisations. There were a few immigrant women's organisations, of which the Turkish HTKB (Hollanda Türkiyeli Kadinlar Birligi) was the most important. Turkish women in the Netherlands set it up in 1974.[7] It ceased to exist in 1995, but the local Amsterdam branch continued under a slightly different name (ATKB). HTKB was a spin-off of HTIB, an organisation composed of left-wing Turkish men in the Netherlands and which had been set up some years earlier.[8] Nihat Karaman ran the men's organisation, and his wife, Maviye Karaman Ince, ran the women's organisation (Onderwater 2008; Robert 2009). In 1988, Nihat Karaman was shot dead in front of his house. According to some, the murder was politically motivated, while others attributed it to problems in the private relational sphere.

HTIB and HTKB were, especially in their early years, left-wing and strongly orientated towards Turkey. The HTKB saw itself as an organisation fighting a class struggle or fighting racism, and less as an organisation fighting for women's rights. Dutch women's organisations, for their part, rarely emphasised what united immigrant and non-immigrant women. Instead, they focused on what they believed divided them. They did little to include immigrant women in their organisations and activities. To the non-migrant women's organisations, migrant women were either invisible or they were victims.[9]

At its height, the HTKB had about 600 members and branch organisations in seven Dutch cities.[10] HTKB had a support group of Dutch women volunteers, as was customary for many Turkish organisations (and those of other minorities) at the time. In the 1980s, the Dutch government decided to specifically target women's immigrant organisations, of which it felt there were too few. A special programme, VEM,[11] was set up to encourage and support immigrant women to organise. VEM ran as a programme between 1982 and 1990. Immigrant women were believed to be doubly disadvantaged because they were women and migrants (or triply disadvantaged if they were also Muslims). Women could ask for subsidies for a place where they could meet 'safely' without men being present. Most initiatives within the VEM programme came from non-migrant women; only some were joint initiatives of migrant and non-migrant women. Turkish and Moroccan women's organisations took very few initiatives. Migrant women tried to gain more influence through creation of new organisations, but they met with opposition from various sides. In the first place, Dutch women within the immigrant or joint organisations refused to give up their positions. Secondly, subsidisers at the local level did not trust Turkish or Moroccan women when they applied for subsidies without the support of Dutch women, and their requests were turned down more often than those of Dutch women within joint organisations. The Dutch women knew the institutions better, they had a better understanding of how to draft a proposal, and they knew the jargon. As a result, the organisations that were created were hybrid in nature. On several occasions, it was pointed out that the organisations of, or for, migrant women, which were successful in getting subsidies, were artificial organisations (Bilgin et al. 1988).[12]

HTKB provided Dutch language classes, sewing classes and programmes aimed at teaching Turkish women how to ride a bicycle or swim. HTKB worked together with other immigrant women's organisations. In 1980, the Dutch Women's Movement (NVB) took the initiative to organise some of the immigrant women's groups under a joint umbrella organisation. Immigrant women's organisations found this initiative patronising.[13] The Amsterdam municipal authorities, however, subsidised joint initiatives. Via subsidies, Dutch authorities forced Turkish migrants to organise as Turks, and not as Kurds, left-wing or right-wing Turks, as workers, or as Muslims. When subsidies for all organisations were reduced, tensions increased amongst the rather artificially created organisations.[14] Subsidies for initiatives that had to do with immigrant women continued.[15] In 1993, this led to a coup at the general meeting of the HTKB. A group of 50 women joined the organisation at the meeting, two of them stood as candidates for the board, and they were chosen by the other new members. An emotional meeting followed. At one point the board called in the assistance of the police because of the threatening presence of Turkish men outside of the building. The parties went to court in order to settle their dispute. This heralded the end of the organisation. The story of HTKB illustrates the role of government subsidies in shaping organisations and their goals. Turkish women were first made dependent on non-Turkish volunteers. Subsidies disempowered rather than empowered them. Eventually the end of the subsidies led to violence and conflict, and the end of the organisation.

## Women from a repressive culture

I have described the issue of dependent residence status at some length elsewhere (Schrover 2009b, 2010a) and will therefore summarise it here only briefly. Dependent residency was an issue not only in the Netherlands, but also in other Western countries (Sterett 1997; Côté, Kérisit & Côté 2001). The issue arose when in 1975 recruitment of guest workers came to an end. Labour migration was replaced by migration in the context of family formation and reunification (Bonjour 2008). Since the guest workers had been mostly men (Wentholt 1967; Chotkowski 2000; Obdeijn & Schrover 2008), it was mostly women who came within the framework of family reunification. In theory, men who joined their wives could also get dependent residence permits, but since most guest workers had been men, in practice it was mostly women who obtained permits that depended on the residency status of their husbands. Dependent residency thus became a women's issue. Dependent residency meant that a woman could be deported if she left her husband (or was left by her husband) within the waiting period of three years after her arrival in the Netherlands. Dutch women's organisations took up the issue, expanding the framework within which the matter of the waiting period was discussed. Stories about women started with an emphasis on the goal of the campaigns – reduction of the waiting period – but continued as stories about abuse and domestic violence, and about persecution in women's countries of origin. Other issues were linked as well, such as forced or arranged marriages of young girls.[16] The linkages made the problem all the more urgent.

From 1979 onwards, Dutch women's organisations (mostly consisting of non-immigrant, white, middle-class women) agitated against dependent residency. Their campaigns personified the issue. Women who epitomised the matter were singled out. Dutch women's organisations sought out women as figureheads for their media campaigns in shelters for abused and maltreated women. Other organisations had followed similar principles to find the figureheads used in campaigns described by Schacher, Oxford, and Walaardt in this volume. The shelters were willing to cooperate because they did not receive state support for foreign women who had left or had been left by their husbands within the three-year period. Since the number of foreign women in the shelters had increased – at the time of the campaigns they made up half of the residents[17] – a solution to the problem of the waiting period would also solve the precarious financial situation of the shelters.[18]

All of the women selected for the media campaigns were Turkish. This choice of cases made the matter both a women's issue and an issue about the repression of women within Islam. In their campaigns, Dutch women's organisations reproduced 19th-century stereotypes about Islam and about women's dependency within it. Rather surprisingly, Dutch newspapers however, at this time seldom used the word 'Islam', but only the word 'religion'. Emphasis was on the backwardness of Turkish society.[19] Women who were divorced would not be able to survive in Turkish society, according to newspapers.[20] The women were said to have shamed and dishonoured their families.[21] Their (former) husbands and family members were likely to take revenge on the women if they were forced to return to Turkey, the newspapers wrote.[22] The arguments and stereotypes used echoed those described by Schacher in this volume for refugees from Turkey decades earlier.

Women's organisations presented three cases of individual women in quick succession. The first woman who was chosen for the campaign got a permit to stay on humanitarian grounds shortly after the start of the campaign.[23] Since no change in policy had been achieved, the women's organisations presented a second case of a woman who was maltreated by her husband and twice ended up in hospital. All Dutch newspapers reported on her situation.[24] Turkish women submitted a petition to the government signed by 2,656 people. Fearing a similar 'success' to that in the first case, the women's organisations added a third case.[25]

In Dutch parliament questions were raised about the number of women encountering such problems, the number of women with a dependent residence status in shelters, and the number of women threatened with deportation. Rather surprisingly, the State Secretary of Justice could not answer any of these questions; data were not available and the activists did not provide them.[26] In response to the question about how many women were affected, newspapers provided information about the total numbers of Turkish and Moroccan women in the Netherlands,[27] implying that all of them were likely to get into this situation. The shelters used general quantifiers ('many' women).[28] The State Secretary of Justice emphasised that women who were in this position would be allowed to stay on humanitarian grounds. There was no need for a change of law, she stressed. The length of the waiting period had been chosen to discourage marriages of convenience. One member of parliament asked if this was a Turkish or Turkish-Moroccan problem, rather than a problem that applied to all migrant women. The answer was no; the women in the shelters were definitely not all Turkish or Moroccan. The fact that this question was raised illustrates the strong association that by then had developed between the issue of dependency and being Turkish.[29] Throughout the campaigns, Turkish women in the Netherlands were presented as dependent and vulnerable, and Turkish society was portrayed as extremely backward. A Turkish women's organisation in the Netherlands pointed out that the association between a dependent residence status and violence could negatively influence the image of foreign (or Turkish) women, and this would, in the long run, be to the detriment of women. A Turkish social worker later said, 'There were many Dutch volunteers, but it was all very patronising. I was invited to speak [at a meeting of Dutch women] about Turkish women. I immediately noticed that they thought all Turkish women were backward and pathetic. They wanted to hold on to that image' (Tinnemans 1994: 182). Dutch women's organisations pushed forward with their campaigns along the lines criticised by Turkish women.

In 1983, there was a change in policy; women still had to be married at least three years, but they only needed one year of residency in the Netherlands before they could apply for an independent residence permit. The policy change was announced by the Secretary of State at the end of a conference on sexual violence against women and girls, thus linking dependent residence status, the vulnerable position of migrant women, and violence.[30] In two of the three cases presented by the campaigners, the women did not meet the criteria of the new law. Therefore, even under the new law they would not have been allowed to stay. For them personally the change of law was of little relevance since they had already been allowed to stay on humanitarian grounds. On a general level, and combined with the fact that it was never clear from the beginning how many women were disadvantaged by the old law, this makes the success of the campaigns questionable. It did, however, strongly present Turkish culture as backward, which in the long run disadvantaged Turkish women in the Netherlands.

## Honour killings

Introduction of the term 'honour killings' was preceded by newspaper reports in 1972 about severe riots in Rotterdam, which the Dutch newspapers labelled 'race riots' (Schrover 2011).[31] The riots started over a housing issue and lasted seven days. Underlying the conflict was Dutch government policy regarding family reunification. Guest workers were only allowed to bring their families if they had suitable housing. Since rental homes were very difficult to get, Turkish guest workers bought cheap houses in rundown neighbourhoods. Turks also bought houses, which they converted to boarding houses for their fellow countrymen. The riots started when a Turkish homeowner tried to evict a Dutch woman with three young children. Dutch neighbours protested, and Dutch rioters cruised the neighbourhood and smashed the windows of the homes of Turks. Their furniture was thrown onto the street and set on fire.[32] Turkish families were forced to flee. A Turk stabbed several Dutch people in self-defence. They had to be treated in hospital. The Dutch rioters complained that Turks were taking over the neighbourhood. They expanded the issue by adding that Turks were harassing Dutch girls, some of whom were no older than 12 or 13. Two Dutch girls were harmed by the Dutch rioters because they were friendly with Turks. The police were photographed standing by idly during the riots, while laughing and doing little to protect Turks. Police, however, did block street entrances to make sure Turks in the neighbourhood did not get support from Turks from elsewhere.[33] Turkish women and children turned to the Turkish consulate for support and advice. The consul and the Turkish minister of foreign affairs intervened, calling upon the Dutch government to protect the Turks and their property.

Newspapers described the Turks efforts to organise to defend themselves and their calls for support. Turkish thugs, according to one of the papers, armed with guns planned to take revenge.[34] One Turk was quoted as saying he would behead the whole neighbourhood. Turks who had fled to the roofs of their houses threw roof tiles onto rioters several floors below them.[35] Four Turks were arrested, as well as about 60 Dutch rioters.[36] Dutch groups, which came out in support of the Turks, stated that the young Dutch rioters did know what they were getting themselves into. The Turks were hard to restrain, they said. Despite the support group's efforts, they might very well become violent and might cut the rioters into seven pieces.[37] Newspaper articles supported this view; Turkish women and children had left the neighbourhood, but Turkish men hid in backrooms, listened to the muffled thuds of stones landing in their front rooms, the scattering of glass and the splintering of wood, and waited to crack the skull of every Dutch guy who dared climb the stairs.[38]

Overall the tone in the newspapers was one of surprise and outrage at the eruption of violence and racial hatred. But the articles also fed an atmosphere of fear. Shortly after the outbreak of the riots, a Turkish man stood to allow a young Dutch woman to sit on a packed train. The woman misunderstood his intentions and started to scream. Somebody pulled the emergency chain, forcing the train to stop, and the chivalrous Turk was arrested.[39]

The effect of reports about the riots was twofold. In the first place, a possible violent nature of the Turks was emphasised. This idea was reinforced by endless reports in the Dutch newspapers about Turkish atrocities against Greeks in Cyprus in 1974, and reports about riots in the Netherlands in 1976. Those riots had started after a Turkish man stabbed a Dutch man to death at a fair. During the 1976 riots an extremist right-wing party – the *Nederlandse Volks-Unie* – started a racist campaign. Secondly, there was the surprising nature of the riots. British, French and Turkish newspapers reported on the Dutch race riots. They were quoted at length in Dutch newspapers. The foreign papers expressed surprise that this could happen in a nation like the Netherlands, which was known for its tolerance and hospitality to foreigners.[40] Dutch newspapers tried to explain the eruption of violence. The Dutch were perhaps not the hospitable or tolerant people they believed themselves to be, according to the papers, but there were also too many Turks and too many Turkish boarding houses in poor neighbourhoods.[41] In offering this explanation, the papers implicitly shifted part of the blame away from the Dutch to the Turks. 'Too many' implied 'too different'. The emphasis on cultural difference was perfectly consistent with the ideas of multicultural policy. It was also consistent with how the issue of honour killings developed.

Generally, culture is invoked to explain forms of violence against immigrant or minority women, while it is not similarly invoked to explain forms of violence that affect non-migrant or non-minority women. In the USA, for instance, the media framed the murder of an Indian woman within an assumed old Indian tradition of dowry murders, rather than presenting the murder as a response to domestic violence common in the USA (Volpp 2001: 1187). In the case of honour killings, violence is allegedly used to restore the honour of the family. The murderer is believed to be chosen by the family at a family conference, after which he plans his murder (which makes it premeditated murder and not manslaughter); he turns himself in after the murder and does not show remorse (Siesling 2006: 24). The assumption is that honour-related violence is tolerated or excused by the members of the family or community.

In the case of honour killings, perpetrators availed of a so-called 'cultural defence' (Siesling 2006 103-126). Cultural defence was seldom used in practice, but it did have a strong influence in public and political discourse. Cultural defence is not a doctrine in Dutch law (nor in US law) (Siesling 2006: 66; Korteweg & Yurdakul 2009). Cultural defence implies recognition that customs or mores might differ between countries (or cultures) and that an accused may be aware of differences, but not able to comply with the rules of the country of settlement because of an internalisation of the mores of the country of origin or pressure from a community in the country of settlement. The accused is seen as having no free will and as not accountable for his actions (diminished responsibility). Attorneys seek sentencing in line with the personal characteristics of the defendant (as in the case of mentally handicapped or children, who cannot be held responsible for their actions). The defence is similar to the *battered woman syndrome defence*, in which it is claimed that women are not accountable for killing their husbands after they suffered years of maltreatment. Culture, however, is different from mental state or age. Cultural cases move the responsibility away from the individual, but also from society. The behaviour of migrants results from their culture (which is presented as static), and that is not something the country of settlement can remedy.

In cultural defence cases there is an emphasis on shame; men are assumed to have killed their daughters, wives or sisters because the women shamed the family with their assumed loose moral behaviour. The culture of the country of origin of the perpetrator (or his forefathers) is contrasted with the more individualistic societies in which he lives and which are believed to care less about honour and shame. In the discourse, a distinction is made between backward cultures (often called 'traditional') and modern cultures. Both are seen as static. Rather surprisingly, little reference is made to the connection between the need to avenge shame on an individual level and the absence of strong central government or that individual-level revenge in the form of feuds and duels was common in European countries from the Middles Ages until the 19th century (Le Vaque-Manty 2006). Avenging shame is presented only as part of the traditions of non-European countries.

Authors have pointed out that advocating use of the cultural defence is problematic because it focuses on the rights of the defendant and fails to protect the victims and the public at large. The argument that 'his culture made him do it' does little to deter others from committing the same act or even to deter the defendant himself from repeating his offence. Nor does it assure victims and other potential victims that society is willing to protect them or to punish the defendant for the harm done by his act (Lambelet Coleman 1996: 1136).

Non-migrant women in the Netherlands are also killed by their husbands, brothers and fathers because of shame or jealousy, but these murders are never discussed in the same way as the so-called honour killings. In 1959, a Dutch man avenged his sister, according to Dutch papers, by killing a man who had slapped her in the face.[42] Generally when a Dutch man kills his wife, sister or daughter, it is described as a crime of passion or a family tragedy. Furthermore, in the Netherlands (and Germany) honour killings are characterised as a Turkish issue, while in the UK they tend to be associated with the Pakistani community. Honour killings were reported in Greece in the late 1960s (Safilios-Rothschild 1969), but murders among Greeks in the Netherlands were not explained from that perspective.

In the 1970s, before the term 'honour killing' was introduced, there were murders in which the perpetrator was Turkish and which took place in the relational sphere.[43] In some cases newspapers used the word 'honour', but not the term 'honour killing'. Some cases had characteristics which later might have been described as 'honour killing'. In 1972, a 14-year-old Turkish boy shot and killed a 36-year-old Turkish man. The boy lived with his father, mother and brothers. According to the police, the man was probably the lover of the boy's mother.[44] In 1973, the public prosecutor in a murder case said that a Turkish drama should be regarded from a Turkish perspective. A Turkish woman had killed her Turkish lover. According to the public prosecutor the Turkish husband should have killed both his wife and her lover, according to Turkish 'adat'.[45] The Turkish man was a coward, the public prosecutor was quoted as saying in a newspaper. Rather than killing his wife and her lover himself, he had provided his wife with a gun so she could kill her lover, save her honour and prove her loyalty to her husband. The whole affair was called a guest-worker drama, not an honour killing.[46] In 1975, a Turkish man fatally shot a compatriot, who he believed had raped his wife. The killer declared he had done so to save his honour as a man.[47] The public prosecutor declared this argument to be absurd and false.[48] Shortly afterwards, a 18-year-old boy fatally shot his uncle, who had knocked his mother unconscious and tried to take his younger siblings away.[49] The conflict within the family had started the previous year, when the father had gone to Turkey to find a bride for his son. He had returned with a 16-year-old girl, whom the son regarded as his wife from then on. The father had, however, started an affair with the girl. According to the public prosecutor, his wife and his son had been shamed by these events. The father had gone to Turkey with this young woman, and some time later had summoned his son to join him there. When the boy refused, his father and uncle threatened to kill him. At this point, the court called upon a lawyer from the Turkish consulate in the Netherlands who was an expert in Turkish common law. The expert explained that the family came from Eastern Turkey, were violence occurred when honour was impugned. The boy, who became the head of the family after his father's departure, was bound to protect his mother and younger siblings. The expert referred to a Turkish proverb, which said that soiled honour could only be restored by blood. The public prosecutor did not accept this defence.[50] One month later, a Turkish man shot and killed his 13-year-old daughter.[51] A year later, a Turkish

woman killed a Turkish man who had followed her by car while she
walked to the post office. He had tried to convince her to come with
him. When she refused and he persisted, she shot him.[52] Shortly afterwards a Turkish man shot his wife, who was planning to leave him;[53] a
young Turkish man died after a fight for an unknown reason;[54] and a
Turkish woman shot her husband dead in the street, because she suspected him of having an affair.[55]

Newspapers, as rule, do not report every murder. Overall the number of murders in this period was about 1 per 100,000 people per year
(Leistra & Nieuwbeerta 2003: 21). With a Turkish population of about
100,000 (or 150,000 if children born of Turkish parents in the Netherlands are also included), the percentage was slightly higher than average in the 1970s. Precise statements are difficult to make, because there
is no registration according to ethnic group, and murder rates are influenced by the demographic profile of a group. The chance of becoming
either a victim or a perpetrator are higher for the age group 18 to 45, and
this group was larger among Turks than among the Dutch population
as a whole. Newspapers in this period did not compare crime statistics
of Turks and non-Turks, but detailed reporting and standard reference
to the ethnic background of victims and perpetrators emphasised the
idea that there was something specific about the murders that called for
an explanation.

The term 'honour killing' was first used in the Netherlands in 1976
when a Turkish boy killed the man who had raped his sister (Ferwerda
& Van Leiden 2005). In 1977, a Turkish man was convicted of manslaughter. He had killed another Turkish man to avenge the repeated
rape of his 13-year-old daughter. The girl had given birth to a child,
thus shaming the family. She would have no other future than work
as a prostitute, the father declared in court.[56] In 1978, a Turkish man
smashed the skull of his heavily pregnant wife with a cognac bottle. The
murder followed marital problems, because the wife refused to obey
the Koran, especially regarding subservience, newspapers wrote.[57] In
1979, a boy was convicted of murdering his half-sister. His motives were
never revealed in court, but he did refer to family honour, which had
been violated. The judge was not convinced by this cultural defence
(Siesling 2006: 200). That same year, a Turkish woman and mother
of four was convicted and sentenced to seven years of imprisonment
for killing a distant cousin. He had raped her a few years before and
spread gossip about her in the Turkish community. The public prosecutor demanded a severe sentence, precisely because he did see this
as honour killing and wanted to deter those with similar plans.[58] A few
days later, two Turkish brothers killed their brother-in-law because he

maltreated their sister, his wife. According to the newspapers this was an honour killing.[59] A public prosecutor declared that cases of honour killings were likely to increase in the Netherlands. He based this statement, according to Dutch newspapers, on a Dutch academic study by A.H. Nauta. Nauta was of the opinion that the recent killings were the tip of the iceberg.[60] The study related to Turkey, but was used to explain murders in the Netherlands.

In 1985, there was a murder during a wedding party whereby reference was made to shame and honour. In all of these cases the perpetrators were Turkish. All murders received a lot of publicity. A strong association developed between the phenomenon and migrants from Islamic countries. In 1999, a Turkish woman was killed by her husband, in the presence of her children. The husband suspected her of adultery. The attorney asked that his client be charged with manslaughter, rather than with premeditated murder, because of his cultural background. The judge called the case revolting, particularly because the defendant showed no remorse. Rather than reducing his punishment on cultural grounds, the judge decided to increase the sentence in order to set an example to Dutch society and the Turkish community within it (Siesling 2006: 202). Two other cases followed. In 2003, a Turkish girl was shot by her father, and in 2004, a woman of Turkish origin was killed by her husband. She had fled to a shelter but her husband had managed to find her. The judges did not consider these cases honour killings, but in public and political debates the murders were presented as such, and demonstrations were held and political measures were called for, although it is not clear what the measures should be.

Overall over the past three decades, six court cases were heard in which honour killings played a role. In one case (1999) that fact led the judge to increase the sentence by five additional years. In two cases (2003 and 2004), the judge did view the cases as honour killings. In the three early cases (1976, 1979 and 1985) it is not clear whether the mention of honour had any influence on the outcome of the trial, positive or negative. However, repeated use of the term in the press and parliamentary debates and the intense public attention that all cases received created the impression that honour killings occurred frequently within the Dutch-Turkish community.

It is unclear how many cases of honour killings or honour-related violence there have been in the Netherlands. The same is true for other countries (Kurkiala 2003). There are two reasons for this. In the first place, the term is used to cover a wide array of 'crimes'. There is no registration of honour-related violence by the police, social services or women's shelters. Neither is there consensus about what constitutes honour-related violence. Secondly, there is no clarity about numbers because judges may use the term honour-related violence, when the perpetrator or attorney does not. Or a perpetrator or attorney may use the term, but the judge may not acknowledge it. The media frequently refer to crimes as 'honour-related' when neither the perpetrator and attorney nor the judge does so. The result is a gross overestimation of numbers.

The subject of honour killings is very much part of recent Dutch public debates. Stories and studies about honour killings only briefly acknowledge that it is unclear how many honour killings actually take place. Reports use vague quantifiers, such as 'many', 'often' and 'frequent', to emphasise that they are common, and they include detailed descriptions of older cases from other countries (mostly Germany). That obscures the fact that these acts did not take place in the Netherlands or that they occurred years ago. The definition of what is an honour killing is currently stretched beyond useful. Honour killings are redefined as honour-related violence, or the physical or physiological violence that stems from a collective mentality and which is a response to (the risk of) the violation of the honour of women, of which the outside world has knowledge or is likely to acquire knowledge. Some researchers stretch the definition so that it includes murder, and also domestic violence, verbal threats, abductions, (extreme) control of men over the mobility of women or girls, forced or arranged marriages, and women being forced into a traditional women's role. Suicides by women and girls are sometimes described as honour-related violence, because the women and girls are believed to have been pushed into suicide by male family members (Bakker 2003).

In 2007, 107 Imams in Turkish mosques in the Netherlands spoke out against honour killings. Their collective stance received wide media coverage. Honour killings are discussed frequently by the media and in parliament. In recent years, numerous books have appeared in the Netherlands about honour killings (Van Eck 2001; Hilterman 2001; Simsek 2006; Van der Zee 2006; Ermers 2007; Özer 2007; Vreeswijk 2008). The press currently labels any violent crime involving men or women of Turkish origin as honour-related. When, in August 2009, a woman who worked at a day-care centre in Amsterdam was murdered, all newspapers wrote about it as an honour killing.[61] The only reason it was classified as such was that she was of Turkish origin as was the perpetrator.

## Conclusion

This chapter described, on the basis of an analysis of immigrant organisation archives, parliamentary debates and newspaper articles,
three parallel and interwoven issues: changing ideas about multiculturalism, campaigns against dependent resident status and honour killings. Multicultural policy was initially shaped by assumptions about
the temporariness of guest-worker migration. Underlying ideas were
acceptable because of ideas about living apart together, which had characterised Dutch society until the 1960s. Some groups were targeted by
multicultural policy more than other groups. As a result, these groups
were more strongly subjected to processes of othering. The most disadvantaged groups could profit more from their supposed victimisation
via subsidies in the short run, but they found it difficult to shed that
victimhood identity in the long run. Subsidies shaped how migrants
presented themselves as communities, led to quests for authenticity,
emphasised differences between migrants and non-migrants, and stimulated organisation on the basis of ethnicity. The portrayal of migrant
or minority women – especially lower-class, Muslim women – was important in securing and continuing government subsidies. Reduction
of subsidies for organisations that did not specifically target women
made the Turkish HTKB the target of a hostile take-over, which signalled its end, and drove other organisations to push women's issues
even more to the foreground. Gender was crucial to how multicultural
policy worked out. Fossilisation of ideas and of initiatives – symbolised
by the endless subsidies for swimming and cycling lessons for Turkish women, which came to be ridiculed by the radical right – fed the
opposition to multiculturalism. Because multiculturalism and racism
are both based on essentialist ideas, the shift from one to the other is
not surprising. The campaigns against dependent resident status, like
multicultural policy, endlessly emphasised victimhood, difference and
backwardness of Turks and Turkish society. In addition, intense attention to so-called 'honour killings', in the first place, created the idea that
they were very common among Turks, and secondly that honour killings were something very different than Dutch family dramas or crimes
of passion. This solidified the othering and static ideas about culture
that had resulted from multicultural policies and the campaigns against
dependent residence status.

The radical right could easily appropriate gender equality, because of
the essentialist assumptions underlying multicultural policy and rhetoric that for decades had constructed migrants or minorities as collectiv-
ist, authoritarian, patriarchal and honour-bound (compare Akkerman

& Hagelund 2007; Roggeband & Verloo 2007). The radical right did not have to prove that immigrant women – especially Muslim women – were oppressed. This had, after all, been the justification for decades of Dutch government subsidies and intervention.

This chapter showed that the purpose of the problematisation of what were seen as Turkish issues in the Netherlands shifted over time. Initially the aim was to generate support for the Turkish migrants. Othering was the outcome. This othering later served to substantiate claims that there were unsolvable problems, and this fed into anti-immigrant and racist discourse. This chapter showed how labelling moved from one discourse to another. Multiculturalism, dependent resident status and honour killings were nodal points in the debates. These points, on which discussions focused, were connected to one other in mutually reinforcing debates.

## Notes

1  The chapter is part of my NWO Vici project (277-53-002).
2  My student assistant Daan Loeff helped me to collect the newspaper articles. I thank him for his work.
3  International Institute for Social History (Amsterdam), Archive Hollanda Türkiyeli Kadinlar Birligi 1974-1995 10815458_EAD. The archival research was done in part by my master's student Jerney Robert, whom I thank here for her work.
4  Proceedings Lower House, session 2003-2004, 28 689, nos. 8-9 Onderzoek integratiebeleid (*Eindverslag van de commissie Blok*).
5  Proceedings Lower House, session 2003-2004, 28 689, no. 12, p. 137.
6  Proceedings Lower House, session 2003-2004, 28 689, no. 12: Onderzoek Integratiebeleid, Onderzoeksrapport, Aanvullend bronnenonderzoek Verwey-Jonker Instituut, 79.
7  Internationaal Institute Social History (Amsterdam) Archive: Hollanda Türkiyeli Kadinlar Birligi 1974-1995 10815458 EAD.
8  Hollanda Türkiyeli Isçiler Birligi.
9  The same relationship between non-migrant and migrant women's organisations has been found in other countries (Scuzzarello 2008: 16).
10  Amsterdam, Rotterdam, Leiden, Nijmegen, The Hague, and Utrecht and a more or less independent branch in Eindhoven (Eindhoven Türkiyeli Kadınlar Birliği).
11  VEM stands for *Vrouwen en Minderhedenbeleid* (Women and Minority Policy).
12  Proceedings Lower House, session 2003-2004, 28 689, no. 12, p. 184.
13  IISG, HTKB, map 241, Stukken betreffende congres Buitenlandse Vrouwen, notulen werkgroep Buitenlandse Vrouwen, 27-09-1981. IISG, HTKB, folio 242, Stukken betreffende het Congres van Buitenlandse Vrouwen in Nederland. 1980, notulen van discussiegroep Nederlandse vrouwen.
14  *De Volkskrant*, 21 April 1995, p. 6.
15  Proceedings Lower House, session 2003-2004, 28 689, no. 12, p. 253.

16  *NRC*, 24 September 1980, p. 3.

17  *De Volkskrant*, 7 June 1983.

18  *Trouw*, 24 September 1980, p. 10.

19  *Het Vrije Volk*, 24 April 1982.

20  *Trouw*, 24 September 1980, p. 10; *NRC*, 24 September 1980, p. 3.

21  *Trouw*, 10 March 1980, p. 9; *Het Parool*, 13 August 1981.

22  *De Volkskrant*, 17 September 1981, p. 7.

23  Proceedings Lower House, session 1981, appendix, p. 573.

24  See, e.g., *Het Vrije Volk*, 21 May 1982, *Het Parool*, 21 May 1982, *NRC*, 21 May 1982.

25  *Het Parool*, 12 July 1982.

26  Proceedings Lower House, session 1980-1981, 16102, no. 9, pp. 1-6.

27  *Trouw*, 10 March 1981, p. 9.

28  *NRC*, 10 March 1981, p. 3.

29  Proceedings Lower House, session 1980-1981, 16102, no. 9, pp. 1-6.

30  *Algemeen Dagblad*, 9 June 1982.

31  *Het Vaderland*, 18 August 1972, p. 1, *Trouw*, 18 August 1972, p. 1.

32  *NRC*, 11 August 1972, p. 12.

33  *Het Vaderland*, 11 August 1972.

34  *De Telegraaf*, 12 August 1972, p. 1.

35  *Het Vrije Volk*, 10 August 1972, p. 1; *Het Vaderland*, 11 August 1972, p. 6.

36  *NRC*, 10 August 1972, p. 2.

37  *Leeuwarder Courant*, 14 August 1972, p. 19; *Nieuwsblad van het Noorden*, 14 August 1972, p. 2.

38  *De Groene Amsterdammer*, 15-22 August 1972, p. 2.

39  *De Telegraaf*, 16 August 1972, p. 5.

40  *The Times*, 12 August 1972; articles in Turkish papers were quoted in *Het Vaderland* 15 August 1972, p. 5.

41  *Het Vaderland*, 12 August 1972, p. 3.

42  *Leeuwarder Courant*, 18 August 1959.

43  *Zierikzeesche Nieuwsbode*, 16 April 1964, p. 5; *Het Parool*, 4 June 1969, p. 1; *Vrije Volk*, 4 June 1969, p. 1; *Zierikzeesche Nieuwsbode*, 5 June 1969, p. 7; *Zierikzeesche Nieuwsbode*, 12 November 1979, p. 2; *Zierikzeesche Nieuwsbode* 8 June 1972, p. 7; *Nieuwsblad van het Noorden*, 28 June 1972, p. 2; *Nieuwsblad van het Noorden*, 27 July 1972, p. 5; *Nieuwsblad van het Noorden*, 28 November 1972, p. 1; *Nieuwsblad van het Noorden*, 7 February 1973, p. 3; *Nieuwsblad van het Noorden*, 27 February 1973, p. 3; *Leidse Courant*, 25 October 1975.

44  *Leidse Courant*, 25 October 1972; *Zierikzeesche Nieuwsbode*, 26 October 1972.

45  *Adat* is a Malayan word for tradition and was used in the Dutch East Indies as the word for traditional law. The Dutch were familiar with the word. The Turkish equivalent is *adet*.

46  *Nieuwsblad van het Noorden*, 29 August 1973, p. 3.

47  *Nieuwsblad van het Noorden*, 21 May 1975, p. 3.

48  *Nieuwsblad van het Noorden*, 3 June 1975, p. 1.

49  *Leeuwarder Courant*, 28 July 1975; *Parool*, 28 July 1975, p. 1.

50  *Parool*, 1 November 1975, p. 4.

51  *Leeuwarder Courant*, 26 August 1975.

52  *Nieuwsblad van het Noorden*, 17 November 1976, p. 3.
53  *Leeuwarder Courant*, 28 February 1977.
54  *Nieuwsblad van het Noorden*, 14 March 1977, p. 11.
55  *Nieuwsblad van het Noorden*, 16 December 1977, p. 17.
56  *Leeuwarder Courant*, 17 November 1977.
57  *Leeuwarder Courant*, 11 July 1978; *Nieuwsblad van het Noorden*, 11 July 1978, p. 7.
58  *Nieuwsblad van het Noorden*, 6 April 1979, p. 3.
59  *De Telegraaf*, 17 April 1979, p. 3.
60  *Leeuwarder Courant*, 17 August 1979.
61  *Algemeen Dagblad*, 12 August 2009.

## References

Akkerman, T. & A. Hagelund (2007), '"Women and children first!" Anti-immigration parties and gender in Norway and the Netherlands', *Patterns of Prejudice* 41 (2): 197-214.

Bakker, H. (2003), *Eerwraak in Nederland: Een quickscan van de stand van zaken* Utrecht: TransAct.

Betts, A. (2006), *Conceptualising interconnections in global governance: The case of refugee protection*, Oxford: RSC Working Paper 38.

Bhabha, F. (2009), 'Between exclusion and assimilation: Experimentalizing multiculturalism', *McGill Law Journal* 54: 45-90.

Bilgin, S., A. Kouwenhoven, R. Latumahina & J. Westhoek (1988), *Met één hand kan je niet klappen: Een onderzoek naar organisaties van vrouwen uit etnische minderheidsgroepen in Nederland*. Utrecht & Leiden: Rijksuniversiteit Leiden, Centrum door Onderzoek Maatschappelijke Tegenstellingen.

Bonjour, S. (2008), 'Ambtelijke onmin rond gezinnen van gastarbeiders: Beleidsvorming inzake gezinsmigratie in Nederland, 1955-1970', *Tijdschrift voor Sociale en Economische Geschiedenis* 5 (1): 101-127.

Chotkowski, M.B. (2000), '"Baby's kunnen we niet huisvesten, moeder en kind willen we niet scheiden": De rekrutering door Nederland van vrouwelijke arbeidskrachten uit Joegoslavië, 1966-1979', *Tijdschrift voor Sociale Geschiedenis* 26 (1): 76-103.

Cillia, R. de, M. Reisigl & R. Wodak (1999), 'The discursive construction of national identities', *Discourse & Society* 10: 149-173.

Côté, A., M. Kérisit & M. Côté (2001), *Sponsorship ... for better or for worse: The impact of sponsorship on the equality rights of immigrant women*. Ottawa: Status of Women Canada.

Dijk, T.A. van (1992), 'Discourse and the denial of racism', *Discourse & Society* 3: 87-118.

Dijk, T.A. van (1989), 'Race, riots and the press: An analysis of editorials in the British press about the 1985 disorders', *Gazette* 43: 229-253.

Dijk, T.A. van (1988), 'The Tamil panic in the press', in T.A. van Dijk (ed.), *News analysis: Case studies of international and national news in the press*, pp. 215-254. Hillsdale: Lawrence Erlbaum.

Dijk, T.A. van (1983), *Minderheden in de media: Een analyse van de berichtgeving over etnische minderheden in de dagbladpers*. Amsterdam: Socialistische Uitgeverij Amsterdam.

Doezema, J. (2001), 'Ouch! Western feminists' "wounded attachment" to the "third world prostitute"'. *Feminist Review* 67 (Spring): 16-38.

Eck, C. van (2001), 'Door bloed gezuiverd: Eerwraak bij Turken in Nederland'. PhD thesis, University of Amsterdam.

Entman, R.M. (1996), 'Reporting environmental policy debate: The real media biases', *Harvard International Journal of Press/Politics* 1 (3): 77-92.

Ermers, R. (2007), *Eer en eerwraak: Definitie en analyse*. Amsterdam: Bulaaq.

Ferwerda, H.B. & I. van Leiden (2005), *Eerwraak of eergerelateerd geweld? Naar een werkdefinitie*. The Hague: Ministery of Justice.

Foucault, M. (1984), 'Polemics, politics and problematisations: An interview with Michel Foucault', in P. Rabinow (ed.), *The Foucault Reader*, pp. 381-390. London: Pantheon Books.

Gorp, B. van (2005), 'Where is the frame? Victims and intruders in the Belgian press coverage of the asylum issue', *European Journal of Communication* 20 (4): 485-508.

Hilterman, K. (2001), *Eerwraak*. Houten: Van Holkema & Warendorf.

Hoving, I., H. Dibbits & M. Schrover (eds) (2005), *Veranderingen van het alledaagse. Cultuur en migratie in Nederland*. Den Haag: SDU.

Korteweg, A. & G. Yurdakul (2009), 'Islam, gender, and immigrant integration: Boundary drawing in discourses on honour killing in the Netherlands and Germany', *Ethnic and Racial Studies*: 32 (2): 218-238.

Kurkiala, M. (2003), 'Interpreting honour killings: The story of Fadime Sahindal (1975-2002) in the Swedish press', *Anthropology Today* 19 (1) (February): 6-7.

Laclau, E. & C. Mouffe (1985), *Hegemony and socialist strategy*. London: Verso.

Lambelet Coleman, D. (1996), 'Individualizing justice through multiculturalism: The liberals' dilemma', *Columbia Law Review* 96 (5) (June): 1093-1167.

Leistra, G. & P. Nieuwbeerta (2003), *Moord en doodslag in Nederland (1992-2001)*. Amsterdam: Prometheus.

Le Vaque-Manty, M. (2006), 'Dueling for equality: Masculine honor and the modern politics of dignity', *Political Theory* 34 (6): 715-740.

Lutz, H. (1997), 'The limits of European-ness: Immigrant women in fortress Europe', *Feminist Review* 57, *Citizenship: Pushing the Boundaries* (Autumn): 93-111.

Matthes, J. & M. Kohring (2008), 'The content analysis of media frames: Toward improving reliability and validity', *Journal of Communication* 58: 258-279.

McKerl, M. (2007), 'Multiculturalism, gender and violence', *Culture and Religion* 8 (2): 187-217.

Obdeijn, H., & M. Schrover (2008), *Komen en gaan: Immigratie en emigratie in Nederland vanaf 1550*. Amsterdam: Bert Bakker.

Okin, S. Moller (1999), 'Is multiculturalism bad for women?', in J. Cohen, M. Howard & M. Nussbaum (eds), *Is multiculturalism bad for women?* pp. 9-24. Princeton: Princeton University Press.

Onderwater, P. (2008), 'Wij zijn geen "zielige vrouwtjes"! Een onderzoek naar de houding van de Turkse vrouwenbeweging in Nederland ten opzichte van het seksedebat tussen 1970-2008'. Master's thesis, Utrecht University.

Özer, N. (2007), *Hatice: Een Turks drama.* Amsterdam: Bulaaq.

Penninx, R. & M. Schrover (2001), *Bastion of bindmiddel: Organisaties van immigranten in historisch perspectief.* Amsterdam: Institute for Migration & Ethnic Studies.

Prins, B. (2002), 'The nerve to break taboos: New realism in the Dutch discourse on multiculturalism', *JLMI/RLMI* 3 (3 & 4): 363-379.

Rhodes, R.A.W. (1997), *Understanding governance: Policy networks, governance, reflexivity and accountability.* Buckingham: Open University Press.

Rijkschroeff, R., J.W. Duyvendak & T. Pels (2003), *Bronnenonderzoek integratiebeleid.* Utrecht: Verwey-Jonker Instituut.

Robert, J. (2009), 'De opkomst en ondergang van Hollanda Türkiyeli Kadinlar Birligi (Turkse vrouwenvereniging in Nederland) 1974-1995: Ruim dertig jaar strijd om mondigheid! Waar ging het mis?' Master's thesis, Leiden University.

Roggeband, C. & M. Verloo (2007), 'Dutch women are liberated, migrant women are a problem: The evolution of policy frames on gender and migration in the Netherlands, 1995-2005', *Social Policy & Administration* 41 (3) (June): 271-288.

Safilios-Rothschild, C. (1969), '"Honour" crimes in contemporary Greece', *The British Journal of Sociology* 20 (2) (June): 205-218.

Scheufele, D.A. (1999), 'Framing as a theory of media effects', *Journal of Communication* 49 (1): 103-122.

Scholten, P. (2007), *Constructing immigrant policies, research-policy relations and immigrant integration in the Netherlands (1970-2004).* Arnhem: University of Twente.

Schrover, M. (2011), *Om de meisjes, voor de meisjes: Een historisch perspectief op problematisering en bagatellisering van onderwerpen die te maken hebben met migratie en integratie.* Leiden: Leiden University.

Schrover, M. (2010a), 'Why make a difference? Migration policy and making differences between migrant men and women (the Netherlands 1945-2005)', in M. Schrover & E.J. Yeo (eds), *Gender, migration and the public sphere, 1850-2005,* pp. 76 96. New York: Routledge.

Schrover, M. (2010b), 'Pillarization, multiculturalism and cultural freezing, Dutch migration history and the enforcement of essentialist ideas', *BMGN/LCHR* 125 (2/3): 329-354.

Schrover, M. (2009a), 'Differences that make all the difference: Gender, migration and vulnerability', in M. Orly, G. Brunet, V. Barusse De Luca, & D. Gauvreau (eds), *A Female demography: Migration, work, fertility, family,* pp. 143-168. Bern: Peter Lang.

Schrover, M. (2009b), 'Family in Dutch migration policy 1945-2005', *The History of the Family* 14: 191-202.

Schrover, M. &. E.J. Yeo (2010), 'Introduction: Moving the focus to the public sphere', in M. Schrover, & E.J. Yeo (eds), *Gender, migration and the public sphere in interdisciplinary perspective 1850-2005,* pp. 1-13. New York: Routledge.

Siesling, M. (2006), *Multiculturaliteit en verdediging in strafzaken: Een onderzoek naar de manieren waarop in het Nederlandse strafrecht ruimte wordt gevonden voor het verwerken van de culturele achtergrond van de verdachte.* Utrecht: Boom.

Simsek, J. (2006), *Alle ogen op haar gericht, eerwraak: Traditioneel geweld tegen Turkse vrouwen en meisjes: een handleiding voor hulpverleners*. Utrecht: Inspraakorgaan Turken in Nederland (IOT).

Snouck Hurgronje, C. (1916), *Mohammedanism: Lectures on its origin, its religious and political growth, and its present state*. Leiden: Project Gutenberg.

Sterett, S. (1997), 'Domestic violence and immigration in Britain', *Polar* 20 (2): 63-69.

Scuzzarello, S. (2008), 'National security versus moral responsibility: an analysis of integration programs in Malmö, Sweden', *Social Politics* 15 (1): 5-31.

Tinnemans, W. (1994), *Een gouden armband: Een geschiedenis van Mediterrane immigranten in Nederland (1945-1994)*. Utrecht: Nederlands Centrum Buitenlanders.

Volpp, L. (2001), 'Feminism versus multiculturalism', *Columbia Law Review* 101: 1181-1218.

Volpp, L. (1996), 'Talking "culture": Gender, race, nation, and the politics of multiculturalism', *Columbia Law Review* 96: 1573-1617.

Vreeswijk, H. (2008), *Eerwraak*. Antwerpen: Manteau.

Wentholt, R. (1967), *Buitenlandse gastarbeiders in Nederland*. Leiden: Spruyt.

Zee, R. van der (2006), *Eerwraak in Nederland*. Antwerpen/Amsterdam: Houtekiet.

# 11 Conclusion

Gender, migration and cross-categorical research

*Marlou Schrover and Deirdre Moloney*

States differentiate explicitly between *categories of migrants* (e.g., colonial, refugee, labour and family) and implicitly according to *categories of analysis*, such as gender, class, religion and ethnicity. This volume focused on this dual relationship between gender and categorisation. Categories of migrants are like communicating vessels: migrants can and do change categories. We analysed how, when and why this happens, and how this differs according to gender, as well as to class and ethnicity. Defining (the true refugee, the family member or difference) is directly related to enumerating migrants. Numbers (real or inflated) are vital to justify measures or new policies. Categorisation is not only important for allocating or withholding rights, but also for substantiating claims, particularly the claim that there is a problem. The numbers game plays out differently for migrant men and women: men are *a* risk, women are *at* risk.

In the introductory chapter, we summarised the large literature on gender and migration. With this volume, we have added to that literature in six significant ways.

In the first place, we moved away from taking stock of differences, and from the over-studied sectors of domestic work and prostitution, with their stress on victimisation, feminisation and problematisation. We explained the functionality of making differences.

Secondly, we focused on the public sphere (political debates and media coverage), where boundaries are redrawn, rather than on the private sphere, and we showed that issues move between both spheres.

Third, we illustrated not only that class and ethnicity intersect with gender, but that religion does so as well. Christian support groups advocated for their co-religionists, and as part of that strategy emphasised that Christian women were at risk of being harmed by Muslim men. The aim of anti-veiling campaigns was partly to protect Muslim women from repression by Muslim men. What is labelled a crime of passion when it involves non-migrants becomes a culturally-based honour killing when it involves Islamic migrants. The intersection between class and gender is often strongest as part of problematising 'their' poverty as 'our' problem. Poor men applying for asylum are more likely to be suspected of not being 'true' refugees than poor women. Poor men are also more likely to be suspected of being labour migrants who are abusing family migration policies.

Fourth, we illustrated differences in the labelling of countries of origin of migrants. Some are more easily declared to be failing states than others. Possibilities for labelling are influenced by economic, political and postcolonial dependencies. The outcome for migrants from these countries differs according to gender, as well as to religion, class and sexuality.

In the fifth place, we emphasised the importance of looking at both men and women, as well as both femininity and masculinity. As Walaardt indicates in his chapter on the Netherlands, some asylum seekers sought to substitute masculinity for femininity in employing victimhood discourse. Advocates and lobbyists simultaneously and successfully redefined roles, so that asylum seekers could be heroes and victims at the same time. In some countries – Morocco, for instance – migration has become a rite of passage from boyhood to manhood. Those who do not manage to migrate remain in perpetual boyhood. That principle does not apply to women. In fact, the opposite is true. Women migrants are viewed as girls, long past the age of girlhood, and married migrant women are grouped alongside children into one broad category of dependents, which suggests they are economically unproductive.

Finally, we demonstrated how understanding the way that women and men crossing borders contributes to our understanding of citizenship and rights, as well as definitions of family, social welfare and religion in a transnational context. We challenged much of the existing literature on gender and migration by proposing that the typical binaries reflected in the scholarship, such as labour migrant and refugee, the West and the Rest, public and private spheres, equality versus difference, democratic versus authoritarian, deserving and non-deserving, and men and women, intersect more than these simple dichotomies suggest. Scholars should not uncritically reproduce dichotomies that are used in the public sphere. Furthermore, we brought out a dilemma: emphasising difference works to gain attention and rights in the short run, but it creates disadvantages in the long run. An alterity discourse can be useful to policymakers and lobbyists, but it disadvantages migrants in the long run, and that, too, often differs by gender.

## Contribution to theory: Introducing the transferral model

In our introductory chapter we pointed out that since there are many differences between migrant men and migrant women, there is not *one* theory that adequately explains all aspects of the relationship between gender and migration. We offered a large number of theories related to gender and migration. With this volume we contribute to theory by explaining when and why categorisation changed and when, how and why differences according to gender (as well as other categories of analysis) have been labelled, detected or deemed important within the public sphere.

Refugees and asylum seekers, family migrants, postcolonial migrants and labour migrants are not mutually exclusive categories, although policymakers tend to regard them as such. In practice, migrants can and do move between these categories.

**FIGURE 11.1** *Migrants can and do move between the different categories*

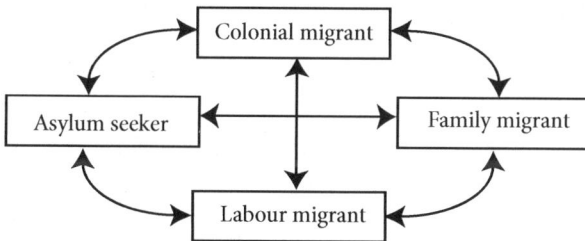

We emphasised the ability of men and women to move between categories of migrant. We further analysed how ideas about gender intersect with other categories of analysis (such as ethnicity, religion and class) to shape debates in the media and politics. We focused on three areas of continued intense debate, in which at least differences according to gender were deemed important and which relate to different categories of migrants. These three areas are who is a 'refugee', who is 'family', and 'multiculturalism'. These questions are frequently seen as separate. We showed that they are not. We described and analysed distinctions made between categories of migrants in France, the USA, Canada, the Netherlands, Sweden and Denmark, and how political debates justified these distinctions.

Scholars tend to appropriate the categorisation framework used by policymakers and reproduced by politicians and journalists. In this volume we sought to move away from that perspective, and its moral overtones, by examining the ways in which migrants and policies move between and across categories. Categories such as gender, class and ethnicity intersect, but not all categorisations are equally important in all contexts or at all times. We aimed to explain when and why differences were labelled, detected or deemed important. New categories were introduced to emphasise the novelty of a phenomenon, and to thus establish the need for new policies. To label phenomena (migrations, policies or debates) as new and different is part of the process of problematisation.

Policymakers, as a rule, seek to interpret categories of migrants narrowly and to exclude people who do not fit their definitions. In contrast, support groups tend to stretch categories and generate sympathy for those who seem to be inhumanly harmed by the government's rigour. Categorisation is not static, but it is frequently presented as such because such a representation eases governmentability. We pointed out similarities over time and between countries. Schacher described the case of Armenian refugees in the USA. The strategy used there was similar to the strategies pursued by Canadian advocates on behalf of Mexican refugees, as described by Boyd & Nowak, and for homosexual refugees in the USA, as described by Oxford. As illustrated by Schacher, Walaardt, and Oxford, state policies, and the policies of advocates, NGOs and lobbyists, continuously interacted, influenced and shaped one another. As Schacher discussed, many Armenian-American social workers in the USA, eager to promote the respectability of the Armenian community, opposed the harsh impact of immigration laws. But they nonetheless accommodated them in practice.

Our emphasis on categorisation highlights when, where and why analytical categories were absent. Gender was, for instance, initially not understood as relevant in refugee policy, as Walaardt showed for the Netherlands, Boyd & Nowak demonstrated for Canada, and Oxford for the USA. In fact, in 1951, when the Refugee Convention was drafted, there was little awareness that women could be refugees. Refugees were assumed to be men and masculine. Only later did women appear on the scene. Only then could refugees – both men and women – be viewed as feminine and vulnerable. Homosexual men have recently become more visible as potential refugees, but as Oxford indicates, lesbian women almost never claim asylum in the USA. Advocates often aim to make categories of migrants visible, although they need not be new. There is a thin line that separates visibility from categorisation. Changes in migration patterns influence visibilities, but high-profile court cases can do so as well, such as that of the caregiver and father Abdellah Berrehab described by Van Walsum, Jones & Legêne for the Netherlands. Possibilities for visibility differ according to gender.

Categorisations apply to migrants, but also to their countries of origin. Categorising democratic countries as failing states proved difficult, as described by Walaardt for Portugal and the USA, and by Boyd & Novak for Mexico, and this influenced the chances of migrants from these countries for gaining asylum. The difficulty of categorising certain states as failing states results not only from a lack of information, but also from a lack of potential political gains. The benefits that Western governments stood to obtain from granting asylum were no longer clear after the end of the Cold War, as indicated by Boyd & Novak and by Walaardt. The discourse of political gains was replaced by a discourse focusing on economic costs, and threats to society were defined in both cultural and safety terms. This is true for all countries described in this volume. Perceptions of costs, gains and threats differed according to gender. Men are more often portrayed as useful to the labour market, but also as (political) threats to society.

Categorisation, furthermore, relates to ideas about what belongs in the private sphere and what in the public sphere. Rather surprisingly, highly personalised and dramatised stories from the private sphere – mostly about women – were found to be instrumental in redrawing boundaries in the public sphere. This was true for the Armenian refugees in the USA, for Muslim migrants in the Netherlands, Denmark and Sweden, and for Mexican migrants in Canada, as well as for homosexual migrants in the USA. At the same time, however, when authorities could successfully relegate an issue to the private sphere they could justify keeping it outside of the public sphere, and refrain from introducing new policies or changing existing policy. For instance, the dominant narrative of 'queer' persecution for gay men and transgendered women is one of sexual family violence, as Oxford discusses for the USA. That which is categorised as 'private violence' – violence within the family sphere – is regarded as something that occurs in all societies. As a result, such incidents are defined as outside the realm of an asylum claim. Asylum claims lose power if persecution can be redefined as maltreatment or classified as belonging to the private sphere.

In the case of family migration, the opposite occurs. Very private aspects of family life – biological parenthood – have been made part of public debates and formal testing. Furthermore, the connotations of categorisations can change. 'French by law' was a legal category, but Sarkozy used it to categorise those who were 'not really French' and associated it with Islam, non-integration, polygamy and, by extension, illegality, as Raissiguier showed.

We described the efforts of supporters and lobbyists to create precedents, while authorities emphasised uniqueness. Among authorities, there was a universal fear of establishing precedents. This was true for all countries studied, as well as for all categories of migrants. Refugee claims were more successful when presented as exceptions, though they had to be transformed into precedent cases to advance the overall cause of a migrant group. We emphasised the strong tendency towards victimisation narratives in seeking to find the 'true' refugee (whether in the Netherlands, in the USA or in Canada), as well as in claiming rights to family migration and in defending selective exceptionalism within multiculturalism (in the Netherlands, Sweden and Denmark).

Personification was one of the main strategies used by lobbyists, as we discussed. Strategies and their success differed according to gender. Personal stories and gruelling details were invoked to strengthen the claims of Armenians and homosexuals in the USA, Mexicans in Canada, and Muslim women in the Netherlands, Sweden and Denmark. Advocacy groups instructed asylum claimants so that they could make a successful appeal. The strategy worked in favour of the migrants in the short run, but led to victimisation in the long run. It also holds true for migrant women within a multiculturalism framework, as shown for the Netherlands, Sweden and Denmark. Victimisation was a successful strategy for claiming rights, but the price of this success was that migrants came to be seen as vulnerable and in need of protection by the state, especially if they were women. More importantly, they came to be regarded as fundamentally different. It proved difficult to escape a victimhood identity. Victimisation played a role in the construction of a counter-identity of the 'Western' advocates who formed the support groups. This othering worked as a disadvantage in the long term by limiting economic and political roles for migrant women and men. Advocates invoked strong tropes, such as those that referred to the Second World War or the Holocaust, as discussed by Walaardt for refugees in the Netherlands, and by Oxford for the USA, fully aware that overuse of such tropes risked ultimately diminishing the power of the argument. But use of the tropes was effective in the short run, and thus attractive.

We demonstrated that discourses are reproduced and copied between categories of migrants, and between countries. Indeed, discourses travel. They shift from anti-colonial and civil rights movements, to family rights, refugee rights and gay rights movements. For the first time, the authors in this volume provide specific empirical evidence on how and why strategies have travelled, and how gender has influenced the transferral of those strategies. The evidence presented indicates how, in very different circumstances and with very different goals, many the same strategies were deployed. We highlighted the passage of discourses and concepts across time and space (between countries) and between categories of migrants. In the process, migrants could and did switch roles and move from one category to another (e.g., from asylum seeker to labour migrant).

We introduce here what we call the *transferral model* to summarise and explain categorisation in relation to gender, class and ethnicity, based on the evidence in the preceding chapters (Figure 11.2). Five factors constitute the model.

**FIGURE 11.2** *Transferral model: Factors that explain the relationship between categorisation and gender, class and ethnicity*

- Characteristics of the immigrant population (size of the group gender, class, ethnicity, religion, number, skill, sex ratio and country of origin)

- Economic situation, geopolitical situation, perceptions of gain and costs, urgency and reciprocity (between countries)

- Credibility, rights attached to 'equality'

- Recognisability, perceptions of 'sameness'

- Migrants' rights discourse combined with other emancipatory goals

The first factor is the characteristics of the migrants, as these determined whether migrants could switch between categories. Foremost among these are their gender, ethnicity, class, the sex ratio within the group, the numbers of migrants, their countries of origin, and their religion.

Secondly, categorisations and therefore migration policies depended on particular economic situations and geopolitical circumstances (such as the end of the Cold War). High unemployment rates removed one avenue for switching categories. Perceptions regarding costs and gains (political, economic and security) influence possibilities for relabelling. Perceptions of costs and gains are influenced by linkage possibilities: Can marriage fraud be linked to migrant illegality? Can migrant illegality be linked to security threat? Urgency is important for relabelling. Cases that relate to women (and children) can be presented as more urgent (from the perspective of a need to save those involved). Such circumstances render it easier to change labels and categorisations, and for migrants to move across and between categories. Lawmakers, policymakers, politicians, journalists and lobbyists are often influenced by what occurs in other countries. Since policymakers, as a rule, look to neighbouring countries in order to synchronise polities and prevent migrants from 'shopping' for rights, they also study the arguments and strategies used elsewhere. They adapt and adopt these when useful or possible, while immigrant support organisations do the same. Leniency (or rumours about leniency) in one country work as a magnet (some fear), and restrictions divert migrants away from a country (some hope). Policymakers respond to what they believe will be the consequences of their decisions on the policies of and practices in neighbouring countries (reciprocity). Criticism about the relative leniency or stringency of policies in neighbouring countries is only valid and effective if it is matched by policies in one's own country.

Thirdly, whether discourses can effectively travel from one category of migrants to another is influenced by credibility, we argue here. Credibility plays an important role in refugee cases. Questions about whether a person is a true refugee or whether democratic countries (such as Mexico, or NATO partners, including the USA and Portugal) can even produce refugees, are central to the implementation of refugee policy. The question 'is this a man or a woman?' illustrates the problem of credibility: who is asking, who is answering and why is the question being asked? Credibility questions are also important to other categories of migrants, not simply asylum seekers: Is this person really migrating for love and marriage, and not for work? Can wearing a veil ever be a choice? Is this a real marriage, a real child, a real spouse? Is this migrant willing and capable of adapting? The answers to these questions differ according to gender, as well as to sexuality, age, class, skill, countries of origin, age and religion. If it can be proven that people are not what they claim to be – a true refugee, a family member, a spouse, or potentially a Dutch, Danish, Swedish or French citizen – rights can be denied accordingly. Multiculturalism had to be declared a failure and had to be attached to all sorts of behaviour, labelled deviant, strange and culturally-determined, in order to exclude migrants and deny their children rights. This happened in each of the countries examined in this volume. When equality comes with many rights, as is true for most Western countries, it is important to set high barriers for access to that 'equality'. Important to the discourse is how 'we' profit from believing or denying claims. A smooth transition from colonialism to postcolonialism, the recruitment of suitable workers, the claim to moral superiority, or the opportunity to pitch the enlightened West against a backward Rest, can be sufficient to change categorisations, as we showed.

In the fourth place, strategies, concepts and debates travel across time, between countries and across and between categories of migrants when new categorisation is built on old categorisations. That process makes new categorisations acceptable. Recognisability, we argue, is a factor that stimulates and enables the transfer of ideas and policies. Transfers between categories, between countries and over time can only take place if those who are instrumental to these transfers believe that the situations, or the migrants, are 'the same'. Debates about multiculturalism are much more closely related to debates about who is a refugee and who is family, than might be apparent at first glance, or has been suggested in earlier literature. As in the quest for the 'true' refugee and 'true' family members, multiculturalism takes an essentialist view. Static ideas about culture legitimise categorisations. Since equality – or sameness – comes with rights, it is important to prove difference, as was done in multiculturalism, or fraud, as was key in debates about refugees or family members. The shared essentialist basis makes it possible for discourses to travel.

Lastly, similar archetypes figure in many of these debates. The 'eksik etek' – the 'short skirted', intellectual, unmarried us women, who came out in support of the Armenian refugees, as described by Schacher, were similar to the Dutch women who supported Turkish women decades later, as Schrover described. The people who supported gay rights, also came out in support of refugee rights in several of the countries examined. Strategies that proved to be successful in one context were copied, adapted and applied in other contexts. This was especially true if they could serve a multiple cause: advocating immigrants' rights combined with non-migrant emancipatory goals. The refugee war resisters of the 1970s, as described by Walaardt, were important in the anti-Vietnam or anti-'colonial' war movement. Gay refugees were important to the LGBT movement of the 1990s.

The testing and use of this transferral model in new contexts provides ample scope for future advances in the field.

# About the authors

*Rikke Andreassen* is a researcher, teacher and consultant in the fields of media, discrimination and equality, addressing racial and ethnic and gender equality issues. She earned her PhD from University of Toronto, Canada in 2005 and is an associate professor at Roskilde University, Denmark. Andreassen has participated in various public debates about immigration and gender and published a number of articles as well as the books *Menneskeudstilling: Fremvisninger af eksotiske mennesker i Zoolgisk Have og Tivoli* (2011) and *Der er et yndigt land: Medier, minoritieter og danskhed* (2007). She was part of the EU project VEIL (2006-2009), which focuses on European debates and legislation concerning head and body coverings of Muslim women (www.veil-project.eu). She is the coordinator of the Nordic Nordforsk-funded network TheoryNord on re-developing international theories of media and migration in a Nordic context (2011-2013).

*Monica Boyd* joined the University of Toronto in 2001 as a professor of sociology. She holds the Canada Research Chair in Immigration, Inequality and Public Policy. She is an associate editor of the *International Migration Review* and a member of the editorial board of the *American Sociological Review*. Her current research projects are on immigrant inequality in the labour force with a continuing focus on immigrant women, the migration of high-skilled labour and related re-accreditation difficulties, and the socio-economic achievements of the children of immigrants. Among her recent publications are 'Finding a place in stratified structures: Migrant women in North America' (with Deanna Pikkov), in Nicole Piper (ed.), *New Perspectives on Gender and Migration: Livelihoods, Rights, and Entitlements* (London Routledge 2008); 'Falling out of safety nets or saved by family fies? Poverty among Elderly immigrants in Canada' (with Lisa Kaida), *Canadian Journal on Aging* 30: 1 (2011); 'Social networks and international migration' (with Joanne Nowak) in Marco Martiniello and Jan Rath (eds), *An Introduction to International Migration Studies: European Perspectives* (Amsterdam University Press 2012).

*Maja Cederberg* is a senior lecturer in sociology in the Department of Social Sciences at Oxford Brookes University, where she previously worked as a post-doctoral researcher. Her research interests are in international migration, gender, ethnicity, 'race' and racism, and social inequalities. Other related interests include work and employment, labour market and welfare policies, social theory and qualitative research methods. Maja Cederberg's work is published in the journals *Sociology, Acta Sociologica*, the *Journal of Ethnic and Migration Studies* and *Studi Emigrazione/Migration Studies*.

*Guno Jones* is a researcher at the VU University Amsterdam, specialised in post-Second World War political discourses on migration, citizenship and belonging of 'postcolonial citizens' (in particular, in the Netherlands, Belgium and the UK) and in memory and remembrance of the Second World War and of Dutch transatlantic slavery. His recent publications include 'Dutch politicians: The Dutch nation and the dynamics of postcolonial citizenship', in Ulbe Bosma (ed.), *Post-colonial Immigrants and Identity Formations in the Netherlands* (Amsterdam University Press 2012) and 'De Slavernij is *onze* geschiedenis (niet): Over de discursieve strijd om de betekenis van de NTR-televisieserie *De* Slavernij. ('Slavery is (not) *our* history: On the public debate and divergent meanings of the NTR television series Slavery')' *BMGN Low Countries Historical Review* 127: 4 (2012).

*Deirdre M. Moloney* is Director of Fellowships Advising at Princeton University. She is the author of *National Insecurities: Immigrants and US Deportation Policy since 1882* (University of North Carolina Press, 2012), *American Catholic Lay Groups and Transatlantic Social Reform in the Progressive Era* (University of North Carolina Press, 2002) and 'Women, sexual morality, and economic dependency in early deportation policy' in the *Journal of Women's History*. Her recent research was supported by a fellowship at the Woodrow Wilson International Center for Scholars in Washington, DC.

*Joanne Nowak* is a doctoral candidate in sociology at the University of Toronto. Her research interests include the intersection between international migration and development, gender and migration issues, (im)migration policy, as well as the politics of migration. She is the co-author with Monica Boyd of 'Social networks and international migration', in Marco Martiniello and Jan Rath (eds), *An Introduction to International Migration Studies: European Perspectives* (Amsterdam University Press, 2012).

*Connie Oxford* is an assistant professor of gender and women's studies at the State University of New York, Plattsburgh. She received her PhD in sociology and a doctoral women's studies certificate from the University of Pittsburgh in 2006. She is working on an ethnographic study of gender-based asylum claims titled *Fleeing Gendered Harm: Seeking Asylum in America*. That manuscript is based on her dissertation fieldwork in Los Angeles and was supported by fellowships and grants from the National Science Foundation, the Social Science Research Council International Migration Program, and the Andrew W. Mellon Foundation. She is currently doing supplemental research for this project in New York City. Amongst her publications are 'Protectors and victims in the gender regime of asylum', which appeared in the *National Women's Studies Association Journal*, 'Acts of resistance in asylum seekers' persecution narratives', in *Immigrant Rights in the Shadows of United States Citizenship*, and 'Changing the research question: Lessons from qualitative research', in *Research Methods Choices in Interdisciplinary Contexts*.

*Catherine Raissiguier* teaches women's and gender studies at New Jersey City University. She is the author *Becoming Women/Becoming Workers: Identity Formation in a French High School* (SUNY Press, 1994) and *Re-Inventing the Republic: Gender, Migration, and Citizenship in France* (Stanford University Press, 2010). Her current research looks at various processes of border formation in France and the new forms of citizenship politics they elicit.

*Yael Schacher* teaches American Studies at the University of Connecticut. She recently completed her doctoral dissertation, 'Exceptions to exclusion: The prehistory of asylum in the United States, 1880-1980', in Harvard's History of American Civilization Program. She served on the editorial board of *A New Literary History of America* (Cambridge, MA: Harvard University Press, 2009) and was a research assistant for Harvard's digital archives on immigration to the United States (http://ocp.hul.harvard.edu/immigration/).

*Marlou Schrover* is a professor of migration history and social differences at Leiden University. She recently concluded a large (NWO vici) project on gender and migration. Recent publications include *Illegal Migration and Gender in a Global and Historical Perspective* (Amsterdam University Press, 2008) (with Joanne van der Leun, Leo Lucassen and Chris Quispel), *Komen en Gaan: Immigratie en Emigratie in Nederland vanaf 1550* (Bert Bakker, 2008) (with Herman Obdeijn), and *Gender, Migration and the Public Sphere 1850-2005* (Routledge, 2010) (with Eileen Janes Yeo).

*Tycho Walaardt* is a researcher at the Economic and Social History Department of Leiden University. After graduating in 2000, he worked for the Dutch Immigration and Naturalisation Service and the United Nations High

Commissioner for Refugees in Ghana and Eritrea. His main fields of interest relate to the immigration and the selection of immigrants. He has published a number of articles on the Dutch asylum procedure and the arguments and actors that were decisive in them. Recent publications include 'The good old days of the Cold War: Arguments used to admit or reject asylum seekers in the Netherlands, 1957-1967', *Continuity and Change* 26: 2 (2011); 'Patience and perseverance: The asylum procedure of Tamils and Iranians in the Netherlands in the mid-1980s', *Tijdschrift voor Sociale en Economische Geschiedenis* 8: 3 (2011); and 'From heroes to vulnerable victims: Labelling Christian Turks as genuine refugees in the 1970s', *Ethnic and Racial Studies* (forthcoming, 2013). His dissertation 'Geruisloos inwilligen: Argumentatie en speelruimte in de Nederlandse asielprocedure, 1945-1994' (Silently giving in: Arguments and margins in the Dutch asylum procedure, 1945-1994) was published by Verloren in 2012.

*Sarah van Walsum* is a professor of migration law and family ties at the VU University Amsterdam. Her main fields of interest are migration law, gender and migration law, family migration policies, migrant domestic workers, transnational ties and migration law. She is author of *The Famiy and the Nation: Dutch Family Migration Policies in the Context of Changing Family Norms* (Cambridge Scholars Publishing, 2008).

*Other IMISCOE Research titles*

Birgit Glorius, Izabela Grabowska-Lusinska and Aimee Kuvik (eds)
*Mobility in Transition: Migration Patterns after EU Enlargement*
2013 ISBN 978 90 8964 392 6

Joan Font and Mónica Méndez (eds)
*Surveying Ethnic Minorities and Immigrant Populations: Methodological Challenges and Research Strategies*
2013 ISBN 978 90 8964 543 2

Marek Okólski (ed.)
*European Immigrations: Trends, Structures and Policy Implications*
2012 ISBN 978 90 8964 457 2

Ulbe Bosma (ed.)
*Post-Colonial Immigrants and Identity Formations in the Netherlands*
2012 ISBN 978 90 8964 454 1

Christina Boswell and Gianni D'Amato (eds)
*Immigration and Social Systems: Collected Essays of Michael Bommes*
2012 ISBN 978 90 8964 453 4

Maurice Crul, Jens Schneider and Frans Lelie (eds)
*The European Second Generation Compared: Does the Integration Context Matter?*
2012 ISBN 978 90 8964 443 5

Bram Lancee
*Immigrant Performance in the Labour Market: Bonding and Bridging Social Capital*
2012 ISBN 978 90 8964 357 5

Julie Vullnetari
*Albania on the Move: Links between Internal and International Migration*
2012 ISBN 978 90 8964 355 1

Blanca Garcés-Mascareñas
*State Regulation of Labour Migration in Malaysia and Spain: Markets, Citizenship and Rights*
2012 ISBN 978 90 8964 286 8

Albert Kraler, Eleonore Kofman, Martin Kohli and Camille Schmoll (eds)
*Gender, Generations and the Family in International Migration*
2012 ISBN 978 90 8964 285 1

Giovanna Zincone, Rinus Penninx and Maren Borkert (eds)
*Migration Policymaking in Europe: The Dynamics of Actors and Contexts in Past and Present*
2011 ISBN 978 90 8964 370 4

Michael Bommes and Giuseppe Sciortino (eds)
*Foggy Social Structures: Irregular Migration, European Labour Markets and the Welfare State*
2011 ISBN 978 90 8964 341 4

Peter Scholten
*Framing Immigrant Integration: Dutch Research-Policy Dialogues in Comparative Perspective*
2011 ISBN 978 90 8964 284 4

Liza Mügge
*Beyond Dutch Borders: Transnational Politics among Colonial Migrants, Guest Workers and the Second Generation*
2010 ISBN 978 90 8964 244 8

Rainer Bauböck and Thomas Faist (eds)
*Diaspora and Transnationalism: Concepts, Theories and Methods*
2010 ISBN 978 90 8964 238 7

Cédric Audebert and Mohamed Kamel Dorai (eds)
*Migration in a Globalised World: New Research Issues and Prospects*
2010 ISBN 978 90 8964 157 1

Richard Black, Godfried Engbersen, Marek Okólski and Cristina Pantîru (eds)
*A Continent Moving West? EU Enlargement and Labour Migration from Central and Eastern Europe*
2010 ISBN 978 90 8964 156 4

Charles Westin, José Bastos, Janine Dahinden and Pedro Góis (eds)
*Identity Processes and Dynamics in Multi-Ethnic Europe*
2010 ISBN 978 90 8964 046 8

Rainer Bauböck, Bernhard Perchinig and Wiebke Sievers (eds)
*Citizenship Policies in the New Europe: Expanded and Updated Edition*
2009 ISBN 978 90 8964 108 3

Gianluca P. Parolin
*Citizenship in the Arab World: Kin, Religion and Nation-State*
2009 ISBN 978 90 8964 045 1

Maurice Crul and Liesbeth Heering (eds)
*The Position of the Turkish and Moroccan Second Generation in Amsterdam and Rotterdam: The TIES Study in the Netherlands*
2008 ISBN 978 90 8964 061 1

Marlou Schrover, Joanne van der Leun, Leo Lucassen and Chris Quispel (eds)
*Illegal Migration and Gender in a Global and Historical Perspective*
2008 ISBN 978 90 8964 047 5

Corrado Bonifazi, Marek Okólski, Jeannette Schoorl and Patrick Simon (eds)
*International Migration in Europe: New Trends and New Methods of Analysis*
2008 ISBN 978 90 5356 894 1

Ralph Grillo (ed.)
*The Family in Question: Immigrant and Ethnic Minorities in Multicultural Europe*
2008 ISBN 978 90 5356 869 9

Holger Kolb and Henrik Egbert (eds)
*Migrants and Markets: Perspectives from Economics and the Other Social Sciences*
2008 ISBN 978 90 5356 684 8

Veit Bader
*Secularism or Democracy? Associational Governance of Religious Diversity*
2007 ISBN 978 90 5356 999 3

Rainer Bauböck, Bernhard Perchinig and Wiebke Sievers (eds)
*Citizenship Policies in the New Europe*
2007 ISBN 978 90 5356 922 1

Rainer Bauböck, Eva Ersbøll, Kees Groenendijk and Harald Waldrauch (eds)
*Acquisition and Loss of Nationality: Policies and Trends in 15 European Countries*
*Volume 1: Comparative Analyses*
2006 ISBN 978 90 5356 920 7
*Volume 2: Country Analyses*
2006 ISBN 978 90 5356 921 4

Leo Lucassen, David Feldman and Jochen Oltmer (eds)
*Paths of Integration: Migrants in Western Europe (1880-2004)*
2006 ISBN 978 90 5356 883 5

Rinus Penninx, Maria Berger and Karen Kraal (eds)
*The Dynamics of International Migration and Settlement in Europe: A State of the Art*
2006 ISBN 978 90 5356 866 8

*IMISCOE Textbooks*

Marco Martiniello and Jan Rath (eds)
*An Introduction to International Migration Studies: European Perspectives (Vol. 2)*
2012 ISBN 978 90 8964 456 5

Marco Martiniello and Jan Rath (eds)
*Selected Studies in International Migration and Immigrant Incorporation (Vol. 1)*
2010 ISBN 978 90 8964 160 1